# The Global Environment and World Politics

## 2nd Edition

**Also available from Continuum**

*International Law and International Relations*, J. Craig Barker
*International Conflict Resolution 2nd Edition*, Charles Hauss

# The Global Environment and World Politics

## 2nd Edition

### Elizabeth R. DeSombre

continuum

**Continuum International Publishing Group**

The Tower Building 80 Maiden Lane
11 York Road New York
London NY 10038
SE1 7NX

**British Library Cataloging-in-Publication Data**
A catalogue record for this book is available from the British Library.

ISBN: 0826490514 (hardback)
9780826490513
0826490522 (paperback)
9780826490520

**Library of Congress Cataloging-in-Publication Data**
DeSombre, Elizabeth R.
The global environment and world politics / Elizabeth R. DeSombre. – 2nd ed.
p. cm.
ISBN-13: 978-0-8264-9051-3 (hardcover)
ISBN-10: 0-8264-9051-4 (hardcover)
ISBN-13: 978-0-8264-9052-0 (pbk.)
ISBN-10: 0-8264-9052-2 (pbk.)
1. Environmental policy – International cooperation. I. Title.

GE170.D473 2007
363.7'0526–dc22

2006023297

Typeset by Ben Cracknell Studios

# Contents

# Acknowledgments

In writing both first and second editions of this book I have benefited from the help of many students and colleagues at Colby College (where I used to teach) and at Wellesley College (where I teach now). Colby students who served as my research assistants over the years I worked on topics related to this book include Kate Litle, Katie Wasik, Stephanie Graber, Carolyn Szum, and Jen Dakin. Lauren Gritzke at Wellesley helped me find sources for the second edition. More importantly, my students both at Colby and Wellesley have challenged me constantly to think through how to present information on global environmental politics in a way that is both rigorous and accessible. They have also inspired me to continue working on the issues presented here, and to teach students how to think about the global environment in the hopes that they may help to improve it. My colleagues both at Colby and at Wellesley are a source of inspiration as well, for demonstrating that excellent teaching and important research can (indeed, must) go hand-in-hand.

I have benefited greatly from the intellectual community provided by the "teaching global environmental politics" (gep-ed) listserv run by Mike Maniates at Allegheny College, and the Environmental Studies Section of the International Studies Association. In both these arenas scholars are generous with their resources, experiences, and ideas. I am grateful to work in such a cooperative field.

I also appreciate the support the Political Science Department at the University of Florida provided in my sabbatical year during which I wrote the second edition. I am especially grateful to Aida Hozic for the use of her office during the period I was working on this book. Others, such as Lynda Warwick, Jen Stiles, and Sophie and Molly, rescue me from too much work and help me remember that a concert (ideally by Tracy Grammer or Crooked Still) or a good game of fetch is necessary in the process of figuring out how to save the world.

Finally, highest thanks are due to Sammy Barkin, who reads and comments on everything I write. My ideas are better for discussing them with him, my examples are more extensive, and errors that would be in this book are not because of his help. I could not do what I do without his support, both practical and moral.

# Abbreviations

| | |
|---|---|
| AOSIS | Alliance of Small Island States |
| CBD | Convention on Biological Diversity |
| CFC | chlorofluorocarbon |
| CITES | Convention on International Trade in Endangered Species of Wild Fauna and Flora |
| CPR | common pool resource |
| DFN | debt-for-nature |
| EANET | East Asian Acid Deposition Monitoring Network |
| FAO | Food and Agriculture Organization |
| FCCC | Framework Convention on Climate Change |
| GEF | Global Environment Facility |
| GHG | greenhouse gas |
| IPCC | Intergovernmental Panel on Climate Change |
| IR | international relations |
| ISO | International Organization for Standardization |
| IWC | International Whaling Commission |
| LMO | living modified organism |
| LRTAP | Convention on Long-Range Transboundary Air Pollution |
| MNC | multinational corporation |
| NGO | non-governmental organization |
| ODS | ozone-depleting substance |
| ODP | ozone depletion potential |
| OECD | Organization for Economic Cooperation and Development |
| OPEC | Organization of the Petroleum Exporting Countries |
| UNEP | United Nations Environment Programme |
| VOC | volatile organic compound |
| WMO | World Meteorological Organization |
| WTO | World Trade Organization |

# 1 Introduction

Politically, the world is composed of states. International relations at its most traditional examines how states interact with one another in an anarchic world; one that does not have an overarching authority to impose political order on individual sovereign states. Environmentally, the world is made up of ecosystems. The rainforest that forms the watershed of the Amazon river stretches from Brazil to Peru and Ecuador and up through the Guyanas. The ozone layer that circles the stratosphere exists above states; the thinning of this layer over the South Pole affects states like Chile and Australia despite the fact that the main producers of ozone-depleting substances were in the United States and Europe.

This disconnect between ecological and political systems makes addressing environmental issues at the global level both difficult and necessary. On the one hand, the fact that states cannot address many environmental problems successfully on their own impels international cooperation, and there are many situations in which all parties can benefit (in the aggregate, at least) from working together to prevent or fix an environmental problem. But states are also pluralistic entities, and within them, some actors will benefit more or be harmed more by action taken to protect the global environment. And even in situations when all states benefit from environmental protection, some may benefit more than others, and most would benefit from taking no action at all and leaving environmental protection to others. Such is a recipe for complete inaction. States must learn – and they have, to a large extent – how to avoid this tragedy of the commons.

Successful mitigation of environmental problems at any level is not easy: the geographic disconnect combines with a temporal disconnect as well, as politicians respond to electoral cycles that do not include the future generations that will likely benefit from potentially costly measures taken now to protect resources. Add to that a multiplicity of states, with their own concerns and decision-making structures and a variety of competing domestic interests, and the fact that the dumping of the most toxic pollution into the ocean has ceased, that many ozone-depleting substances are no longer used, and that many migratory endangered species are surviving is impressive indeed.

# 2 The Global Environment and World Politics

This volume examines the process of addressing problems that face the environment internationally. Global environmental politics is a discipline that brings together a wide variety of traditions examining the way states and other actors interact internationally. It draws from traditional international relations theory in addressing concerns and actions of states, and in reflecting the conflict that takes place over how to protect the global environment. But it also brings in a variety of new perspectives to explain issues that are unique to environmental politics or more prominent in them than in other international issues.

These issues are explored through the lens of theoretical concerns and case studies of issues relevant to understanding the politics of the global environment. There is no grand unified theory of global environmental politics. What exists forms a patchwork of different theoretical approaches and concerns. This volume explores four of these theoretical issues in depth: the process of international environmental cooperation; the issue of science, uncertainty, and risk; the role of developing states; and the role of non-state actors in international environmental politics. While these are not the only theoretical issues facing those who attempt to respond to global environmental problems, they are among the most important.

Environmental cooperation is one of the most prominent and innovative forms of international cooperation generally. The study of this phenomenon can both usefully draw from and contribute to the examination of international organization and international cooperation more broadly. Cooperation in addressing issues of the environment faces some similar issues to international cooperation more broadly, such as the role of powerful states and the difficulty of negotiation. But international agreements have evolved a set of practices, most importantly the process of creating framework conventions to which protocols are later added when states are willing to undertake more serious regulation, that help address the issues of uncertainty and the generally multilateral nature of environmental cooperation. Similarly, issues of who has negotiating power, which states need to be brought into an international agreement, and how you determine whether the agreement is effective, all take slightly different – and more complicated – forms when addressing environmental issues.

What we don't know about the global environment impacts political action to address environmental problems in significant ways. Uncertainty and risk pervade discussions of the environmental problems and the ways to mitigate them. Uncertainty about environmental problems, their consequences, and the costs and effectiveness of mitigating them impacts political willingness to address them. Studies of risk suggest that people, and thus policy makers, do not approach risk in an economically rational way, and the implication of that observation for environmental policy making is important. Information and science are essential in this process but are likely to become politicized themselves, as those who are affected by the environmental problems attempt to spin the science or represent the uncertainty in ways that best address their interests.

Developing states are central actors in international environmental politics. They are frequently not the primary cause of the problems that affect the global environment (though their population growth and industrialization process may make them important contributors to these problems in the future) and may have different interests in international environmental cooperation than the wealthier states in the international system. Despite their varying vulnerabilities to different environmental problems, the solidarity of developing countries in international environmental negotiations has been notable, as they attempt to achieve common recognition of their sovereign rights to develop and control their own resources and frequently seek financial assistance as a *quid pro quo* for agreeing to participate. The structure of environmental problems is such that developing countries, by making a credible threat to remain outside of cooperative efforts, are able to gain major concessions in negotiations.

Another important element of international environmental problems is that action that causes environmental problems or action to mitigate them most frequently comes from those other than states. For that reason, non-state actors have had a higher degree of influence than in other realms of international politics. The boundaries between what action is taken by international organizations, states, and non-governmental actors is particularly porous in this discipline. Most importantly, the way these actors act on issues of the global environment challenges many of the most state-centric approaches to international relations, and even the traditional view of the interaction between domestic politics and international relations.

Since the proponents of various theoretical perspectives have often focused on different cases or different elements of environmental politics, it can be difficult to determine where these disparate approaches are compatible or in conflict. It is through the examination of particular issue areas that it is possible to see where various perspectives fit together or clash, and what those experiences contribute to further generation of theory. The cases presented here are chosen to be representative of various types of global environmental issues. They include issues that are primarily addressed by developed countries and those that involve primarily developing countries; issues that take place in the global commons of the atmosphere and the oceans and those that have a directional, non-commons, component. There are those that have been addressed by interstate cooperation and those that have been most effectively addressed by non-governmental actors. There are issues that have been addressed through cost–benefit analysis and those that are debated through ethical arguments. This group of cases provides information about much of the spectrum of global environmental issues.

Climate change and ozone depletion, both issues of the global commons and of long-scale ecological processes, have met with varying levels of success in efforts to prevent global environmental damage. While they share the similarity that their harm is truly global and not influenced by the location of damaging emissions, they also present different political problems. Both the science and the economic structure of industry relating to ozone depletion are simpler than is the case in climate change. In particular, the states most concerned about ozone depletion were those most responsible for causing it, and also the most capable of taking action to prevent it. The same cannot be said for climate change, where the industry is varied and dispersed, the impacts vary widely and are still uncertain, and many people have not yet been convinced that taking action is politically feasible.

Whaling is among the oldest type of environmental problem: the harvesting of a natural resource that becomes less sustainable when improved technology and increasing population make harvesting more efficient. It also provides an important additional view into the ethical issues of environmental politics: while some who want to restrict whaling seek to do so for the reasons that motivated the origins of the International Whaling Commission – the protection of the whaling industry through successfully managing the level of harvesting – others are concerned about the intrinsic value of whales. The combination of these two approaches allowed the creation of a moratorium on commercial whaling, but they are uneasy bedfellows both in whaling and in other environmental issues. Ethics plays a role in addressing the global environment, but there is no clear consensus on who is deserving of consideration or how to act on behalf of nonhuman entities. The whaling case also demonstrates more mundane but essential political lessons about the ease of cheating on international obligations, and the difficulty of regulating a large number of actors. It also suggests that, even when an industry has a collective interest in protecting the resource upon which it depends, it may fail.

Examining biodiversity, especially in the context of the Amazonian rainforest, suggests the true interconnected nature of environmental resources as well as their interactions with political structures. The harms to the rainforest come both locally and globally, and from resource harvesting, pollution, and subsistence farming. The loss of biodiversity and harm to Amazonian ecosystems also have both local and global effects, including ones that we are unlikely to fully realize until the damage is irreversible. Nevertheless, it is in the area of addressing biodiversity that some of the most innovative strategies have been attempted. Local political action can have global impacts in these cases. The fact that the environmental problems happen in physical locations gives political power to the states where biodiversity of concern is located, and suggests that, when properly motivated, they may in fact be able to use their sovereignty to protect resources. Efforts via debt-for-nature swaps, bioprospecting agreements, and ecotourism may not be the panaceas that they were initially believed to be, but they are creative ways to address local concerns with global resources in a way that may ultimately protect what some consider to be the common heritage of humankind.

Finally, acid rain presents in some ways a traditional problem: industrial pollution that harms lakes, forests, and the associated resources, as well as destroying cultural artifacts. It followed a traditional path for addressing environmental problems as well, with the discovery of a local environmental problem motivating the search for its cause, and eventual regulation of the activities that caused it. But acid rain also differs from the model many intuitively apply to environmental politics in that its effects are directional. How much an area suffers from the problem is determined not only by its natural ecological resistance to acidifying substances but also by its position in windflow. States thus face a quite different situation in negotiations to address acid rain than they do in traditional commons problems like fisheries or ozone depletion, and those that are net importers of pollutants have a greater necessity, but lesser ability, to address the problem. What is notable in this situation is that addressing acid rain in Europe has nevertheless involved even the major polluters in reasonably serious efforts to mitigate the problem. The same is less true in North America, where the United States, which causes more harm than it suffers in acidifying pollutants, was able to resist action for a decade.

Environmental politics poses challenges to a lot of traditional thinking about international relations. At its most basic, environmental politics challenges the idea of sovereignty – states can no longer realistically protect their own territory and populations from harm by actions they take alone. Thinking about the environment expands the sphere of concern of international relations beyond state-centric security-dominated approaches; many recent discussions within international relations theory have their origins in efforts to understand international environmental politics. In examining a number of new paradigms that help explain global environmental politics, however, it is important not to forget the lessons that traditional IR theory can provide. Those who focus on the involvement of non-state actors and the potential for cooperation based on new scientific understanding should not forget that environmental politics can be a realm of conflict, both domestic and international. It should not be assumed, for instance, that all states have the same goals in approaching environmental problems, or even that the issue of relative gains is unimportant. Nevertheless, the challenges to traditional approaches that come from efforts to protect the global environment can be instructive as we work to understand international relations more broadly.

# International Environmental Cooperation

2

It is through international environmental cooperation that most global environmental problems are mitigated or at least managed. The amount of cooperation internationally to address environmental issues has grown exponentially in the last century, with much of it reaching maturity in the last thirty-five years. In addition to an increase in raw numbers of instruments of cooperation, the number of states that participate internationally and the sophistication of international agreements has grown as well. Certainly there are gains to be made from international cooperation, but that alone is not sufficient to bring it about or to ensure that all actors participate in and comply with international agreements. Moreover, one of the difficult lessons of the last century of international environmental cooperation has been that simply negotiating an agreement, even if all relevant states participate and live up to their obligations, may not be sufficient to address the environmental problem. Despite this difficulty, however, great strides have been made in understanding and creating international environmental cooperation.

# 8  The Global Environment and World Politics

This chapter examines explicitly state-based international efforts to manage international environmental issues; later chapters examine the types of actions undertaken by individuals, non-governmental organizations, or business actors. It should also be noted that this chapter, and the book as a whole, focus primarily on environmental problems that themselves cross international borders. It thus gives short shrift to what Ken Conca has called "physically local but globally cumulative socioecological controversies,"[1] such as desertification, access to fresh water, and other environmental problems that may result at least in part from global economic forces but are felt primarily domestically. These environmental problems are important and are discussed in passing when considering the concerns of developing states and examining the politics of Amazonian biodiversity, but addressing them fully is beyond the scope of this volume.

The first essential element to keep in mind in examining international environmental cooperation is that no state can ever be required to join an international agreement or to undertake a particular regulation. The international system is anarchic in that there is no overarching authority (in this case, world government) that can dictate to individual states, or actors within those states, what they must do. And although there are international courts and tribunals, no state can ever be forced to appear before them, or to accept punishment from them. What this structure means is that states must want to make environmental policy on the international level, and they must be willing to comply with the policies they have made, or submit to dispute resolution procedures to address problems that come up as a result of their actions or inaction. Under what conditions might they be willing to do so?

Theories of international cooperation in a variety of issue areas impact our understanding of international environmental cooperation; more importantly, international environmental cooperation can help support or challenge some of these broader approaches. Cooperation to address environmental issues is clearly a growth field. By the time of the United Nations Conference on Environment and Development in Rio in 1992 there were more than 900 instruments of international cooperation to address protection of the environment.[2] Some estimate that at least five agreements focusing directly on international environmental cooperation have been added each year since then.[3] Others put the numbers even higher: Ronald Mitchell suggests that there are at least 1,700 international environmental agreements and probably considerably more.[4] Examining international efforts to address global environmental issues allows us to apply well-developed theories about international cooperation to the environmental issue area, where it becomes clear that environmental issues provide difficult laboratories that challenge the conventional wisdom not only about what makes cooperation possible, but about how even to study the conditions under which it will come about or succeed.

What is clear is that states have turned primarily to international agreements to address global environmental problems, and that sometimes these agreements have been effective at changing state behavior and ultimately impacting the environment in a beneficial way. In other cases, success – either in the creation of international mechanisms, or in their influence on behavior of states or individuals and ultimately their ability to improve the condition of the environment – is less certain. It is through these experiences that we can learn both what may make for effective international environmental cooperation, and, more importantly, how to understand why.

# Recent History of International Environmental Cooperation

Despite the difficulty of international environmental cooperation, international action to address environmental policy has developed in both depth and breadth since its beginnings. Early environmental cooperation addressed issues pertaining to wildlife. In particular these instruments focused on such things as migratory birds, which would be threatened if not protected in the various areas through which they migrated, and (though it would not have used this terminology at the time) sustainable hunting of species. One of the most effective early treaties of this sort was the 1911 Fur Seal Convention which attempted to use biological indicators to make sure that seals were not overharvested.

Although states have been cooperating to manage natural resources for more than a century, the modern era of international environmental cooperation is generally traced to the United Nations Conference on the Human Environment, held in 1972 in Stockholm. This international conference addressed the collective human responsibility for environmental protection on a global scale and put forth the idea that environmental protection was important for human social and economic development. More than 100 states participated in the conference, and more than 400 non-governmental and international organizations attended. The main results of the conference were the Declaration on the Human Environment and an Action Plan for how to implement its principles. The United Nations General Assembly, after the conference, accepted a central recommendation from the Action Plan and created the United Nations Environment Programme (UNEP), which has taken on an important coordinating and leadership role in international environmental policy since its inception.[5] The publicity and enthusiasm generated by the Stockholm conference led to the negotiation of a number of international environmental treaties in the early 1970s. These treaties addressed such issues as acid rain in Europe, ocean dumping, the regulation of trade in endangered species, and the protection of wetlands. Although intended to be inclusive, these treaties primarily reflected the concerns of the developed countries that initiated their negotiations.

Environmental cooperation in the early 1980s continued and deepened the focus on international problems of the global commons. What is notable, however, is a shift in emphasis toward the end of the decade to some issues – the transboundary movement of hazardous waste, for example – that were driven by developing country concerns. In addition, developing countries began to recognize their importance to, and thus negotiating power in, global environmental agreements. Treaties such as the 1987 Montreal Protocol on Substances that Deplete the Ozone Layer included measures to help address the development concerns of developing countries. At the same time, as evidenced by the Montreal Protocol, environmental issues began to be seen as even more clearly global in scope and elusive in character. Issues like ozone depletion and global climate change could potentially bring environmental disaster, but action to prevent them would have to be taken before actual damage from human activity became apparent. And all countries, rich or poor, would have to be involved in the prevention of these problems.

Twenty years after Stockholm, the United Nations Conference on Environment and Development, held at Rio in 1992, addressed the intersection of environment and development issues more explicitly. The declaration negotiated at that conference included the idea that the needs of the least developed countries should be given special priority and that developed countries bore a special responsibility for working toward sustainable development. Treaties signed in the wake of the Rio conference addressed issues such as biodiversity, global climate change, and desertification, all of which have significant North–South equity implications. The Rio Declaration on Environment and Development, as well as Agenda 21, the action plan of the conference, reiterated states' rights to sovereignty over their natural resources and to development. These texts also emphasized the "polluter pays" principle, the idea that those responsible for causing pollution should also be responsible for paying the costs of cleaning it up, and the precautionary principle, the idea that regulations to prevent possible environmental harm should not

*Not have to wait for scientific certainty.*

have to wait until there is full scientific certainty on all aspects of the issue, particularly if the problem would be serious or irreversible.[6] Recent treaties generally include differential obligations for developed and developing states, and include funding mechanisms or provisions for technology transfer. The role of developing states in global environmental politics is discussed further in Chapter 4.

More recently international environmental cooperation has moved further into the realm of regulating hazardous substances with transboundary implications. These include trade in hazardous chemicals and pesticides, regulated by the Rotterdam Convention on the Prior Informed Consent Procedure for Certain Hazardous Chemicals and Pesticides in International Trade (1998), and persistent organic pollutants, regulated under the Stockholm Convention on Persistent Organic Pollutants (2001).

# Instruments of International Environmental Cooperation

*regime*

Any sustained effort at international environmental cooperation can be considered a "regime," within the international relations literature, generally designated as "principles, norms, rules, and decision-making procedures around which actor expectations converge."[7] This designation indicates that international cooperation can take place both formally and informally, within and outside of international institutions, and can happen even without high-level state-run negotiations. Nevertheless, it is useful to look at the specific aspects of international regimes that constitute cooperation to address environmental issues.[8]

*treaties*
*↓*
*2 variation*

The main instrument of international environmental policy is international treaties, sometimes bilateral but most often multilateral. These treaties can be regional or global depending on the scope of the environmental problem and the desires of the actors involved. There are different approaches to the making of international environmental treaties. The two main variations are first, treaties in which regulatory authority is delegated to a committee or organization, and second, convention/protocol processes. In practice, however, many treaties contain aspects of both. In addition, customary international law, legally binding principles that have not been agreed to in any specific negotiation, play a role in international environmental cooperation, as do non-binding international declarations.

The regulatory type of treaty involves empowering a treaty organization (composed of representatives of states) to make regular policies, generally through decisions requiring a supermajority of votes. These decisions, while they bind the states that are members of the treaty, do not require formal ratification and thus allow policy to respond quickly to environmental conditions. Most fisheries treaties and the International Convention for the Regulation of Whaling make annual "schedules" of catch regulations this way. Similarly, the Convention on International Trade in Endangered Species of Wild Fauna and Flora (CITES) uses this type of procedure for changing the status of and therefore also the regulations pertaining to endangered species. But because states can never be bound by international law without their consent and this process allows for regulations to be made with which a minority disagrees, states would not join such an agreement without the possibility to opt out of the decisions made by the group. Generally there is a specific procedure, sometimes called an "objection" or "reservation" procedure, by which a state can indicate its intention not to be bound by a regulation passed in this manner. Unfortunately, states that benefit most from whatever activity is being regulated may be most likely to opt out of the regulations, thereby free riding on the actions taken by other states. These procedures also allow for other states to opt out of the regulation once an initial state has done so, so that states will not have to put up with free riding if they do not want to. This policy sometimes results in a situation in which none of the relevant actors are bound; for example, there are times when all the states whaling in a certain region opted out of the regulations they would have been bound by.[9] Although many complain about opt-out provisions in regulatory treaties, the fact that no state can be bound by international law against its will makes them a necessary evil in this type of treaty. Without them few states would agree to regulation created by less than unanimous voting. When states do opt out, it is possible that scientific evidence, domestic pressure, or diplomatic pressure can persuade them to remove their objection to the regulation in question.

The most common approach to recent environmental treaty-making is the convention/protocol format, in which an initial convention is first negotiated and then followed by the negotiation of protocols and amendments. Often the initial agreement is what is called a framework convention, because it includes a general approach to the issue without requiring specific obligations to reduce environmental damage. It may call for cooperation on research to increase the understanding of the problem, and may include a plan for negotiating binding controls. These protocols, negotiated later, must be fully agreed to by all state representatives and ratified by states, thus making the process more time consuming than the regulatory approach discussed above. But because these conventions and protocols are fully negotiated they also generally are not subject to opt out procedures. On the other hand, states may sign or ratify protocols and amendments at different speeds, so a situation can still exist in which different states are held to different standards. Either the recently popular convention/protocol approach or the regulatory process has an advantage, however, over earlier forms of treaties in which a completely new treaty would be negotiated any time circumstances changed. In international environmental policy understanding of an environmental problem can change rapidly, so treaties that can adapt to new scientific information or new willingness on the part of states to protect the environment are important.      *international law.*

Customary international law is an often overlooked form of international regulation, because it does not come about by a standard negotiation process. Two things are required for a principle to become customary international law: states must act in a way consistent with the principle (by either undertaking an action or refraining from undertaking an action), and they must do so because they believe they are legally obligated to. Evidence that states have through time acted on and recognized a certain set of obligations can be used in international court cases or dispute settlement procedures. An example of this type of law is the obligation that a state may not "use or permit the use of its territory in such a manner as to cause injury ... in or to the territory of another."[10] This principle was deemed customary international law and used to settle a transboundary air pollution dispute between the United States and Canada as early as 1935; it has been frequently cited as a principle of international law despite not being negotiated into a formal treaty.

Also important in international environmental policy is what is known as "soft law,"[11] so called because it is not technically legally binding but nevertheless *soft law.* takes on the character of international law. International organizations may adopt "codes," such as the International Maritime Dangerous Goods Code which determines which products are considered hazardous for shipping and sets up processes for labeling and documenting these goods. Although codes such as this one are not obligatory, they are often taken seriously, amended regularly, and lead to a change in the behavior of the states involved. Declarations made by international organizations such as the United Nations General Assembly can also constitute soft law. For example, UN General Assembly Resolution 44/225 recommended a moratorium on "all large-scale pelagic driftnet fishing on the high seas by 30 June 1992." Although this recommendation was not a legal obligation, many states took action to change their own activities to meet this moratorium and encouraged or persuaded others to do the same.

Large international conferences such as those in Stockholm and Rio (as well as many others that received less international attention) also contribute declarations that, while they do not bind states legally, indicate states' intentions. The Rio Declaration on Environment and Development, for example, proclaims a responsibility by states to "cooperate in a spirit of global partnership to conserve, protect, and restore the health and integrity of the Earth's ecosystem," but does not assign specific requirements by which to do so. More importantly, it declares that "the developed countries acknowledge the responsibility that they bear in the international pursuit of sustainable development in view of the pressures their societies place on the global environment and of the technologies and financial resources they command."[12] Evidence that these types of resolutions are taken seriously can be found both in the seriousness with which they are negotiated, and in the activities of states to ensure their view of what they have agreed to is understood. In this case, the United States released "interpretive statements" on several of the Rio Declaration principles, including the seventh one, quoted above, indicating that it did not accept any international obligations or liabilities stemming from the declaration.[13] The use of soft law allows states to indicate their intentions to act collectively to address international environmental problems (and sometimes some principles about the way in which they will do so) when they may not yet be ready to accept binding obligations.

## Negotiation

The creation of international environmental agreements can be contentious and the outcome uncertain. Nevertheless, a long history of international negotiations has suggested that particular factors are likely to influence the success and outcome of negotiations in potentially predictable ways. Factors examined generally include the interests and power of the actors involved, the number of actors, and characteristics of the problem, including the structure of the issue under negotiation. Problem characteristics take on particular importance in the context of environmental negotiations. In addition, specific types of tools, such as issue linkage, side payments, and threats, can be important in the process of negotiations to protect the global environment. Other decisions to be made in the process of negotiation include whether to approach the issue broadly and with widespread participation, or to focus either on a narrower version of the issue or on states that are more likely to be able to agree.

Examining the process of negotiation involves both an analytical and a prescriptive discussion; what, empirically, are the effects on negotiations of a variety of factors, and given those effects, how should one approach international environmental negotiations? It is also important to acknowledge that most studies of the negotiation process of international environmental agreements look at agreements that have been successfully negotiated. Fewer studies examine negotiations that do not lead to agreements, and fewer still consider issues where negotiation is never even attempted.[14] For that reason, a discussion of how negotiations to address global environmental issues take place should bear in mind the implicit selection bias that underpins most of the existing research, and consideration should be given to whether these features persist in instances when negotiation did not succeed or was not even attempted.

## Interests of Actors

The interests of the individual states involved with an international problem is likely to have an impact on the extent and type of regulation. These interests collectively can shape both the extent to which a cooperative outcome is likely and the particular form of an agreement that does emerge. Realist international relations theory at its most basic, seeing any international cooperation that does emerge as epiphenominal, would suggest that the interests of the individual states are paramount. This phenomenon is, if anything, more likely in issues relating to the environment. Detlef Sprinz and Tapani Vaahtoranta see states as rational self-interested actors. They suggest that the worse the condition of the environment (in an individual state), "the greater the incentives to reduce the ecological vulnerability" of a state. Specifically, they expect states that are the victims of pollution to seek international environmental protection, and those that are net contributors to the problem to resist.[15]

This formulation still leaves room for a determination of how states define their interests, which may not only be as unitary actors or with unchanging preferences. Certain forms of international cooperation that, for example, demonstrate the severity of a problem may alter a state's preferences if it determines it is more harmed by the environmental problem than it believed or discovers that the cost or effectiveness of abatement measures would be different than it thought. Similarly, concerns of sub-state actors for or against international cooperation, and their domestic political power, may influence a state's negotiating position. These factors can still fit within the interests framework, but allow the definition of interests to be broadened.

## Power of Actors

The power of individual actors involved in international negotiation, especially relative to others in the negotiation, is likely to play a role in the outcomes observed. Some argue that international cooperation is unlikely to take place absent a powerful hegemon whose interests an international agreement serves.[16] Notably, such cooperation would therefore be unlikely if it were not in the interests of the hegemonic actor. In addition, international negotiation on issues that require near universal participation to be effective gives negotiating power to actors not typically thought of as being powerful in international relations. In particular, large developing countries, not responsible for causing most of the environmental damage in question but capable of causing it in the future, gain negotiating influence due to their "power to destroy" a resource.[17] They can refuse to participate until an agreement is reached on their terms, and thus demonstrate power on environmental issues when they would not have such power in many other international issues where their participation is less necessary.

Related to this concept is the question of whether cooperation is easier when actors are homogeneous (as is frequently assumed in formal examinations of cooperation theory) or heterogeneous. Conventional international relations theory would hold that heterogeneity of actors (in terms of size, power, and interests) makes cooperation more likely, in part because of the possibility that a powerful actor (a hegemon) can undertake the provision or coordination of a cooperative outcome that can then benefit others. Those who study local commons, on the other hand, find that homogeneity of actors is more conducive to cooperation.[18] The advantages of a hegemon in international relations may be outweighed by the advantages of actors with similar interests and a shared community in a local commons. What is yet to be determined is which factor weighs more heavily in addressing issues of the international commons.

## Number of Actors

The above issues are not unrelated to the number of actors involved in a negotiation. The number of actors addressing a collective action problem is thought in general to have an impact on the likelihood and type of cooperation emerging to address it. The effect of different numbers of actors, however, is the subject of some disagreement. Most analysis suggests that collective action is more difficult with larger numbers of actors than with small numbers. The increased difficulty of cooperation with greater numbers of actors comes from increased difficulty of monitoring, ensuring compliance,[19] and increased transactions costs more broadly.[20] Duncan Snidal points out, however, that those who study local common pool resource issues do not tend to find a strong effect from increasing numbers of actors, although even these studies suggest that cooperation may be easier with smaller groups.[21] It is worth noting that while the number of states may be different in different efforts at cooperation, they are not the only relevant actors when considering numbers.[22] When dealing with environmental issues there may be large numbers of domestic actors that have to change their behavior to address a problem. This assessment of the effect of number of actors may be even more important than the number of states in analysis of negotiation and of the success of international cooperation.

In part because of the role that numbers of actors may play in international negotiations, one aspect that needs to be considered in deciding how to negotiate a treaty is whether to involve all possible states or limit the number to those specifically interested in the issue or willing to take strong regulatory action. Since international treaties are negotiated such that all involved must agree to their provisions before signing, they often fall prey to the "least common denominator" level of regulation that is acceptable to those involved. Some therefore advocate including only those states that are willing to undertake serious commitments, or those that contribute to the problem. Two potential problems result from limiting the number of states involved in a treaty negotiation. If a state not participating is an important actor in the issue area but unwilling to take serious action, a treaty without that state will have little positive effect on the environment. And if the states not involved are developing countries or those that may contribute little to the problem or care little about it, but have the potential to contribute to the problem in the future, excluding them from negotiations may make it more difficult to gain their participation later. From their perspective it is only fair to have a say in rules they might ultimately be expected to abide by. More importantly, because they cannot be bound without their consent, big developing states that are not included in the negotiating process of an international convention may stay outside the process and refuse to modify their impact on the global environment.

Limiting participation works best when the issue in question is not a global commons problem but is instead geographically bounded; the Mediterranean Action Plan is an example of a regional agreement to protect a variety of aspects of the Mediterranean Sea that involves all the major states in the region. There is no particular reason to involve those outside of the region and doing so would probably have hampered negotiation. In fact, negotiators intentionally limited how they defined the problem in order to limit the number of states that would be involved in the negotiation and increase the likelihood of substantive cooperation.[23] Nonenvironmental cooperative efforts, such as that of the North Atlantic Treaty Organization (NATO), however, reaffirm the belief that the way a problem is defined and the issue of which states to involve are not inherent aspects of an issue but rather constructed socially and simultaneously.[24] Even in reasonably clear-cut cases like Mediterranean pollution or European acid rain any decision to keep a negotiation limited comes from greater consideration than simple environmental characteristics of the regime. In the Mediterranean example, in fact, the exclusion of states from which water reaches the Mediterranean Sea but that are not contiguous to the sea itself actually makes addressing some of the pollution in the region more difficult. But the relationship among the states that were included in negotiations was perhaps more amenable to cooperation. The more we learn about the complexity and reach of environmental problems the harder it may be to achieve small-scale negotiations.

## Issue Structure

Several important characteristics of environmental issues influence negotiations on international environmental issues. The extent to which an environmental issue is excludable – whether or not states can keep others from enjoying the benefits of a protected environment – affects the potential negotiating positions of relevant states. If no one can be excluded from use of a protected resource, even if that individual or state did not contribute to protecting it, actors benefit from free riding on the provision of that environmental protection. If a large number of actors, realizing they do not have to contribute to the protection of a resource in order to enjoy access, fail to contribute, insufficient resources will be mustered and the resource will not be protected at all. If enough actors with enough resources care about provision of the good, however, they can get together to create it, even though they will not be able to exclude those who did not help provide it from benefiting from it.[25] Similarly, if the resources to be protected *are* excludable, such as species resources that reside in a particular state, protection may be more easily accomplished by excluding access of outsiders if the state in question is sufficiently motivated to protect the resource. But if it is not, those outside the area may have even less ability to influence its protection.

The extent to which a resource is subtractable – whether or not use of the resource by one actor diminishes that resource's value to another actor – affects the extent to which all actors must be brought into an international negotiation. For a subtractable good like a fishery, any fish that is caught is not available for use by others (or for reproduction in the ocean). If states or fishers cooperate to agree to limit their fishing, they may nevertheless fail to protect the resource if there are others not part of that cooperative agreement that can come in to take fish. This "power to destroy" gives those actors that use the resource but that might not want to participate in protecting it a lot of power. Because they are needed in any cooperative arrangement for it to succeed in protecting the resource, they can often extract large concessions in order to be persuaded to join.

|  |  | Excludable | |
|---|---|---|---|
|  |  | Y | N |
| Subtractable | Y | Private goods | Common Pool Resources → *Envt.* |
|  | N | Club Goods | Public Goods |

*subtractable?*

Figure 1. Types of goods

*public good.*

The ways that these characteristics combine give structure to an issue. Environmental problems are often defined as public goods,[26] though in reality few fit the true definition. A public good is not subtractable and not excludable. It is for this reason that public goods are underprovided, since states cannot be kept from the benefits of the cooperation undertaken by others and therefore are tempted to free ride. Though much of the international cooperation literature focuses on the provision of public goods, the subtractable nature of almost all environmental issues prevents them from fitting into this category, and means that cooperation over environmental issues faces challenges not faced in other types of international cooperation.

The most appropriate description for most environmental issues is that they are common pool resources. In addition to being nonexcludable (and hence underprovided), they are also subtractable, which means that one actor's use of them *does* influence the ability of other actors to use them.[27] At first glance environmental resources may not look like they would be subtractable – after all, one person's use of a healthy ozone layer does not influence someone else's ability to benefit from the UV protection it provides. But what is subtractable in this case is the ability to pollute without causing harm, and the influence that has on the ability of others to use the resource in that way. The relevant issue is the provision of a healthy ozone layer, and if one state chooses to destroy the ozone layer there is nothing others can do to prevent that.[28] This subtractability is easier to understand in resource issues. Hunting is a classic example of the danger of subtractability: the number of elephants killed by poachers directly impacts the number of elephants someone else can kill, or that remain for nonconsumptive uses or reproduction.

*Elephant Example. Subtractability.*

This element of subtractability is one of the things that can make protecting the environment difficult and can influence the negotiating power of a subset

*→ projected ability to do harm.*

of states willing to hold out on cooperation. Unlike public goods that can be provided by one or several actors who care enough and have sufficient resources to provide them, common pool resources cannot necessarily be provided by a subset of relevant actors. The subtractability exhibited in common pool resources means that any one actor may have the ability to destroy the resource, even if others want to protect it. In a fishery, one fisher that refuses to limit fishing while others do can alone prevent the resource from being sustainably managed. So the actor that is willing to destroy (or simply unsustainably consume) the resource, or to threaten credibly to do so, can gain concessions from those who want instead to protect the resource. Subtractability of an issue is therefore one source of power for some states in international negotiations, and one source of variation across issues.

It is possible for environmental issues to have characteristics of excludability, while remaining subtractable, which would classify them as private goods. Species that do not migrate across borders are an example of an excludable resource, since states can deny access to those species to actors from other states. Even those species that do migrate might be excludable to those outside of the areas where the species are located. Imposition of 200-mile Exclusive Economic Zones (EEZs) was an effort to create excludability for a set of resources; states gained control over the ocean resources within 200 miles of their coastlines. This effort was imperfect for a number of these resources, since some fish species swim further out to sea or into a neighbor's EEZ, and undersea oil fields may straddle EEZs. But this policy change was nevertheless an effort to change the character of the issue.

The level of excludability changes the dynamics of the bargaining situation, by giving influence to states that can exclude others from their resources. This change can be seen in one of the proposed solutions to Hardin's tragic commons. It is suggested that privatizing the commons, which makes them excludable, could prevent ruin.[29] In the example of the cow pasture, if the land were divided among the herders then an individual herder could keep everyone else's cows off privately held land. Others could not harm the land, nor could they reap its benefits. The herder with excludable rights could demand compensation for access to the resources, and short of using physical force, others would have no choice but to give it or forego access.

Finally, though it may seem that club goods – those that are both excludable and not subtractable – would have little relevance to the discussion of international environmental issues, the way states choose to regulate internationally may be able to transform common pool resources into club goods at the point of regulation. Recent efforts in several different regional fishery management organizations acknowledge that while the fishery itself is a common pool resource, a club good can be made out of the market for fish products. States within a given fishery organization agree only to buy and sell fish products with other states that are also within the fishery organization. The market in fish products is therefore transformed into a club to which states may be willing to agree to fishery conservation to be able to gain access.[30]

These variables can be considered as binary (an issue is either excludable or not; subtractable or not), but in reality they are more likely to form a sort of spectrum. Among issues that are considered subtractable – fisheries and forests, for instance – there can be varying degrees of subtractability. A forest, which can be completely harvested and then replanted, may be considered as less subtractable than a fishery, which cannot be recreated once harvested past the level at which fish can reproduce. Similar variation can be seen across excludability. Moreover, some elements of excludability are not necessarily given in a resource but may be created, as the EEZ example and the fish trade restrictions suggest. But, most importantly, they influence the different incentives faced by actors attempting to negotiate international cooperation on environmental issues.

## Problem Characteristics

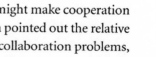

There are many additional aspects of any problem for which international cooperation might be appropriate that will impact the ease of negotiations to address it. Many of the characteristics relevant at the negotiations stage emerge as well when addressing compliance with and effectiveness of negotiated measures. The variety of these factors and their impact on different stages of international cooperation make it particularly difficult to evaluate what leads to effective international cooperation.

There are certain types of problem characteristics that might make cooperation easier. Early international relations theories on cooperation pointed out the relative ease of addressing coordination problems compared with collaboration problems, largely because of the implications for compliance.[31] Once a solution has been found to a coordination problem (right of way in international airspace, for instance) no one has a reason not to uphold it, whereas in collaboration problems (such as the prisoners' dilemma or the tragedy of the commons, discussed further below) an actor can always improve individual utility by not living up to the agreement. While this might appear to be an issue only of compliance, discussed further below, it is likely that states will be more willing to negotiate agreements when they believe that actors will uphold the deals they make. On the other hand, arriving at the initial agreement may be more difficult in situations structured

coordination – collaboration  ?

as coordination games, because although all actors benefit from bringing their behavior into agreement, some may lose more than others from the coordinated arrangement that is reached. Take, for example, the decision of an international language for air traffic control. Once the language has been chosen – in this case, English – no pilot would choose to fly internationally without being able to understand the common language. But before it was chosen, states had a strong incentive to push for their language to be chosen, and an incentive to hold out on agreeing to a language that would require additional training for their pilots. So while they will likely live up to a chosen standard afterward, they may put up a bigger fight in the actual creation of the standard.

Other characteristics of the problem may be particularly important in environmental issues. Who causes and who suffers from the environmental harm will certainly have implications for how issues are negotiated. This is an aspect of what Oran Young identifies as asymmetries in the environmental issue.[32] While this can refer to any number of differences between actors pertaining to the environmental problem, one major aspect is the difference between true commons problems, in which all parties contribute to the harm and all suffer from it (though outside the game-theoretic world parties rarely do so equally) and directional transboundary problems, in which some states may simply be net polluters and others net recipients of pollution. A true commons problem provides greater incentives for all individuals to be involved in negotiations, since all will benefit from collective regulation that prevents a tragedy. A directional transboundary issue, such as acid rain or river pollution, provides little incentive in and of itself for polluters at the head end of the directional problem to participate. But some of these problems may be overcome by issue linkages, including simple payoff schemes.

Others, as discussed further in the section on effectiveness, come up with additional characteristics on which to classify the differences between environmental issues and how easy or hard they are to address. Some of these include such issues as whether conflicts in the environmental problem are about means, values, or relative or absolute gains.[33] Others focus more on the different preferences of the actors.[34] In any case, it is clear that some environmental problems will lead to easier negotiation than will others.

## Issue Linkage

Many international relations theorists see issue linkage as an important tool in international negotiations[35]; states may choose to link their agreement on one issue (within or outside a specific negotiation) to action others take on other issues within the negotiation or even outside of the issue area. Given the potential for issue linkage in negotiation on environmental issues, a question that arises is whether it is more beneficial to negotiate a multi-issue treaty or stick fairly narrowly to one specific issue. The most common example of a multi-issue treaty is the United Nations Convention on the Law of the Sea, which addresses almost every issue relating to oceans. Multi-issue treaties allow for direct issue-linkage within the negotiating process, so that states that might have different priorities can trade off their positions and agree to something they might not want in return for a different regulation that is important to them. In addition, many environmental problems *are* linked to each other, and addressing one aspect without including all can lead to a situation of proliferating regulations that do not take into consideration the effect of their rules outside their narrowly defined issue area. For example, regulations on forestry will have an impact on biodiversity and global climate change and vice versa, and if these issues are addressed separately these links may not be taken into account. On the other hand, the Law of the Sea Convention took eight years to negotiate and ultimately was so politicized that it was not ratified by some of the most important states in the process for decades. At least in part for this reason, narrowly defined environmental treaties are now the most common type.

## Environmental Aid and Economic Sanctions

Within the international relations literature, aid, particularly within the context of convincing states to join treaties, can be seen as essentially a side-payment, which is also a type of issue-linkage. A state's behavior in one area (a treaty) that it may not be particularly concerned about is linked to something else (a type of aid) that it is. Using side-payments is a well-known strategy for encouraging international cooperation. Aid can also been seen within an international relations framework as an effort to change a state's preferences – changing the payoffs, in a game-theoretic structure. If a state's preference ordering is changed from preferring to stay out of a cooperative arrangement to preferring to join, due to aid, cooperation becomes more likely.

The threat and imposition of economic harm has similarly long been a foreign policy tool used to convince states to change their behavior. It is also used to change a state's calculation of interest in taking a particular position. Although persuading states to join environmental treaties is likely to meet with far less resistance than some of the other purposes for which sanctions are threatened, it is a controversial tool in international environmental negotiation. It nevertheless has been used to persuade states to negotiate internationally or to agree to measures they might not otherwise have chosen to accept.[36]

Some of the tools used to bring states into international environmental agreements have potential problems. Environmental aid presents the possibility of moral hazard.[37] If states only take a desired action when they receive aid, will they only continue to take that action as long as aid is provided? Will it be possible to convince them of the benefit of undertaking the action in question, or will they simply do it for the payoff? Moreover, paying states to take a beneficial action may have longer-run effects if states learn that they do not have to take action to protect the resource. It is conceivable that states that might have taken some action on their own will discover that if they hold out they can get side-payments, raising the cost of negotiating agreements and the likelihood that they will not be completed. Economic threats, while occasionally effective, can be seen as internationally illegitimate, and may conflict with international obligations or aspirations for free trade. These tools are all used, however, in negotiation of agreements to protect the environment, and may make them possible where they otherwise would not have been.

## Implementation, Compliance, and Enforcement

It is obviously not sufficient for states to agree to take action to protect the global environment if they do not then put these regulations into practice. The situation may be worse where states agree to environmental measures but then do not implement them than when they do not agree to cooperate in the first place, because public pressure may decrease if people believe that the issue has been addressed. It is therefore important to determine what increases the chances that states will change their behavior in accord with international environmental agreements they have negotiated, and how to best create agreements that will not only achieve compliance, but increase the likelihood that we can detect and address non-compliance. The theoretical connection between issues of negotiation and compliance becomes clear as well. Many of the factors that increase the chances of negotiating an agreement likely relate to the chances that it will be implemented and upheld. While that is useful information for those involved with addressing these problems, it provides more difficulty for those studying them, since the two stages cannot be studied entirely independent of one another.

Aside from possible (and potentially serious) difficulties determining what states or sub-state actors are doing, compliance with international environmental agreements should be a reasonably simple proposition. In most cases, states will benefit if all states live up to the obligations they have taken on, because environmental conditions will improve. So why might states not comply with international environmental agreements? How much of a concern does that pose, and what can be done about it?

The question of why states might not comply with international environmental agreements takes us back to one of the central articles in environmental studies and the idea of the "tragedy of the commons." Garrett Hardin in 1968 observed the difficulty of achieving environmental cooperation, with an analogy to medieval cow herders who all kept their cows on commonly-held land. He observed that each herder gains the full positive utility of every new cow put onto the common pasture, but that the negative utility (also seen as environmental externalities) of each new cow is shared by all, with that cow's herder thus only bearing a fraction of the cost of the additional cow. Even if there is a set number of cows the pasture can support, each individual herder, doing a cost–benefit analysis, will always find it advantageous to add another cow. Moreover, this logic remains even if a given cow herder knows that the next cow added to the pasture will push the ecosystem past its carrying capacity and thus ruin the commons for everyone. As long as one herder cannot be sure that another herder will add the extra cow, the first herder will have an incentive to do so. Practicing restraint can lead to the worst possible outcome: if you decide to forego the benefits of adding an extra cow but someone else does; you have thereby not gained the benefits of the extra cow and you still bear the cost of the destroyed ecosystem.[38]

While some have pointed to the lack of inevitability in this formulation (and the historical inaccuracy of the analogy),[39] it is nevertheless a useful starting point for understanding the difficulties of cooperation, and the incentives to cheat on agreements even once they have been made. This analogy is nearly identical to the game-theoretic formulation of the prisoners' dilemma, used by so many to explain both the difficulties and advantages of international cooperation.[40] Work on this subject suggests that international cooperation is, of course, possible, and made more likely under certain conditions, such as when actors can be made to care more about gains in the future than in the present, and when the interaction is likely to be repeated.[41]

When applied particularly to global environmental issues, some of these factors change slightly. For instance, the role of free riders takes on increased significance in common pool resource problems, for reasons explained above. In these situations, in which the environmental good is both nonexcludable and subtractable, a state that does not comply risks undermining the entire system,[42] as does the cow herder who adds the final cow to the tragic commons.

This aspect makes compliance with, and participation in, international environmental agreements more important than in some other situations of international cooperation.

In order to determine when a state is complying with an international environmental agreement, it would seem reasonable to examine the obligations of the agreement, examine the behavior of states, and determine whether they coincide. While that may certainly constitute evidence of an agreement's influence, it should not immediately be seen as an indication of compliance per se. When state behavior reflects internationally negotiated agreements, there are several possible interpretations of the situation. It may be, as is likely the case with Scandinavian states in the Convention on Long-Range Trans-boundary Air Pollution,[43] that these states are doing what they would have done even in the absence of an international obligation to do so, most likely because their actions have localized benefits, or because domestic pressure demands action. It may be that the same action that inspired the regulation independently inspired actors to change their behavior. An example of this relationship may be seen within the United States when information about ozone depletion was publicized in the early 1970s. Laws passed by Congress ending the use of cholorofluorocarbons in nonessential aerosols coincided with a public demand for alternative products. The law and the decreased public consumption can be seen as both deriving from new scientific information, rather than one directly causing the other. While they are related, it is not clear that the law was the primary determinant in the change of behavior. In other words, determining when states change their activities to coincide with international environmental obligations may be difficult. If we want to learn how to make strong international environmental institutions, we need to figure out what it is that makes states change environmentally damaging behavior.

## Conditions for Compliance

In his classic observation about international law, Louis Henkin suggests that "almost all nations observe almost all principles of international law and almost all of their obligations almost all of the time."[44] Examination of international cooperation generally and cooperation to address environmental issues specifically suggests certain conditions that may increase the likelihood of compliance with international agreements. Characteristics of states – the extent to which a state has control over the actions of its sub-state actors, for instance, or its general regulatory approach – are likely to make a difference,[45] as are aspects of the international agreement itself, such as monitoring or enforcement provisions or who has to make changes to implement the agreement.

Discussion of how to gain compliance leaves open two important questions. The first is whether we actually need complete compliance, and the second is what general approach is likely to lead to the greatest degree of compliance. To the first question, the answer is a somewhat qualified no: most systems of cooperation can survive less than complete compliance by at least some of the members some of the time. While the problem with free riders is more serious for commons problems than other types of issues, and certainly full-scale non-compliance by particularly important actors would make a difference, perfect compliance by all actors is unlikely to be necessary.

Moreover, when a state's behavior does not appear to be in complete alignment with international accords, it should not necessarily be taken as an indication that the agreements are not influencing international behavior. As an analogy, think of speed limits on highways. At any given point, a large percentage of cars are going faster than the posted speed, and thus are in technical non-compliance with the regulation. At the same time, the speed of almost all cars on the road is likely influenced by the speed limit. Their behavior, while not living up to the standard exactly, is likely closer to the regulated speed than it would be if there were no limit or if the limit were different. It is thus possible to have rules with a very low level of compliance, strictly defined, that nevertheless have a dramatic influence on behavior. This change in behavior may be sufficient to impact the underlying concern.

The question of what creates the greatest degree of compliance leads to a debate between what have been called the managerial and enforcement models of international law. The idea that international cooperation requires enforcement is the more traditional approach, at least from international relations scholars. There is certainly evidence of states or sub-state actors attempting to cheat on their international obligations; usually, if they choose to do so they succeed. As discussed in chapter 7, the former Soviet Union systematically assisted its whalers in non-compliance with the International Convention for the Regulation of Whaling. Other information that has come to light since the fall of the Soviet Union suggests that the USSR did not comply with other international environmental obligations: the military dumped not only oil waste but also high-level nuclear waste at sea.[46] The enforcement model looks to ways in which states can be made to live up to their international obligations, either by imposing specific penalties for non-compliance (which may be as diffuse as the increased difficulty of finding cooperation partners in the future if you cheat on your current obligations or as specific tit-for-tat retaliation for those who do not do what they have agreed to do), or by "systems for implementation review" that may point out when states are not living up to their agreements.[47] It is worth noting, however, that in international environmental agreements the use, or even inclusion, of formal compliance mechanisms is rare; states, for a variety of reasons, are hesitant to coerce others to follow the rules they have agreed to. Important exceptions to this observation exist, although (as with the U.S. threats of economic sanctions used to compel action in the case of whaling, discussed in chapter 7) they are frequently about gaining participation rather than compliance.

The managerial approach, while discussed through much of the history of examining international cooperation, gained a higher profile from the work of Abram and Antonia Chayes. This perspective suggests that non-compliance is often unintentional rather than calculated. States may not comply because they are not aware of what sub-state actors are doing or because they do not have effective control over their borders or the funding to put toward environmental priorities. By logical extension, the best way to avoid non-compliance would be through consultation and assistance, rather than by using strict enforcement mechanisms.[48] The "systems for implementation review" identified by David Victor, Kal Raustiala, and Eugene Skolnikoff most frequently take this form; when states were found to be in non-compliance with their obligations under the Montreal Protocol on substances that deplete the ozone layer and were required to go through the official non-compliance procedure under the agreement, they ultimately were granted financial assistance and more time to comply.[49] There are certainly potential difficulties with the managerial model. As indicated, states that choose not to comply with international environmental agreements are likely to continue to do so, despite assistance; Soviet whalers who withheld true catch statistics from the International Whaling Commission would not have been deterred by aid or technical assistance, but might have been if an international observer system had been in place to detect their lack of compliance. Most recent work on compliance in international environmental law implicitly approaches the topic with a managerial bias,[50] although there is evidence for the advantages of both approaches under different circumstances.

One link between the two approaches may be action taken by sub-state actors. In some cases states may legitimately want to change their environmental behavior, but have difficulty controlling the action of those whose behavior must actually change for the state to comply with international environmental agreements. Brazil, for instance, has difficulty upholding species and timber regulations in the Amazon rainforest, where it is difficult to monitor what individual actors are doing.[51] Likewise, post-Soviet Russia has much less control over its borders than it did during the era of centralized political authority.[52]

Of relevance to this question, Ronald Mitchell has demonstrated that the point of regulation in international environmental agreements can have an enormous influence on compliance through regulating actors whose behavior it is easier to monitor. He found that regulations on how much oil an individual oil tanker can discharge into the ocean were far less successful than equipment regulations imposed on the far smaller number of shipyards that build oil tankers, primarily because it is much easier to monitor the behavior of a few big actors than many small dispersed ones.[53]

The focus on compliance also brings up the possibility that international *[binding vs non binding]* environmental cooperation can best be achieved through nonbinding agreements rather than, as many have assumed, treaties. Victor et al. suggest that while compliance may be higher with legally binding treaties, implementation – behavior change and thus ultimate effect on the environment – may be more significant in some cases with nonbinding measures. Such measures may tend to be more ambitious and therefore have a lower level of compliance, but the actual degree of behavior change under them may be greater. The case that provides the best support for this conclusion is the international regime to regulate trade in pesticides and chemicals through the process of prior informed consent (PIC). Prior to its integration into the Rotterdam Convention on the Prior Informed Consent Procedure for Certain Hazardous Chemicals and Pesticides in International Trade, an informal regime existed. Victor argues that there was no evidence of non-compliance with this regime and that its informal nature allowed it to adapt to changing circumstances and adopt stricter regulations than would have been possible with a binding agreement.[54] Nevertheless, that the states involved decided to create a legally binding treaty rather than continue with the informal process suggests that some find binding obligations valuable.

## Effectiveness

Ascertaining effectiveness of international environmental cooperation is difficult for a number of reasons. First is definitional: what should be considered to constitute an effective international environmental agreement? Until recently, a focus within international relations on issues of compliance led to a bias in favor of examining the influence of an international regime on the actors (both state and sub-state) it was intended to regulate. This aspect is important and should not be overlooked; if international cooperation cannot succeed in changing the behavior of actors whose original behavior has been causing environmental problems, it is reasonable to consider it ineffective. Behavioral effectiveness also has the advantage of being relatively easy to measure. Although there are difficulties in determining what it is that individual actors are doing (and, more importantly, why they are doing it), it is a much more straightforward way to try to determine the impact of a regime than other methods. Many studies simply examine whether actor behavior lines up with that prescribed by the regime.

What most people would really like to know about an international regime's effectiveness, however, is whether it actually has a positive impact on the environment: is the natural environment better because of international regulatory efforts than it would have been otherwise? Although few large-scale studies have been able to address this issue, due to problems discussed below, the trend in the literature is at least to pay lip service to the idea that what should really be examined is the effect of cooperative efforts on environmental quality. Some progress has been made in determining how effective specific environmental regimes have been at protecting the environment.

The most important difficulty in determining effectiveness is logistical: how would you know whether a regime has succeeded at protecting the environment? On the face of it, evidence that the environmental problem has improved would tend to suggest that the cooperative effort has been effective, and evidence that it has not would suggest otherwise. But it is entirely possible to have improvement in the environment, happening at the same time as international regulation, that is nevertheless not caused by the regulation. The improvement may be a coincidence, or (similarly) due to some natural fluctuation in an environmental resource that has nothing to do with what human action has produced. Fish stocks, some of which go through large cycles that people do not fully understand, may have a beneficial upswing at the same time that international cooperative effects emerge to protect them, for example.[55]

Similarly, a decrease in environmental quality does not necessarily indicate that cooperative efforts are not succeeding. The same natural cycles may – and empirically, often seem to – bring together increased regulatory efforts and natural declines in environmental quality. As the environmental problem gets worse, regulation becomes more likely, and thus international environmental cooperation may begin at a particularly low point for the natural resource. Related is an issue of measurement. If there is a time lag in mitigating the problem, even if it will ultimately improve, there may be increased levels of environmental degradation from the point at which cooperation began. The volume of ozone-depleting substances in the upper atmosphere has not only not dropped but is increasing. The annual thinning of the ozone layer over Antarctica is still getting larger every year.[56] Does this mean that human activities to protect the ozone layer are ineffective? Not likely. Some ozone-depleting substances have residence times in the atmosphere of up to a century. Even if the response to the earliest hypothesis in the 1970s about the possible human impact on the ozone layer had resulted in an immediate cessation of all use of ozone-depleting substances, the ones emitted prior to that point would still be depleting the ozone layer for decades to come. Effectiveness may be difficult to measure – and, likewise, adjust policies to augment – in a simple regulatory time-frame. These time lags in demonstrated effectiveness make it particularly difficult to gain political action to address a problem that will not improve until after the politicians in question have retired from public office, while any potential costs to change behavior come in the short term.

In addition, although still probably evidence of ineffective environmental management, one of the reasons the environment may fail to recover even when cooperative efforts have been undertaken may be that these efforts are too late: a tipping point has been reached, beyond which recovery is unlikely or much more difficult. Species that have become extinct, or even simply too low in population, are not going to be able to recover. A fundamental shift in the climate system is suggested as one of the possible results of climate change; if that happens, no amount of cooperation to reduce carbon emissions may be able to change the climate back to what it once was. In fact, given the difficulty of gaining political support for cooperation to address issues about which there is uncertainty, we may be chronically predisposed to negotiate agreements at points when the environmental problem has shown sufficient evidence of its seriousness that making the situation better becomes harder.

Most importantly, however, a decline in environmental quality coincident with international cooperative efforts can still happen in the face of effective environmental management. What we really need to know is what would have happened to the environment counterfactually – without international cooperation. International regulatory measures may in fact be quite effective at decreasing the amount of damage humans do to the global ecosystem, but not mitigate them completely, even within a particular issue area. In the case of ozone depletion, it is relatively simple to plot the amount of ozone-depleting substances that would have been put into the stratosphere if use of these substances had continued to increase at the rate at which they were already increasing, and infer from that the level of damage to the environment without regulation. Many have shown the much lower level of stratospheric ozone-depleting substances than would have been likely without regulation.[57]

A final difficulty at evaluating effectiveness of international environmental cooperation is the multiple causes there can be for some environmental problems. On the one hand, it may seem foolish to speak of the effectiveness of a program to address an environmental problem that stops only one source of the problem, while others continue to operate and worsen the problem. If the agreements to protect the ozone layer had only regulated chlorofluorocarbons, it could legitimately have been seen as ineffective for leaving out other substances, such as halons, that destroy the ozone layer even more effectively through similar mechanisms. On the other hand, some of the multiple impacts on an environmental problem may be diverse and unconnected. While protection of whales from overharvesting has been difficult enough to accomplish effectively, new evidence has emerged that global climate change may have a serious impact on the well-being of the world's population of whales.[58] In this case, the regime set up to prevent overharvesting of whales from commercial whaling is beginning to consider this possible new cause of harm to whales (though there is likely little it can do as an organization in terms of prevention of damage), but it may be unrealistic to expect any single cooperative process to address all potential causes of an environmental problem. At worst, some environmental cooperation may be no better than rearranging deck chairs on the Titanic. Such actions can even be counterproductive by suggesting that steps have been taken to address a problem when they have not been, and thus leaving the public to believe that the issue is no longer worthy of attention. But as suggested above, an effort that may not be effective at completely eliminating a given problem may still mitigate it to an extent greater than if no cooperative solution had been attempted. In some cases that may be far better than nothing.

## Conditions for Effectiveness

While we may not be entirely clear about how effectiveness is to be measured, there has nevertheless been some progress in ascertaining the conditions under which environmental agreements may be more or less effective. Certainly the structure of an environmental problem has some impact on how effectively it is addressed. Who causes the problem, who is most harmed from it, how difficult are the proposed solutions to undertake, and a wide range of other factors can influence the ease with which cooperative efforts will succeed at addressing environmental problems.

*effective regimes*

Peter Haas, Robert Keohane, and Marc Levy suggest that effective regimes are those that build upon existing concern, work with or create capacity, and take place in a reasonable contractual environment.[59] It is easy to understand why these might be important precursors to effective regimes, but far more difficult to ascertain systematically what degree of each of these factors is necessary for success, or whether a large amount of one factor can outweigh the need for another.

A project headed by Oran Young identifies a number of "causal pathways" by which international environmental regimes can be effective: They can modify the utility of a state by giving it a context (or the information) to care about an environmental issue it might not previously have, or an institutional context that can allow states to avoid collective action problems like the tragedy of the commons. Within this context, cooperation can be effective when it allows for the ratcheting up of obligations. Regimes can also bestow authority, creating rules seen as legitimate and thereby followed by actors who do not necessarily undertake a cost–benefit analysis to determine whether to implement their requirements. They can facilitate learning about the nature of the environmental problems or about ways to mitigate it.[60]

A project led by Edward Miles in Seattle, Arild Underdal in Oslo, and others, also addresses conditions for effectiveness of international environmental regimes, by looking at the role that the structure of the problem plays in effectiveness of environmental regimes. They define effectiveness as both the degree of relative improvement and how far the current situation is from a collective optimum; both difficult to measure, but important aspects of the question. Moreover, the major explanatory variables they examine relate to the type of problem (how benign or malign it is, determined by the extent of symmetry of interests, congruity of goals, and extent or nature of cleavages), and characteristics of the regime itself, described as problem-solving capacity and including organizational structures and political capabilities. Ultimately they conclude that most of the regimes they studied made a difference in actor behavior and environmental conditions, but fell short of providing ideal solutions. Moreover, they find that even malign problems, while scoring lower on both elements of effectiveness, have been improved by the regimes to manage them. While their study supports their hypotheses that problem and regime characteristics influence effectiveness, they also find that there are pathways to effective environmental regimes they do not account for.[61]

A related effort, often referred to as the "Oslo–Potsdam Solution," attempts to formalize the evaluation of effectiveness, measuring effectiveness on a scale of zero to one across many different agreements. It examines the counterfactual of what would be expected if there had been no regime, evaluates the performance of the regime that exists, and compares it to a potential collective optimum that could potentially be reached.[62] The most complicated aspects of this effort are determining a no-regime counterfactual and calculating the collective optimum, which different scholars have done by game-theoretic modeling and consultation of experts, among other approaches. These approaches have been criticized for ignoring the possibility of multiple non-cooperative solutions within game theory and for how empirical evaluations of very different issues are translated into a comparable score.[63] But any effort to determine the effectiveness of international environmental agreements will have to be able to compare across issue areas and also to determine effectiveness relative to what would have happened without agreement.

Among the most important large-scale evaluations of international environmental agreements is a project by Ronald Mitchell that attempts to characterize all existing international environmental agreements. The project is working to code characteristics of existing agreements and make possible a comparison of treaties and their provisions with environmental conditions and state (and non-state actor) behavior over time. He observes that effectiveness in agreements comes less from the inclusion of certain types of provisions for monitoring and enforcement, and more from "ensuring that agreements contain provisions that are responsive to the type of problem being addressed."[64]

Efforts to explain true environmental effectiveness of international cooperation is of necessity in its infancy, as most of the major international agreements have been around for less than three decades, and the environmental problems they address are long-lived and complex. Attempts to understand what factors make international environmental cooperation more or less effective is likely to be one of the most important aspects of research into the politics of the global environment.

## Conclusion

Overall, the extent and variety of efforts at international environmental cooperation are impressive. States have been willing to undertake potentially costly action to prevent or mitigate environmental problems for which there is initially only theoretical evidence. They have created ways to negotiate international agreements that allow them to respond to changing information to modify obligations accordingly. And early evidence suggests that while not all states uphold their obligations all the time, many have acted collectively in ways that either improves or slows the damage to the global environment.

# Notes

1  Ken Conca, *Governing Water: Contentious Transnational Politics and Global Institution Building* (Cambridge, Mass.: MIT Press, 2006), 387.

2  Harold K. Jacobson and Edith Brown Weiss, "A Framework for Analysis," in Edith Brown Weiss and Harold K. Jacobson, eds., *Engaging Countries: Strengthening Compliance with International Environmental Accords* (Cambridge, Mass.: MIT Press, 1998), 1.

3  Sebastian Oberthür and Thomas Gehring, "Reforming International Environmental Governance: An Institutional Perspective on Proposals for a WEO," in Frank Biermann and Steffen Bauer, eds., *A World Environment Organization* (Aldershot: Ashgate, 2005), 206.

4  Ronald B. Mitchell, "International Environmental Agreements: A Survey of Their Features, Formation, and Effects," *Annual Review of Environmental Resources* 28 (2003): 429–61.

5  Elizabeth R. DeSombre, *Global Environmental Institutions* (London and New York: Routledge, 2006).

6  Michael Grubb, Matthias Koch, Abby Munson, Francis Sullivan, and Koy Thomson, *The Earth Summit Agreements: A Guide and Assessment* (London: Earthscan, 1993).

7  Stephen D. Krasner, "Structural Causes and Regime Consequences: Regimes as Intervening Variables," in Stephen D. Krasner, ed., *International Regimes* (Ithaca and London: Cornell University Press, 1982), 1.

8  The content of this section is drawn partly from Elizabeth R. DeSombre, "International Environmental Policy," in B. Nath, L. Hens, Compton, and D. Devust, eds., *Environmental Management in Practice: Analysis, Implementation, and Policy* (London and New York: Routledge, 1998), 361–77.

9  Patricia Birnie, *International Regulation of Whaling*, vol. I (New York, London, and Rome: Oceana, 1985), 326.

10  Philippe Sands, *Principles of International Environmental Law* (Manchester and New York: Manchester University Press, 1995), 244.

11  Patricia W. Birnie and Alan E. Boyle, *International Law and the Environment* (Oxford: Clarendon Press, 1992), 26.

12  Rio Declaration on Environment and Development, 1992, Principle 7.

13  Grubb et al.

14  Radoslav S. Dimitrov, *Science and International Environmental Policy: Regimes and Nonregimes in Global Governance* (Lanham, Md.: Rowman and Littlefield, 2006).

15  Detlef Sprinz and Tapani Vaahtoranta, "The Interest-Based Explanation of International Environmental Policy," *International Organization* 41(1) (Winter 1994): 77–105.

16 Robert O. Keohane, *After Hegemony: Cooperating and Discord in the World Political Economy* (Princeton: Princeton University Press, 1984); Duncan Snidal, "The Limits of Hegemonic Stability Theory," *International Organization* 30(4) (1985): 579–615.

17 Elizabeth R. DeSombre, "Developing Country Influence in Global Environmental Negotiations," *Environmental Politics* 9(3) (Autumn 2000): 23–42.

18 Duncan Snidal, "The Politics of Scope: Endogenous Actors, Heterogeneity, and Institutions," in Robert O. Keohane and Elinor Ostrom, eds., *Local Commons and Global Interdependence* (London: Sage, 1995), 47–70.

19 While the issue of compliance with an agreement may seem to be one that emerges after an agreement has been reached, the potential for noncompliance can preclude the ability to reach agreement in the first place.

20 Kenneth A. Oye, "Explaining Cooperation Under Anarchy: Hypotheses and Strategies," in Kenneth A. Oye, ed., *Cooperation Under Anarchy* (Princeton: Princeton University Press, 1986), 18–20.

21 Snidal, 47, 57–62.

22 Robert O. Keohane and Elinor Ostrom, "Introduction," in Keohane and Ostrom, eds., 6.

23 Peter M. Haas, *Saving the Mediterranean: The Politics of International Environmental Cooperation* (New York: Columbia University Press, 1990).

24 See Snidal, 48.

25 Such hegemony has often been seen as a necessary condition for creating global public goods. See Charles Kindleberger, *The World In Depression, 1929–1939* (Berkeley: University of California Press, 1973); Robert O. Keohane, *After Hegemony: Cooperation and Discord in the World Political Economy* (Princeton: Princeton University Press, 1984).

26 See, for example, Susan Sell, "North–South Environmental Bargaining: Ozone, Climate Change, and Biodiversity," *Global Governance* 2 (1996): 97; Andrew Hurrell and Benedict Kingsbury, eds., *The International Politics of the Environment* (Oxford: Oxford University Press, 1992).

27 See Samuel Barkin and George Shambaugh, eds., *Anarchy and the Environment: The International Relations of Common Pool Resources* (Albany: SUNY Press, 1999).

28 David Downie, "Ozone Depletion and Common Pool Resources," in Barkin and Shambaugh, eds.

29 Hardin, 1245.

30 Elizabeth R. DeSombre, "Fishing Under Flags of Convenience: Using Market Power to Increase Participation In International Regulation," *Global Environmental Politics* 5(4) (November 2005): 73–94.

31 Arthur A. Stein, "Coordination and Collaboration: Regimes in an Anarchic World," in Krasner, ed., 115–140.

32 Oran R. Young, *Governance in World Affairs* (Ithaca: Cornell University Press, 1999), 69.

33  See, for instance, Volker Rittberger and Michael Zürn, "Regime Theory: Findings from the Study of 'East–West' Regimes," *Cooperation and Conflict* 26 (1991): 171–72.

34  Arild Underdal, "Patterns of Effectiveness: Examining Evidence from Thirteen International Regimes," paper presented at the International Studies Association Annual Convention, Toronto, March 1997.

35  See, for example, Robert O. Keohane and Joseph S. Nye, *Power and Interdependence: World Politics in Transition* (Boston and Toronto: Little, Brown, and Company, 1977).

36  See, generally, Elizabeth R. DeSombre, *Domestic Sources of International Environmental Policy: Industry, Environmentalists, and U.S. Power* (Cambridge, Mass.: MIT Press, 2000).

37  Robert G. Darst, *Smokestack Diplomacy: Cooperation and Conflict in East–West Environmental Politics* (Cambridge, Mass.: MIT Press, 2001), 46–48.

38  Garrett Hardin, 'The Tragedy of the Commons', *Science* 162 (1968): 1243–48.

39  Susan Jane Buck Cox, "No Tragedy on the Commons," *Environmental Ethics* 7 (Spring 1985): 49–61.

40  See, for example, Robert Axelrod, *The Evolution of Cooperation* (New York: Basic Books, 1984), and Keohane, *After Hegemony*, among others.

41  Oye, 1–24.

42  J. Samuel Barkin and George E. Shambaugh, "Hypotheses on the International Politics of Common Pool Resources," in *Anarchy and the Environment: The International Relations of Common-Pool Resources* (Albany: SUNY Press, 1999), 1–25.

43  Marc A. Levy, "European Acid Rain: The Power of Tote-Board Diplomacy," in Peter M. Haas, Robert O. Keohane, and Marc A. Levy, eds., *Institutions for the Earth: Sources of Effective International Environmental Protection* (Cambridge, Mass.: MIT Press, 1993), 75–132.

44  Louis Henkin, *How Nations Behave: Law and Foreign Policy*, 2nd edn. (New York: Columbia University Press for the Council on Foreign Relations, 1979), 47.

45  See, generally, Brown Weiss and Jacobson, eds.

46  William Zimmerman, Elena Nikitina, and James Clem, "The Soviet Union and the Russian Federation: A Natural Experiment in Environmental Compliance," in Brown Weiss and Jacobson, eds., 313–14.

47  See, generally, David Victor, Kal Raustiala, and Eugene B. Skolnikoff, eds., *The Implementation and Effectiveness of International Environmental Commitments* (Cambridge, Mass.: MIT Press, 1998).

48  Abram and Antonia Chayes, *The New Sovereignty: Compliance with International Regulatory Agreements* (Cambridge: Harvard University Press, 1995).

49  David G. Victor, "The Operation and Effectiveness of the Montreal Protocol's Non-Compliance Procedure," in Victor, Raustiala, and Skolnikoff, eds., 137–76.

50  See, for example, Brown, Weiss, and Jacobson, eds.; and Victor, Raustiala, and Skolnikoff, eds.

51   Murillo de Aragão and Stephen Bunker, "Brazil: Regional Inequalities and Ecological Diversity in a Federal System," in Brown, Weiss, and Jacobson, 475–509.

52   Zimmerman, Nikitina, and Clem, 291–325.

53   Ronald Mitchell, *Intentional Oil Pollution at Sea: Environmental Policy and Treaty Compliance* (Cambridge, Mass.: MIT Press, 1994).

54   David G. Victor, "'Learning by Doing' in the Nonbinding International Regime to Manage Trade in Hazardous Chemicals and Pesticides," in Victor, Raustiala, and Skolnikoff, eds., 221–81.

55   K. Sherman, "Large Marine Ecosystems," in *Encyclopedia of Earth System Science*, vol. II (New York: Academic Press, 1992), 653–73.

56   British Antarctic Survey Bulletin, 19 December 2005, http://www.theozonehole.com/ozonehole2005.htm.

57   UNEP, "BACKGROUNDER: Basic Facts and Data on the Science and Politics of Ozone Protection," November 2005, 5; http://ozone.unep.org/Public_Information/press_backgrounder.pdf.

58   William C. G. Burns, "From the Harpoon to the Heat: Climate Change and the International Whaling Commission in the 21st Century," An Occasional Paper of the Pacific Institute for Studies in Development, Environment, and Security, 2000.

59   Peter M. Haas, Robert O. Keohane, and Marc A. Levy, "The Effectiveness of International Environmental Institutions," in Haas, Keohane, and Levy, eds., 3–24.

60   Oran R. Young and Marc A. Levy (with the assistance of Gail Osherenko), "The Effectiveness of International Environmental Regimes," in Young, ed., *The Effectiveness of International Environmental Regimes* (Cambridge: MIT Press, 1999), 1–32.

61   Edward L. Miles, Arild Underdal, Steinar Andresen, Jørgen Wettestad, Jon Birger Skjaerseth, and Elaine M. Carlin, *Explaining Regime Effectiveness: Confronting Theory With Evidence* (Cambridge, Mass.: MIT Press, 2001).

62   Jon Hovi, Detlef F. Sprinz, and Arild Underdal, "The Oslo–Potsdam Solution to Measuring Regime Effectiveness: Critique, Response, and the Road Ahead," *Global Environmental Politics* 3(3) (August 2004): 74–96.

63   Oran Young, "Inferences and Indices: Evaluating the Effectiveness of International Environmental Regimes," *Global Environmental Politics* 1(1) (February 2001): 99–121.

64   Mitchell, "International Environmental Agreements," 430.

# 3 Science, Uncertainty, and Risk

Uncertainty – of what other states will do, of how serious a threat is – underlies international relations broadly, but is nowhere more important than in the area of the global environment. The causes of many environmental problems are uncertain, as are the effects of a wide variety of proposed solutions. Environmental problems are often addressed as uncertainties are resolved, though in some types of cases resolving uncertainty may make international cooperation more difficult. International agreements are often designed to include research that will help gather the information needed for continued regulation. The designing of international regulation to allow for changes in agreements as uncertainties are resolved is a hallmark of international environmental policy-making. And scientific cooperation may in some cases drive political cooperation, to an extent often not present (or at least not examined) in other international issue areas.

Related, but important to distinguish, is the concept of risk. Risk relates to the probability of the occurrence of an event. In some cases (the chance that a flipped coin will come up heads, for example), probability is easy to determine. The reason that risk and uncertainty are so frequently confused stems from the fact that determining probabilities for many environmental, or political, events is fraught with uncertainty. Risk is a statement about likelihood, but in most cases relevant to this topic the likelihood is fundamentally uncertain. They are thus separate but intertwined issues. Examining risk demonstrates primarily that people, and politicians, do not evaluate risk in the same way that economists or risk assessors do. That disjuncture leads both to a certain predictability about the concerns that will attract the greatest public pressure, and to a concern that the public does not value risk correctly and thus that attention and resources are not allocated in the best possible way.

The role of science and scientists within this framework is also essential, but complicated. A view of science as an objective search for truth must be balanced against an examination of science as politics – what we think we know may depend on who asks what questions. Scientists themselves play political roles, intentionally or not. International agreement may be more likely when there is a community of scholars who share similar approaches and agree on the basic components of a problem. Within the study of environmental politics an objective role for science has been questioned, but within global environmental issues such a role also appears inescapable.

## Uncertainty

Uncertainty can be defined as incomplete information or disagreement between information sources. It occurs in any discipline and is certainly important in any aspect of international relations. Policy makers want to know what other actors will do in order to be able to decide what they should do. The issue becomes more complicated in environmental politics, however, as political uncertainty intersects with scientific uncertainty. It is suggested that "in environmental regulatory affairs we are confronted with data for which neither the level of precision nor the level of accuracy is particularly high."[1]

Scientific uncertainty is given as an underlying cause for the failure to reach prompt international agreements, particularly with respect to environmental issues. Oran Young suggests that science may play a role in influencing the success or failure of the creation of international regimes.[2] The role of science and uncertainty of this sort is essentially functionalist, in that science is seen as a nonpolitical, objective, activity that generates additional information that can be used by the policy-making arena to generate cooperative outcomes.[3] This type of uncertainty is almost always seen to be detrimental to international cooperation. Within international environmental politics there are a number of examples of agreements that have become possible once uncertainty has been diminished. The history of the Montreal Protocol on Substances that Deplete the Ozone Layer is a good example, as increased understanding of the damage caused to the ozone layer, of the increasing numbers of substances that could be held responsible for it, and of the effects of this damage, caused states to agree to stricter controls over time. Likewise, learning that acidifying substances could travel long distances in the air, and the discovery during national assessments of damage that had not previously been noticed, made some states more willing to undertake substantial changes in their emissions of the pollutants that contribute to acid rain.

There are circumstances, however, in which uncertainty may be beneficial. When states considering cooperation to address a problem about which there is uncertainty find out that they do not suffer net harm from a pollutant, these states might be less willing to negotiate mitigation measures. Lawrence Susskind argues that a similar phenomenon was at work in negotiations for the Antarctic Treaty. States were unaware of the existence or extent of mineral wealth in Antarctica, which helped facilitate the negotiation of a minerals regime; if it were demonstrated that valuable minerals were present states would have had a harder time bargaining over who would have access or rights to them.[4] Seong-lin Na and Hyun Song Shin suggest that coalitions to address international environmental problems are easier to form before the resolution of some uncertainties. They argue that information about an environmental issue can help policy makers make more informed decisions, but nevertheless find that "cooperation is more difficult to achieve when the likely winners and losers are known when negotiation takes place." They demonstrate, in a game-theoretic framework, that outcomes achieved with more information are less beneficial overall than are those made under uncertainty.[5] In other words, if we assume that states negotiate strategically to try to get the best deal for themselves, they will be willing only to undertake the minimum action required to benefit. If they do not know, however, exactly how they will be impacted, they are closer to a Rawlsian veil of ignorance in which they will agree to outcomes that make the entire group better off.[6]

The extent to which uncertainty helps or hinders negotiation has yet to be systematically empirically investigated. In addition, there are different types of things about which actors can be uncertain, some of which clearly benefit from being resolved. There is, for instance, a big difference between not understanding the mechanism by which an environmental effect occurs (or even if actual problems will result from hypothesized impacts), and not understanding the costs of abatement measures or which actors will contribute most to or suffer most from the environmental problem. Radoslav Dimitrov argues that we do not need certainty about the full extent or magnitude of an environmental problem to take international action. Rather, the essential characteristic on which uncertainty must be resolved for international cooperation is knowledge about "negative transboundary consequences." If actors are not clearly aware of the problems caused, across borders, from lack of cooperation, they will not be willing to cooperate internationally to address the problems.[7]

*evidence*

Additionally, evidence abounds of use of uncertainty for political ends. Industries most likely to be harmed by regulations to mitigate a suspected environmental problem are likely to play up the existing uncertainties and fund scientific studies to attempt to call the environmental problem into question. The role of the media in many advanced industrialized countries plays into this strategy, by focusing on disagreement or giving equal time to opposing viewpoints.

*How solutions depend on this*

*✱*

International environmental agreements often address legitimate underlying uncertainties in how the agreement is structured. Many recent global or regional environmental agreements begin with framework conventions to which protocols are later added as the cause and magnitude of the harm become clearer and more widely accepted, and the costs of regulation more clearly understood. Most importantly, these initial framework conventions often contain specific processes for scientific cooperation generally, and for gathering information on the environmental issue and state actions. Parties to the Vienna Convention on the Protection of the Ozone Layer agree to cooperate in a wide range of activities relating to investigation of the nature and extent of the problem of ozone depletion.[8] Parties to the Convention on Long-Range Transboundary Air Pollution agree to "initiate and cooperate in the conduct of research" relating to development of technologies for abatement and measurement of pollutants, models for understanding the transmission of air pollutants, and the effects of air pollutants on human health and the environment, and to implement the "Cooperative Programme for the monitoring and evaluation of the long-range transmission of air pollutants in Europe."[9]

Likewise, one of the most important but easily overlooked aspects of uncertainty that generally needs to be resolved is the actual behavior of states with respect to an environmental issue. Most states in the international system are not so economically centralized that they know exactly how much carbon dioxide or CFCs the state as a whole emits. Before any abatement measures can be undertaken, states need to know their contribution to the problem, both to gain a greater understanding of the scope of the environmental problem and because obligations (for pollutants at least) are frequently given as reduction to a certain percentage of emissions from a certain year. That requires that states find out how much they are contributing to the environmental problem, and continually monitor their behavior afterward. To this end, for example, parties to the Framework Convention on Climate Change agree to "develop … and make available … national inventories of anthropogenic emissions by sources and removals by sinks of all greenhouse gases."[10]

# Precautionary Principle

One of the important international efforts to address environmental decision-making under conditions of uncertainty is the precautionary principle, first elaborated in environmental policy in Europe in the 1970s.[11] The principle suggests that uncertainty should not prevent action to mitigate environmental problems. The most widely quoted version appears as Principle 15 of the 1992 Rio Declaration on Environment and Development: "Where there are threats of serious or irreversible damage, lack of full scientific certainty shall not be used as a reason for postponing cost-effective measures to prevent environmental degradation." As the Rio version suggests, the principle is generally taken to be most applicable to cases where environmental damage, if it occurred, would be impossible or difficult to reverse. In addition, most recent versions of the principle focus to some extent on the cost of the action; not requiring every possible action to be taken, but rather suggesting that scientific uncertainty should not be used as an excuse for not taking any action until the uncertainty has been resolved. Stronger forms of the principle suggest not using any new technology (such as genetically modified organisms) until proven safe. This latter formulation is more controversial and less widely accepted.

This precautionary principle has become enshrined in international environmental law, most prominently as the basis for European environmental law under the Treaty on European Union.[12] It is included in various forms in a wide variety of international environmental instruments, from the non–legally binding 1984 Declarations of the International Conferences on the Protection of the North Sea,[13] to its first treaty appearance in the 1985 Vienna Convention on the Protection of the Ozone Layer,[14] to the 1992 Transboundary Watercourses Convention, and the 1992 Framework Convention on Climate Change, among others. Apart from its use, generally in a permissive sense within treaties or in a variety of nonbinding international declarations (allowing states to take action despite uncertainty), the precautionary principle has likely not quite reached the status of customary international law. More recent statements of the principle (such as in the Rio Declaration) do suggest, however, that states are coming to see it as a standard international legal principle. It is also an important corrective to the traditional delaying tactic of requiring more research before taking any action on environmental problems that politicians would rather not endure costs for beginning to address.

It is one that is difficult to apply in practice, however. Daniel Bodansky suggests that it is "too vague to serve as a regulatory standard."[15] William Burns points out that in most of its uses in international environmental law the instruments in which it appears give no guidance about how to apply it.[16] As it currently stands, the principle is open to interpretation. One study found fourteen different versions of the principle in treaties and multilateral declarations,[17] suggesting at minimum that there is not an international consensus on what it entails. Bodansky, moreover, suggests the real question left unanswered is "what types of precautionary actions are warranted and at what price?"[18] The principle does not suggest whether actions should be taken under conditions of uncertainty to prevent all possible risk of harm, or simply to decrease the risk, nor does it give a clear indication about how to decide how much uncertainty is enough to prevent action.

Others critique the principle on philosophical, rather than practical, grounds. Some see it as damaging the role of science by moving away from the requirement of demonstrating cause and effect before taking regulatory action.[19] It is also worth noting the inevitable tradeoffs: in working to mitigate one uncertain risk, say global climate change, we will inevitably take on other uncertain risks, such as potentially lost jobs or wealth. It is for this latter reason that recent statements of the precautionary principle focus more on the cost effectiveness of the measures taken.

## Risk

The evaluation of risk, and the process of making decisions about how best to prioritize the mitigation of risk, is essential in the process of understanding how to respond to environmental problems globally or locally. Addressing risk is also essential in international relations. The ways different sets of scholars have conceptualized and applied the idea of risk is illuminating in determining what role it plays, or should play, in decisions about global environmental problems. It is clear that political decision makers, led by the individuals who elect them, systematically value risk in ways that appear to be economically irrational. What is less clear is how to address these seeming irrationalities, or whether they in fact are irrational at all.

Much discussion of the difficulties of evaluating risk comes from psychology. Cognitive psychologists Paul Slovic, Sarah Lichtenstein, and Baruch Fischhoff and others provided the empirical foundation of risk perception beginning in the 1970s. Their findings suggested that people are generally not adept at judging the likelihood of hazards.[20] Early such experiments asked people to assess the lethality of forty-one different causes of death, and suggested that we tend to underestimate the likelihood of death due to high-frequency causes (like asthma) and conversely overestimate the likelihood of death due to low-frequency causes (like tornadoes).[21] Such research also indicates that experts tend to be more accurate assessors of risk than are laypeople.[22]

Some of these incorrect assessments of risks can be traced back to uncertainty. Because in most social or scientific situations worth evaluating there is insufficient information to allow people to assess the likelihood of an outcome, they apply certain heuristics to help them approach the process of assessing risk. Scholars have identified some of these frames people use to assess probability. These heuristics have systematic biases that can be anticipated. The "representativeness" frame is the belief that events have similar probabilities because of other similarities they share. Rose McDermott gives as an example of this phenomenon attendance at an arms control lecture in which it is known that three-quarters of the audience is academics and one-quarter artists. When attempting to guess the profession of a questioner from the audience, dressed in black, with an earring and a beret, people simply playing the odds should guess that the questioner is an academic, since three in four audience members are. But since the person up for analysis resembles other people we have perceived to be artists, people are more likely to guess "artist" for that person's profession.[23] Daniel Kahneman and Amos Tversky suggest that "people appear to believe in a hologram-like model of personality in which any fragment of behavior represents the actor's true character."[24] In the political realm, people often use historical analogies for current policy events.[25] They may also see international environmental problems as similar (ozone depletion and climate change, for instance) when they share some similar characteristics but are in other ways fundamentally different.

A second systematic bias is what has been called "availability." Tversky and Kahneman find that availability of information about an uncertain risk makes people overvalue it. That suggests that events with a small chance of occurring (such as shark attacks) appear more likely when the film *Jaws* is released or when there is news coverage of shark attacks. Similarly, we believe that homicide happens more frequently than suicide, because there are more reports about the former, when really the latter is the more common.[26] People may be more concerned about environmental risks that are widely discussed than those (persistent organic pollutants, for example) that are probably more serious but have not received media attention.

A third risk heuristic commonly found is the idea of "anchoring." People tend to stick to their original assessments of probability even when new information would allow them to update their information and make better predictions. Experimental psychology has shown that people even use these anchors in entirely unrelated issues. When people have been told a number and then told it has nothing to do with the question that they are about to be asked (estimating the number of hospitals in the United States, for instance), they are nevertheless likely to come up with an answer that makes use of this unrelated number.[27] This phenomenon suggests that people accept outdated information on environmental problems (including such things as the level of uncertainty of human impacts on the global climate), even when that information has changed.

People also demonstrate overconfidence, being "more confident in their judgments than is warranted by the facts."[28] One piece of evidence suggested for this phenomenon is the propensity by people to begin small businesses despite the knowledge that two-thirds of small businesses fail in the first four years. Dale Griffin and Amos Tversky found evidence for overconfidence in a wide range of professions. They note, however, that overconfidence is not universal. As suggested by Slovic et al. in 1979, there are particular circumstances in which people are likely to be underconfident in their assessments. Griffin and Tversky find that overconfidence happens when the strength of the evidence is high and sample size is small. For example, in determining whether a tossed coin is biased, the percentage of heads is likely to be given far larger weight than the number of coin tosses. Conversely, underconfidence occurs when the strength of the evidence is high and sample size is large.[29] Probability gives us a systematic way to assess these two factors but robust evidence from psychology suggests that people do not follow the rules of probability in determining risk.

People also have a desire for certainty that leads them to insist that uncertainty does not exist, even when evidence suggests that it does. People who live in areas where a disaster has just happened are quick to state that it could never happen again.[30] This characteristic is a central tenet of prospect theory, discussed below. What is important about this particular frame is to note that denial of risk often provokes anger at risk assessors or policy makers who insist on presenting risk assessments in probabilities, rather simply stating whether something is safe or dangerous.[31]

Apart from, but often confused with, the question of our ability to understand how risky various activities are, is the issue of which risks people tend to care most about preventing. In general, people tend to be most concerned about risks that are imposed rather than voluntarily undertaken, risks that are shared unfairly, and human-created risks, including those from exotic technologies, more than those that are natural.[32]

The discussion of how to prioritize decisions based on risk comes from economics, but it is clear that even apart from people's inaccurate risk assessments, the way they value risk is also not reducible to simple economics. Economically rational behavior suggests that a dollar is worth a dollar no matter the circumstances, and assumes that gains and losses are identical. Evidence suggests that people do not behave this way.

Evaluating risk is thus also about loss. Something is considered to be a greater risk not only when it is more likely to happen, but when the value of the loss is greater. Thus risk assessment needs to consider both the likelihood of outcomes and a judgment about their relative subjective utility.[33] One of the first theories to assess risk was the idea of "expected value." This approach suggests that the expected value of an outcome is equal to its payoff multiplied by its probability. Problems with this approach were first noted by Daniel Bernoulli in 1738 when he observed that assuming a direct relationship between expected value and payoff did not accurately predict behavior, since people may have different individual values that they attach to a particular payoff.[34]

The modification suggested initially by Bernoulli adds a utility function to the idea of expected value, acknowledging that outcomes have different utilities to people in different situations, and in particular "increments of utility decrease with increasing wealth." As McDermott suggests, $1 is a lot of money if that is all you have, and you would be unlikely to take a risk of losing the dollar; if you have $101, you would not value that dollar as highly and might be more willing to accept a risk of losing it.[35] This model thus produces a concave risk function (since increments of utility should become less valuable with increases in wealth) and assumes risk aversion. The next major modification of the approach to valuing risk came from John von Neumann and Oskar Morgenstern, who approached the issue from the opposite direction Bernoulli did. They used utility to derive preferences. The only rules they applied were that a person's utility must show transitivity, dominance, and invariance. The first assumes that if a person prefers A to B and B to C then that person prefers A to C. Second, if an option is better in one way, and at least equal in other ways, it will be preferred to other options. Third, a person's preferences will not change based on the way in which the options are posed, as long as they are the same options. This allowed for individual utility functions within certain sets of assumed rules, rather than uniform ones across all people. In this model people act to maximize their subjective utility, even though they may not share the same views of utility.[36] But it turns out that even these sets of assumptions do not accurately describe how people approach risk

## Prospect Theory

The most important new set of insights into decision-making under risk came originally from Kahneman and Tversky's revision of expected utility theory that they termed prospect theory. Their initial article on the topic pointed out several types of situations in which people systematically violate the assumptions of expected utility theory. One is the idea of certainty, discussed above. People will take a smaller certain gain over even a high probability of a bigger gain. A second observation suggests that when a gain is likely, people will choose an option with the higher probability but lower payoff, whereas when gains are highly unlikely they will choose the option with the higher payoff but lower probability. Most importantly, when the idea of gains is replaced by losses, their choices in the above situations completely reverse: people will choose even a high chance of a larger loss over the certainty of a small loss; when losses are probable they will choose to take a smaller risk of a higher loss; and when losses are unlikely they will choose to take a higher chance of a smaller loss. An additional observation Kahneman and Tversky make is that people are more willing to endure higher costs to reduce the probability of a negative outcome to zero than they are to undertake small costs to reduce, but not eliminate, a risk. Finally, they identify what they call "the isolation effect"; the propensity of people to irrationally simplify decision problems by focusing on what distinguishes the sets of decisions from each other, rather than by looking at the entire set of decisions.[37]

To put it more generally, they suggest that people tend to be risk averse when there is a situation of gains, and risk acceptant when there is a situation of losses. This approach returns to the idea of decision curves that are identical for all people; they are simply not identical in all situations. In their new approach they create a system that assigns value to gains and losses rather than to assets, and use "decision weights" to replace probability. They also describe different value functions for these situations: for gains (as consistent with Bernoulli's observations) the value function is concave, for losses it is convex, and it is steeper for losses than for gains. Similarly, what they term "decision weights" differ from actual probabilities; people particularly misapprehend probability at the extreme ends of the spectrum, considering very unlikely events to be impossible and very likely events to be certain. Moreover, these extreme ends take on more psychological importance. People are willing to pay a lot more to reduce a low risk (.01) to zero than to reduce a slightly higher risk by exactly the same percentage (.02 to .01). Consistent with this weighting of decisions is that somewhat low probability events are seen as more likely than they really are, and medium and high probability events seen as less likely.[38]

There are a number of implications of prospect theory for political decision-making generally, and for global environmental politics more specifically. First it suggests that decision-making at the extremes will seem economically irrational. People will be more likely to try to reduce a risk to zero even when doing so is costly, than to simply reduce risk by a large amount. It also means that states are more willing to take chances when it means that they might be able to avoid losses than when they are trying create gains. In essence, entering into a negotiation is a form of risk, because it is not clear what the outcome will be, so negotiation may be easier if it involves preventing a loss.[39] That should be good news for the likelihood of environmental agreements, but other aspects of prospect theory suggest a bias toward the status quo in politics. Because of a preference to avoid losses, people are particularly attached to the status quo. Robert Jervis suggests, for instance, that wars are more likely when each side believes it is trying to defend the status quo.[40] In addition, how people identify whether something is a gain or a loss depends on their reference point,[41] and in political interactions the existing situation is usually the reference point.[42] It is also possible, however, for expectations to take on the role of reference point,[43] which suggests that what the public expects to accomplish out of a negotiation may then come to mean that anything less is seen as a loss.

These factors can help explain such things as the willingness of politicians to persevere in deteriorating situations, such as U.S. President Lyndon Johnson's escalation in Vietnam or Nixon's decision to try to cover up the Watergate break-in.[44] Similarly McDermott argues that the U.S. willingness to attempt to rescue the Iranian hostages despite the high risk can be explained by assuming that the United States perceived itself in a situation of loss, and was therefore more willing to undertake risky action.[45]

While there are few outright disavowals of prospect theory, its usefulness for political situations (since it takes psychological observations about individual decision-making and applies them to situations where people act in groups) can be questioned. In addition, calculation of probability or even decision weights in a political situation is much more difficult than simply assigning numerical values, and must rely on an interpretation of what people say and do[46]; doing so is easier *post hoc*, which can make its use in predictive social science problematic. It is interesting to note that most of the political applications of this theory so far focus on single case studies, rather than drawing broad conclusions about international negotiations. Some also challenge the validity of prospect theory outside the laboratory, and note that even in experimental settings it fails to predict the actions of up to one-third of the individuals involved.[47] Nevertheless, it is clear that prospect theory helps to systematically describe some of the ways that people value risk, and accounts for many of the differences between what concerns average people and what concerns experts.

## Re-evaluating Risk

If people do not assess risk correctly, even if their misassessments can be predicted, the next question is what should be done about the situation. Even if prospect theory may help us better to anticipate the ways in which people are likely to perceive risk, would it not be better if policy could be made to avoid the greatest risks at the lowest costs, rather than spending resources on something that concerns the public but is likely to cause less harm than other problems? Stephen Breyer points out that states do not have unlimited resources to devote to issues of human health or environmental protection and suggests that if we do not allocate funding based on accurate risk assessment, the money "will not be there to spend, at least not if we want to address more serious environmental or social problems."[48]

There are two main suggestions about political approaches to dealing with the public's misevaluation of risk. These two approaches could be characterized as efficiency and democracy, and they differ based on their view of the role of science in decision-making. A third option is the argument that people's assessment of risk is not as irrational as it may seem, and that even though it may differ from that of professional risk assessors (or perhaps, even, because it does) it can be seen as valid in its own right.

Breyer, now a U.S. Supreme Court Justice, sees as the solution to the public's misvaluing of risk the creation of a politically insulated, technically sophisticated, and well-respected bureaucratic elite that would allocate resources to health and environmental problems in a more rational manner.[49] Because politicians have to act on people's concerns or run the risk of not being re-elected, Breyer suggests that the prioritization of risk should be left to experts who cannot be voted out of office. There are logistical questions about how such a risk assessing body could be created (and it is not clear whether it would be harder or easier on the international level than on the domestic level), and whether it could truly insulate itself from political pressures. The main criticism of this approach, which Breyer acknowledges but considers less important than the advantages,[50] is that it is antidemocratic.

A second approach moves in the other direction, calling for greater citizen participation in policy-making processes and what can be called "civic science."[51] Sylvia Tesh argues that environmentalists have emphasized science over unfounded perceptions of risk since the beginning of the environmental movement. The literature on risk (and particularly on inaccurate perceptions) misunderstands the conflict about the dangers of environmental pollution, because it ignores environmental organizations, which reason in the same ways that professional risk assessors do. In her view, then, the answer is not to cut the people out of the political process as Breyer suggests, but to involve them more directly.[52] A similar view is the call for more "grass-roots science," particularly as a way to avoid the capture of risk assessment in the other direction: by industries who have an incentive to skew risk assessment to reflect their interests.[53] Inclusion of people with a wide variety of perspectives in the process of conducting scientific assessments may minimize the likelihood of narrowing alternatives.[54] Some, however, hypothesize that non-governmental actors have little influence on the "less tangible" environmental issues on which there is high uncertainty.[55]

An altogether different response to the issue of different valuation of risk by the public and risk assessors shifts the blame and suggests an alternative to "rational" risk prioritization that has profound implications for policy analysis. This approach suggests that there are good reasons that people value risk they way they do. Part of the reason for this difference between laypeople and experts is that most people bring in a number of subjective characteristics into their assessments of risks.[56] For instance, most professional assessments of risk evaluate an activity based on the likelihood of dying. While that is certainly one of the worst outcomes possible, it is not clear that an activity in which three people die suddenly is worse than one in which no one dies but hundreds become horribly sick for years. Moreover, when you take these additional human harms into consideration, regulations that those like Breyer present as prohibitively costly (such as his argument that the U.S. Environmental Protection Agency's ban on asbestos containing products would have cost between $200 and $300 million to save only seven or eight lives otherwise lost to cancer over thirteen years)[57] seem quite inexpensive. One estimate of the illnesses and non-cancer deaths from asbestos, along with cancer deaths (which the EPA estimated at a higher 202) suggests that this regulation would thus cost only fourteen cents per U.S. citizen to prevent a wide variety of harms not limited to death from cancer.[58] And this estimate does not even consider the advantages beyond the thirteen-year period under consideration.

For those concerned about environmental issues in particular, the focus on human mortality is even more limiting; there are ecological values that are excluded when risk is identified only as risk to human life.[59] Even for those concerned primarily with human well-being, there are a variety of environmental damages that may contribute eventually to a lower quality of life for humans and are not taken into consideration in most risk assessments. The burning of forests may cause few direct human deaths, but it may lead to soil erosion that makes agriculture more difficult and to runoff that decreases water quality. It may also contribute particulate air pollution that has health implications and greenhouse gases that impact the climate in ways that could have much broader effects. Moreover, for those who believe that ecosystems or nonhuman species have value apart from their benefit to humans, it can be important to prevent an oil spill (for example) simply because of the harm caused to nature, not because any loss of human life will result.

There are also distributional issues worth considering. The environmental justice movement suggests that environmental hazards, such as the siting of toxic waste dumps, is more likely to happen in low-income or minority neighborhoods. Even if the risk of loss of human life from these activities is low, or even in the unlikely event it is lower in these locations than in other possible locations, is it acceptable to impose risks upon generally disenfranchised people? Removing asbestos from schools may cause more risk to the asbestos removal workers than it prevents in exposure by schoolchildren, but the asbestos workers knowingly take on the task, wear protective clothing, and receive higher pay than do other workers who incur less risk, whereas children are required to show up for school without regard for the health risks they may encounter. In cases where the relative degree of harm from an environmental problem is determined by natural conditions rather than political decisions, the issue of equity persists. Some low-lying countries may simply cease to exist after the sea-level rise predicted to occur with global climate change, despite their infinitesimal contribution of greenhouse gases to the atmosphere. The Alliance of Small Island States (AOSIS) has had a greater degree of influence in international negotiations on climate change than might otherwise be predicted, largely because people recognize the inherent unfairness of the risks these states face. Being more concerned about risk that occurs to those who did not choose it and cannot control it may not be economically rational, but may be ethically valuable.

Similarly, some of the harshest critics of the public's valuation of risk fail to differentiate based on who is causing the risk. Focusing simply on the amount of risk avoided per unit of cost avoids holding those most responsible for creating risks also the most responsible for preventing, mitigating, or paying for them. There may be advantages to requiring industries to internalize externalities – in other words, to bear the full environmental, health, and safety costs of their activities – even if the risks of disaster are small. If industries knew they could be held responsible for any potential environmental damage their activities caused, would they be more risk-averse?

Victor Flatt also points out the advantage, on which it is difficult to put a price, of being able to make our own decisions. Is it actually irrational to be more concerned with those risks that are imposed on us than those that are voluntarily undertaken? People may choose to value having control more than they value reducing risk, per se. Studies suggest that people are willing to undertake voluntary risks over involuntary risks by a factor of up to 1,000. [60] The suffering that is caused by being exposed to risks not voluntarily undertaken may be greater (though, again, in a calculus that considers more than human mortality) than from those risks we choose.

It is also possible that there is a basis for people's seemingly irrational fears of non-natural phenomenon. Breyer suggests that regulating to prevent ingestion of small amounts of carcinogens from newly created chemicals is irrational in a situation in which people are subjected to similar levels of cancer-causing substances occurring naturally in such substances as peanut butter or mushrooms. As Lisa Heinzerling points out, however, these comparisons overlook the fact that many foods that contain potential carcinogens also contain cancer-preventing substances. [61] Moreover, people have evolved alongside these naturally occurring substances and may have evolved defenses to them in ways that do not exist for newly created chemicals. While both of these potential explanations are subject to a high degree of uncertainty, they do at least suggest rational explanations for otherwise irrational fears.

It is also the case that risk assessors focus on a limited number of factors (though more and more with improving technology) in determining risk; people may in fact be able to include additional factors in their analysis without being aware of it. To return to McDermott's example of the beret-wearing questioner at an arms control lecture, it may be true that if you reduce the audience simply to number of academics versus artists the person is more likely to be an academic. But how many of us honestly believe that the questioner is not an artist? We take a variety of factors, many of which we may not even be able to quantify, into consideration when making those judgments. We may not be wrong.

Certainly, as Mary Douglas and Aaron Wildavsky point out, risks are social constructs and there is no objective way to say that one risk judgment is better or worse than another. [62] Whatever one's perspective on how to correctly value risk, it is likely that communication about risk can be improved. Better information about risk is crucial to allowing people to participate more effectively in the political process. [63]

# Politics of Science

Given the role of risk and uncertainty in decisions pertaining to the global environment, it should not be surprising that scientists are important throughout the process of addressing these issues. Scientists are often the ones who first notice that environmental damage is taking place, or theorize that certain substances may be harmful even before damage has become evident. So the process of addressing international, as domestic, environmental issues may begin with scientists. They become even more important in international issues than in domestic ones, since states must collectively be convinced that there is an environmental problem and that it has anthropogenic causes before they are willing to take costly action. Transboundary scientific investigation contributes to the raising of concern and resolving of uncertainty about environmental problems.

## Epistemic Communities

The school of analysis within international relations that examines the role of scientists and other related actors as an explanation for international outcomes was elaborated by Peter Haas under the term epistemic communities. These are "knowledge-based networks of specialists who share beliefs in cause–effect relations, validity tests, and underlying principled values, and pursue common goals."[64] While such communities are not limited to scientists, nor even to environmental issues, it is argued that they have a profound impact on international cooperation, and most discussion of them occurs in the context of addressing uncertainty in international environmental issues. The theoretical approach suggests that the existence of epistemic communities allows those within them to impact decision makers and policy in the face of uncertainty. A wide array of anecdotal evidence suggests that collections of actors organized around providing knowledge has influenced outcomes in particular environmental issues. Examples most frequently given are the protection of the Mediterranean, the protection of the ozone layer and, more controversially, climate change. The influence of epistemic communities may depend on a variety of factors, including the number and importance of states a given community can persuade on the issue in question, which may relate to the interest of states.[65] (Certainly what seems to be a strong epistemic community on climate change has failed to persuade politicians in the United States.) Uncertainty is given as a reason that policy makers would turn to such communities for advice,[66] and their transnational character can give them added influence on international issues.

Others are less sanguine about the influence of epistemic communities. Martin List and Volker Rittberger acknowledge that "shared knowledge may be a necessary condition of regime formation," but doubt that epistemic communities are alone responsible for creating international regimes, and may in some cases help delay international cooperation.[67] Jutta Brunnée and Stephen Troope suggest that political officials will often not take the advice of scientific and policy experts, partly out of an interest in maintaining control.[68] Jonathan Wiener suggests as an example that negotiations on climate change are not influenced primarily by epistemic communities,[69] although his example of the Intergovernmental Panel on Climate Change as controlled by governments undermines his own logic; most see this group both as an epistemic community, and as one that is willing to act against the wishes of the governments that appoint the scientists. It certainly has been influential (although perhaps not the determining factor) in international cooperation to address climate change. Ozone depletion is a case about which there is considerable disagreement, as well, about the role of an epistemic community. Some, like Karen Litfin, are critical of the idea of objective science and find "discursive practices" a more useful explanation of the ozone case.[70] Others see economic and political interests as the most important factors in producing agreement on protecting the ozone layer.[71] It is clear, nevertheless, that communities of experts play some kind of role in policy-making on global environmental issues. Whether it is the primary role in reaching international cooperation remains to be seen.

## Politicized Science

Science is rarely entirely disconnected from politics. The approaches different states take to operating under conditions of uncertainty, or the different institutional mechanisms for interpreting science within the political process, can lead to differences in policies. Some approaches to the relationship between science and politics see the differences of interpretation of science as arising unintentionally from institutional constraints. Sheila Jasanoff has compared the different ways states approach risk, noting, for instance, that in Europe the policy process is more cautious about accepting risk than is the case in the United States; strangely, these initial early approaches also have allowed the United States to slow down international cooperation with claims of uncertainty.[72]

It is also possible for science to be used in an explicitly political way. Ronald Brickman, Sheila Jasanoff, and Thomas Ilgen illustrate that scientific uncertainty can "make it possible for proponents and opponents of regulation to interpret the scientific basis for ... risk assessment in ways that advance their particular policy objectives."[73] Interested parties or groups, notes Young, "manipulate scientific findings ... in their efforts to promote their preferences" in the creation of new regimes or the operation of existing ones.[74] Litfin's work on science allows for either the intentional or the unintentional use of science for political ends.[75] Susskind argues that the United States uses scientific evidence to argue in favor of the courses of action it prefers but "when we prefer to take a different political course we attack the available data as insufficient, regardless of the strength of the worldwide scientific consensus."[76]

The prevailing view of science's role in diminishing uncertainty would suggest simply doing more science (making climate models more detailed and including more information in them, for instance). Others disagree. A different take on the same issue is the observation that science is socially constructed; what experts give is "varying interpretations of uncertainty shaped by their own and their informants' local contexts and locally colored world views."[77] Dale Jamieson concurs, suggesting that what we take to be uncertain depends on what questions we are asking. He gives as an example his process of selling a bicycle to a friend. Both he and the friend are likely to believe that he owns the bicycle, and thus do not act as though there is any uncertainty about that part of the transaction. But there could be a different situation in which he suffers from either amnesia or kleptomania; if his friend knows he has one of these afflictions, the friend is likely to require proof of ownership before buying the bicycle. In other words, what people even stop to consider the certainty of is influenced by social context.[78]

Jamieson also points to the importance of reference points, similar to but even more fundamental than that explored in prospect theory. When people discuss an increase in global mean temperature, it matters what their frame of reference is (compared to the last decade, century, millennium?), where their measurements are taken, or even that they examine global mean temperature rather than average high temperature.[79] The broader point to take from all of this is that uncertainty is not simply an objective value that can be reduced by more scientific inquiry; social priorities for what issues to value and what questions to ask influence how we make policy about environmental risks under conditions of uncertainty.

The level of uncertainty about the role of science, risk, and uncertainty in addressing global environmental problems thus remains high. As soon as one moves past a simple cost–benefit assessment of risk and a belief that more scientific inquiry will make environmental problems easier to address, it becomes clear not only that we do not fully understand how the global environment functions on its own or intersects with political or economic systems, but even more that we are not even clear about how best to study these phenomena.

# Notes

1 R. W. White, "Introduction," in M. F. Ulman, ed., *Keeping Pace With Science and Engineering: Case Studies in Environmental Regulation* (Washington, D.C.: National Academy Press, 1993), 4.

2 Oran Young, "Science and Social Institutions: Lessons for International Resource Regimes," in Steinar Andresen and Willy Ostreng, eds., *International Resource Management: The Role of Science and Politics* (London and New York: Bellhaven Press, 1989), 12.

3 Jan-Stefan Fritz, "Earthwatch Twenty-Five Years On: Between Science and International Environmental Governance," *International Environmental Affairs* 10(3) (Summer 1993): 185–86.

4 Lawrence E. Susskind, *Environmental Diplomacy: Negotiating More Effective Environmental Agreements* (New York and Oxford: Oxford University Press, 1994), 66–67.

5 Seong-lin Na and Hyun Song Shin, "International Environmental Agreements Under Uncertainty," *Oxford Economic Papers* 50(2) (April 1998) 173–85.

6 See John Rawls, *A Theory of Justice* (Cambridge, Mass.: Belknap Press of Harvard University Press, 1971).

7 Radoslav S. Dimitrov, *Science and International Environmental Policy: Regimes and Non-Regimes in Global Governance* (Boulder, Colo.: Roman and Littlefield, 2006).

8 Vienna Convention for the Protection of the Ozone Layer (1985), Articles 2 through 4 and Annexes I and II.

9 LRTAP 1979, Articles 4 and 9.

10 Framework Convention on Climate Change (1992), Article 4(1)(a).

11 Kenneth R. Foster, Paolo Vecchia, and Michael H. Repacholi, "Science and the Precautionary Principle," *Science* 288 (12 May 2000): 979.

12 Ibid., 979.

13 Michele Territo, "The Precautionary Principle in Marine Fisheries Conservation and the U.S. Sustainable Fisheries Act of 1996," *Vermont Law Review* 24 (Summer 2000): 1356.

14 Vienna Convention (1985) Preamble; cited as the first treaty usage in Philippe Sands, *Principles of International Environmental Law*, vol. I (Manchester and New York: Manchester University Press, 1995), 209.

15 Daniel Bodansky, "Scientific Uncertainty and the Precautionary Principle," *Environment* 33(7) (September 1991): 4–5, 43.

16 William C. G. Burns "Introduction to Special Issue on the Precautionary Principle and Its Operationalisation in International Environmental Regimes and Domestic Policymaking," *International Journal of Global Environmental Issues* 5(1/2) (2005): 1–9.

17  David VanderZwaag, "The Precautionary Principle in Environmental Law and Policy: Elusive Rhetoric and First Embrace," *Journal of Environmental Law and Practice* 8(3) (October 1999): 355–75.

18  Bodansky, 4–5, 43.

19  Patrick Michaels, "Environmental Rules Should be Based on Science," *Insight* (12 April 1993): 21.

20  S. Lichtenstein, P. Slovic, B. Fischhoff, M. Layman, and B. Combs, "Judged Frequency of Lethal Events," *Journal of Experimental Psychology: Human Learning and Memory* 4 (1978): 551–78.

21  Lichtenstein et al., cited in Lola L. Lopes, "Risk Perception and the Perceived Public," in Daniel W. Bromley and Kathleen Segerson, eds., *The Social Response to Environmental Risk* (Boston, Dordrecht, and London: Kluwer Academic, 1992), 60.

22  Sylvia Noble Tesch, *Uncertain Hazards* (Ithaca and London: Cornell University Press, 2000), 82.

23  Rose McDermott, *Risk-Taking in International Politics: Prospect Theory in American Foreign Policy* (Ann Arbor: University of Michigan Press, 1998), 6–7.

24  Amos Tversky and Daniel Kahneman, "Judgments of and by Representativeness," in Daniel Kahneman, Paul Slovic, and Amos Tversky, eds., *Judgment Under Uncertainty: Heuristics and Biases* (Cambridge: Cambridge University Press, 1982), 84.

25  Robert Jervis, *Perception and Misperception in International Politics* (Princeton: Princeton University Press, 1976).

26  McDermott, 7.

27  Ibid., 8.

28  Dale Griffin and Amos Tversky, "The Weighing of Evidence and the Determinants of Confidence," *Cognitive Psychology* 24 (1992): 411.

29  Griffin and Tversky, 411–35.

30  Robert W. Kates, "Hazard and Choice Perception in Flood Plain Management," *Research Paper 78*, Department of Geography, University of Chicago, 1962.

31  Paul Slovic, Baruch Fischhoff, and Sarah Lichtenstein, "Rating the Risks," *Environment* 21(3) (April 1979): 14–20, 36–39.

32  Daniel Goleman, "Hidden Rules Often Distort Ideas of Risk," *New York Times*, 1 February 1994, C1.

33  McDermott, 6.

34  Ibid., 15.

35  Ibid., 16.

36  John von Neumann and Oskar Morgenstern, *Theory of Games and Economic Behavior*, 2nd edn. (Princeton: Princeton University Press, 1947); McDermott, 17.

37  Daniel Kahneman and Amos Tversky, "Prospect Theory: An Analysis of Decision Under Risk," *Econometrica* 47(2) (March 1979): 263–92.

38  McDermott, 30.

39  Jeffrey Berejekian, "The Gains Debate: Framing State Choice," *American Political Science Review* 91(4) (December 1997): 789–805.

40  Robert Jervis, "Political Implications of Loss Aversion," *Political Psychology*, 13 (1992): 187–204.

41  Amos Tversky and Daniel Kahneman, "Loss Aversion in Riskless Choice," *Quarterly Journal of Economics* 41 (1991): 1039–1061.

42  Jack S. Levy, "Loss Aversion, Framing, and Bargaining: The Implications of Prospect Theory for International Conflict," *International Political Science Review* 17(2) (1996): 179–95.

43  Chip Heath, Richard P. Larrick, and George Wu, "Goals as Reference Points," *Cognitive Psychology* 38 (1999): 79–109.

44  Paul A. Kowert and Margaret G. Hermann, "Who Takes Risks? Daring and Caution in Foreign Policy Making," *Journal of Conflict Resolution* 41(5) (October 1996): 611–37.

45  McDermott, 45–75.

46  William A. Boettcher III, "Context, Methods, Numbers, and Words: Prospect Theory in International Relations," *Journal of Conflict Resolution* 39(3) (September 1995): 561–83.

47  Kowert and Hermann, 611–13.

48  Stephen J. Breyer, *Breaking the Vicious Circle: Toward Effective Risk Regulation* (Cambridge, Mass: Harvard University Press, 1993), 18–19.

49  Ibid., 59–63.

50  Ibid, 73.

51  Karin Bäckstrand, "Civic Science for Sustainability: Reframing the Role of Experts, Policy-Makers and Citizens in Environmental Governance," *Global Environmental Politics* 3(4) (November 2003), 24–41.

52  Sylvia Noble Tesh, *Environmental Activists and Scientific Proof* (Ithaca and London: Cornell University Press, 2000), 86–99.

53  Michael K. Heiman, "Science by the People: Grassroots Environmental Monitoring and the Debate Over Scientific Expertise," *Journal of Planning Education and Research* 6 (1997): 291–303.

54  Bäckstrand, 32.

55  Neil E. Harrison and Gary C. Bryner, "Toward Theory," in Neil E. Harrison and Gary C. Bryner, *Science and Politics in the International Environment* (Lanham, Md.: Rowman and Littlefied, 2004), 327–350.

56  Paul Slovic et al.

57  Breyer, 14.

58  Lisa Heinzerling, "Political Science," *University of Chicago Law Review* 62 (Winter 1995): 463–64.

59 Victor B. Flatt, *"Breaking the Vicious Circle*: A Review," *Environmental Law* 24(4) (October 1994): 1707–28.

60 Ibid., 1715.

61 Heinzerling, 461–63.

62 Mary Douglas and Aaron Wildavsky, *Risk and Culture: An Essay on the Selection of Technical and Environmental Dangers* (Berkeley, Los Angeles, and London: University of California Press, 1982).

63 Paul Slovic, "Beyond Numbers: A Broader Perspective on Risk Perception and Risk Communication," in Deborah G. Mayo and Rachelle D. Hollander, eds., *Acceptable Evidence: Science and Values in Risk Management* (New York and Oxford: Oxford University Press, 1991), 62–63.

64 Peter M. Haas, "Banning Chlorofluorocarbons: Epistemic Community Efforts to Protect Stratospheric Ozone," *International Organization* 46(1) (Winter 1992): 187.

65 Emanuel Adler and Peter M. Haas, "Conclusion: Epistemic Communities, World Order, and the Creation of a Reflective Research Paradigm," *International Organization* 46(1) (Winter 1992): 389.

66 Peter M. Haas, "Introduction: Epistemic Communities and International Policy Coordination," *International Organization* 46(1) (Winter 1992): 1–35.

67 Martin List and Volker Rittberger, "Regime Theory and International Environmental Management," in Andrew Hurrell and Benedict Kingsbury, eds., *The International Politics of the Environment* (Oxford: Clarendon Press, 1992), 85–107.

68 Jutta Brunnée and Stephen J. Toope, "Environmental Security and Freshwater Resources: Ecosystem Regime Building," *American Journal of International Law* 91(1) (January 1997): 26–59.

69 Jonathan Baert Wiener, "On the Political Economy of Global Regulation," *Georgetown Law Journal* 87 (February 1999): 749–94.

70 Karen Litfin, *Ozone Discourses: Science and Politics in Global Environmental Cooperation* (New York: Columbia University Press, 1994).

71 Wiener, 772.

72 Sheila Jasanoff, "American Exceptionalism and the Political Acknowledgement of Risk," *Daedalus* 119(4) (Fall 1990): 395–406.

73 Ronald Brickman, Sheila Jasanoff, and Thomas Ilgen, *Controlling Chemicals: The Politics of Regulation in Europe and the United States* (Ithaca and London: Cornell University Press, 1985): 187.

74 Young, "Science and Social Institutions," 20.

75 Litfin, 13.

76 Susskind, 65

77  Sheila Jasanoff, "Pluralism and Convergence in International Science Policy," in *Science and Sustainability: Selected Papers on IIASA's 20th Anniversary* (Laxenburg: IIASA, 1992): 161.

78  Dale Jamieson, "Scientific Uncertainty and the Political Process," *Annals of the American Academy of Political and Social Sciences* 545 (May 1996): 38.

79  Ibid., 39.

# 4 Developing Countries in Global Environmental Politics

> ## Chapter Outline
>
> Terms and Concepts
> Environmental Preferences of Developing Countries
> Issue Structure and Developing Country Influence
> Growing Influence of Developing Country Concerns

Most of the world's population lives in states classified by the United Nations as developing, and developing states outnumber the states in the developed world by a large margin. The relationship of these states with global environmental politics has been complicated and occasionally contentious. This chapter examines the role of developing states as they approach global environmental politics. Although these states are varied in their history and concerns, there are some common experiences they share and some concerns and tactics that differentiate them from the industrialized states that have dominated much of the discussion of global environmental politics.

*reasons for being less interested*

There are some reasons to assume that developing countries will be less interested than industrialized states in addressing global environmental issues. Though their current behavior may contribute to existing global environmental problems, they have not been the primary contributors to many of the types of environmental problems discussed in this volume, most of which result from the industrialization processes of richer states in a previous century. Developing countries fear interference in their domestic decisions about their process of development, and are especially concerned that they will be denied the use of proven technology that enabled the earlier industrialization of other states, or denied sources of income on which they would otherwise rely. While developing states face environmental problems that come from poverty or population growth, these are often not the environmental issues that garner international concern, especially if they are experienced locally. International environmental cooperation may therefore not focus on issues developing states care most about.

There are other reasons to expect strong developing country concern about global environmental problems, however. Many developing countries are particularly vulnerable to global environmental problems, such as climate change. Moreover, states that rely heavily on natural resources and agriculture may be more attuned to environmental conditions and concerned about maintaining a healthy environment. Paul Steinberg demonstrates that levels of domestic environmental concern in developing states as measured by polls often eclipse those in industrialized states.[1] A lack of enthusiasm about the process of governance on these issues should not necessarily be taken as a lack of concern about global environmental problems generally, and presenting a lack of concern may be a strategic negotiating position, in international bargaining situations in which developing countries have become used to their lack of power.

But although developing countries have typically had little ability to influence the process or outcome of international negotiations broadly, their degree of power in some aspects of global environmental governance has been significant. What explains the level and variation of international influence developing states have had in addressing issues of the global environment? This chapter examines how developing states interact with international efforts to protect the global environment, and what that suggests more broadly about the issue of development in conjunction with international environmental issues. The structure of many global environmental problems, combined with high levels of concern about these problems by developed states unable to address the problems without developing country participation, has allowed developing states to demand concessions and receive financial assistance for taking action to mitigate problems of the global environment.

# Terms and Concepts

Before examining the role of developing countries in global environmental politics, some terminological discussions are helpful. There are many different names to apply to the category of countries referred to here as "developing," and complex associations with most of the terms. These states are sometimes called the Third World,[2] to distinguish them, especially in the Cold War era, from the First (industrialized, capitalist) and Second (socialist, Soviet bloc) Worlds; even in the post–Cold War era this terminology is used to emphasize the solidarity of this group of states and the global structure within which they find themselves. They are occasionally known as "less developed countries." Sometimes the distinction is made between industrializing and industrialized states. Another common distinction is between the global South and North, even though not all developing states are south of all industrialized ones. The classification of poor and rich states is also used. The Marxist-derived world systems theory framework refers to the periphery, as distinct from the core.[3] Timothy Doyle is a proponent of the concept of majority world (to refer to developing states) as distinct from the minority (developed) world, used to emphasize the numerical superiority of developing states.[4]

Passionate defenders of each terminological choice denigrate the others as providing problematic value judgments, and none is ideal. In almost all of these options these states are referred to (either explicitly or implicitly) by their distinction from the set of states characterized as developed or industrialized. In some of them assumptions are made about what these states aspire to or should aspire to (development or industrialization) that may or may not be accurate. Although none of these terms is ideal for labeling this diffuse collection of states, if one wants to speak of them collectively, some term must be chosen. This chapter uses the description "developing" most frequently, while recognizing its conceptual shortcomings.

And it is precisely the variety of these states and their goals and approaches that make them difficult to classify. Within this group of states are "least developed" states (which account for more than 40 per cent of developing states by some measures), states with more moderate economic situations, and even those, such as exporters of oil or other high-end commodities, considered to be fairly wealthy.[5] They do not always experience environmental problems in the same way, nor always share the same concerns about global environmental governance. Climate change, for instance, divides developing countries: some are particularly geographically vulnerable (low-lying or island states); the primary income for others comes from exporting fossil fuels. In between are those states with large reserves of fossil fuels available for domestic energy needs (such as coal in China) or other characteristics that make them more or less concerned about climate change or about the changes required to prevent it.

Nevertheless, many argue that the way these countries approach global environmental politics has sufficient similarities, and that these countries have acted in concert frequently enough in international environmental negotiations, to make a distinction between developed and developing countries an analytically useful category. Marc Williams, for instance, argues that the "third world" is a relevant identity, as distinct from an objective description.[6] If states are behaving in a way based on their membership in this group, examining these states as a collective makes sense. Moreover, the history of global environmental negotiations includes much evidence of these states forming coalitions to act collectively.[7]

The Group of 77 (G-77), now containing far more than the original seventy-seven members involved at its 1964 creation in the context of the United Nations Conference on Trade and Development, has played an active role in coordinating the positions of developing countries in global environmental negotiations. Adil Najam argues that the G-77 is unified not by the supposed poverty of its membership but rather by a shared distrust of the prevailing process of global goverance.[8] It is a fairly stable negotiating coalition that clearly goes beyond the narrow self-interest of its members. In negotiations where some (especially large, rapidly industrializing) developing states might have the opportunity to gain more by striking individual deals than by working collectively, the coalition has tended to hold together regardless.[9]

A second conceptual issue is what is meant by *global* environmental politics. While that question is relevant to this book in its entirety, it is especially relevant in this chapter, since one of the arguments frequently made is that developing countries are not concerned about global environmental issues, largely because their local concerns, relating to environment or development, take precedence. As preceding chapters suggest, global or international environmental problems cross borders in some physical way – when activity in one location causes environmental harm in another – or come from causes (such as international trade or finance) that are themselves international. But that definition leaves room for interpretation, especially to the extent that global forces such as colonialism influenced the economic and infrastructural situation of developing states in ways that affect their local environmental issues. Critics contend that the North/South division itself influences what is considered to be a global environmental issue, with those issues of concern to wealthy states defined as global, and those of concerned to the poor defined as simply local.[10]

Nevertheless, this chapter considers primarily environmental issues that reach the level of international environmental negotiation, and examines the experiences of developing countries within that context. It cannot hope to adequately address the voluminous literature on the relationship among poverty, population, and development, or tackle the important local environmental issues that concern developing countries. Examining the role that developing countries play in the process of addressing international environmental problems serves as a window into the concerns of these states, a useful corrective to the perception that international negotiations primarily involve industrialized states, and an indication of aspects of environmental problems that have different implications than other international issues for developing states.

# Environmental Preferences of Developing Countries

It has long been assumed that developing countries are less concerned about environmental issues, and certainly about issues of the global environment, than are wealthier states. Uday Desai suggests that "questions of environmental quality are unlikely to receive careful hearing amid the overwhelming problems of poverty,"[11] and further suggests that "in a choice between economic growth and environmental protection, the environment always loses."[12]

Others disagree. Steinberg points to polls that show that people in developing states not only support environmental protection, but particularly express a willingness to pay higher taxes or volunteer their time to protect the environment, especially when compared to their developed country counterparts.[13] It is also the case that it is the residents of developing countries who are the most harmed by environmental damage. Deaths from water and air pollution occur disproportionately in developing countries, and poverty is associated with poor environmental conditions.[14] Unsustainable resource use, prompted by dire necessity, may perpetuate a cycle in which poor use of agricultural lands leads to erosion and desertification that decreases food supply and makes the need to work marginal lands more pressing. Three-quarters of developing states make at least half of their export income from natural resource exports and are therefore acutely aware of the importance of these resources.[15] Even some environmental problems considered to be international are particularly harmful to those in developing countries. Countries that rely on agriculture are likely to be especially vulnerable to the effects of climate change, and may be particularly harmed by chemical pesticides banned in the developed world but sold or given to developing countries.

Williams suggests that developing states face global environmental negotiations with "shared interests, common ideas, and minimal joint decision-making and policy formulation."[16] Scholars identify a number of these shared interests, including the linking of environment with development and confirmation of the sovereign ability of states to exploit their own resources; the demand for financial assistance in the form of economic aid, technology transfer, and assistance with capacity building; a preference for the creation of new institutions rather than the use of previously existing (and usually North-dominated) ones; a longer time frame within which to take on new rules to protect the environment; and the call for acknowledgment that the states of the industrialized world are most responsible for the creation of global environmental problems, and therefore should be the first to take action to mitigate these problems.

The linking of environment and development is often part of an effort by developing states to ensure that the "right" to develop is not lost in the effort to promote environmental protection. This right has been repeatedly reaffirmed in international environmental conferences, such as the United Nations Conference on Environment and Development in Rio in 1992, whose Rio Declaration noted that "the right to development must be fulfilled so as to equitably meet developmental and environmental needs of present and future generations."[17] One of the most influential concepts in discussing the relationship between environment and development is the idea of "sustainable development." This term, most popularly defined by the World Commission on Environment and Development as development that meets "the needs of the present without compromising the ability of future generations to meet their own needs,"[18] is obviously not only relevant to developing countries. But it is in that context that it has generally been used. The concept, however, provides little guidance on how to actually balance the potentially competing needs of environmental protection and economic development.[19]

A similar concern that developing countries have is their rights to control of their own resources, a standard part of sovereignty. This issue has become particularly important in addressing issues of natural resources that are seen as valuable globally (such as biodiversity). Particularly after the economic, social, and environmental legacy of a history of resource-driven colonialism, developing states are quick to assert the legal right to control their own resources. Though states occasionally lack physical control over their own borders, the legal rights afforded by sovereignty are clear, and developing states have succeeded in reaffirming these rights in international environmental negotiations.

The demand for environmental aid, technology transfer, and other forms of capacity-building by developing states is also pervasive, and increasingly successful. A general concern about the ability of developing countries to participate in global environmental governance comes from the potential imbalance internationally of certain types of resources, be they economic or infrastructural. Apart from general economic development, often seen within the framework of "capacity," the types of environmental capacities developing countries are seen to be lacking include the ability to assess and monitor environmental conditions, and the bureaucratic or institutional capacities within ministries to oversee implementation of international environmental efforts.[20] One of the major approaches to involving developing countries in addressing global environmental problems therefore revolves around the idea of capacity development. This approach is not without controversy. Ambuj Sagar and Stacy VanDeveer suggest that one of the major downsides of existing capacity-building efforts toward developing countries is that they are essentially efforts to make developing states implement "Northern driven" policy objectives.[21]

One aspect of this involves scientific expertise. So much of the discussion of global environmental issues involves scientific understanding and the efforts to resolve uncertainty (see chapter 3) that states without sufficient numbers of trained scientists in relevant fields can be at a disadvantage. The participation of developing-country scientists in international scientific advisory bodies is low.[22] Scientific advisory bodies (such as the Intergovernmental Panel on Climate Change or scientific commissions within treaty governance processes) often attempt to include geographic diversity in their members – though not all do – but the limited number of qualified specialists with the ability to attend international meetings makes this practice imperfect. Sylvia Karlsson argues that this international scientific imbalance has further implications for developing countries in that there is simply less scientific attention paid to the environmental concerns they may have, leading to a decreased likelihood that these problems will reach the international agenda. Similarly, the actual research even on collective problems is likely to be done in developed country conditions rather than those that might be most relevant to developing countries.[23]

Developing states seek, and frequently receive within international environmental agreements, funding to implement obligations of the agreements, access to technology to do so, and general capacity-building funding to assist with other infrastructure and bureaucratic needs. Longer-term capacity needs, like scientific training, may take longer to implement, however. One of the reasons that developing states frequently push for the creation of new institutions to address environmental problems (and especially the capacity-building funding processes within then) is to avoid using existing, northern-dominated processes. In particular they hope to avoid funding institutions created for development assistance, in which the donor states have a disproportionate influence on how the funding is distributed.

An additional way that developed states often seek to bring developing states into international environmental agreements is to promise them additional time to meet the obligations of the agreement. The initial use of this approach, in the Montreal Protocol on Substances that Deplete the Ozone Layer, was not especially successful at persuading developing states to join the agreement, in large part because they were concerned at the costs of meeting the obligations. Since then, however, it has become commonplace to consider additional time between when developed states are required to implement international environmental obligations and when developing states need to. The most important aspect of this approach is seen in the climate change negotiations, in which obligations for developing states in the first commitment period were not even seriously considered.

The broader principle developing states frequently seek to assert is the primary responsibility of developed states for global environmental problems. Though empirically largely true, acknowledgment of this principle has been harder to achieve than gaining financial assistance or a time lag before having to meet international obligations. Developed states are afraid that if they acknowledge this responsibility their commitments to funding all global environmental obligations could be potentially endless. They have therefore been reluctant to accept rhetorical responsibility, while simultaneously agreeing to funding obligations and time lags that tacitly acknowledge their responsibility.

# Issue Structure and Developing Country Influence

How have developing states managed to gain the above concessions in international environmental negotiations? The structure of environmental issues, as discussed in chapter 2, plays an important role in determining the extent of developing country influence in negotiations on international environmental issues and its ability to gain certain types of outcomes in these negotiations. Certain characteristics of international environmental issues influence whether and what kind of power developing states will have in international negotiations. These include the extent to which the issue is subtractable or excludable, as well as the variation and intensity of concern across developing states, which comes at least in part from characteristics of the issue.[24] Under most forms of prevailing realist or liberal international relations theory developing countries are seen as having little chance of influence on the international scene. They tend to lack military might, and they have little economic clout. What they may have, however, is the ability to destroy or the ability to exclude. For some environmental issues, these abilities can be crucial.

## Subtractability and Side-Payments

The extent to which a resource is subtractable – whether or not use of the resource by one actor diminishes that resource's value to another actor – influences the ability of countries to demand compensation or favorable deals for their participation in an agreement, because of the power to destroy. A subtractable good, like a high-seas fishery, needs the participation of all actors that could potentially affect the resource in any cooperative efforts to address it. Those states that do not limit their destruction of the resource in question can prohibit others from successfully protecting it. The participation of reluctant participants is thus essential, and they can often extract concessions or assistance for their agreement to participate.

Developing countries can threaten to take no action to address the environmental problem in question; doing nothing to improve an environmental problem is essentially a threat to destroy the resource, even more so if the process of economic development or population growth will increase the extent of the activity causing the environmental problem. If the environmental issue is a problem with elements of subtractability, inaction by these countries can undo any good done by states that do act to protect the environment, and states that want to address the problem will need to lure the recalcitrant states into international action to protect the resource.

While the ability to destroy and the bargaining power it gives is not limited to developing countries, we do see this threat used much more frequently in that context. Concern about international environmental problems is sufficiently ingrained in the politics of developed country populations[25] that leaders of these states feel constrained in their ability to threaten to destroy the environment, even if only as a bargaining tool. In addition, in many issue areas the developing countries are the ones whose increasing populations and increasing industrialization are likely to give them a greater ability and need to destroy the environment over time, and therefore, absent international agreement, the growth of environmental destruction will be greater in the developing world than among industrialized states. This issue structure suggests that developing states should be most likely to receive special consideration to encourage cooperation on issues that are subtractable, to a much greater degree than on those that are not.

Indeed, developing countries have received enormous concessions for their participation in international efforts to address the most subtractable environmental problems, such as ozone depletion and climate change. As discussed in chapter 6, developing states were allowed extra time before having to phase out their use of ozone-depleting substances, and developed states agreed to contribute

*incremental costs*

to a fund that covers the "incremental costs" to developing states of this phase-out. Most importantly, developing states insisted that they be given central decision-making power in the institutional allocation of this funding, and because they wielded a sufficiently credible threat to remain outside of the agreement unless the institution was created to meet their concerns, they gained many of their primary objectives, contrary to the preferences of some of the more powerful states in the system. There are similarities to be seen in the (also subtractable) issue of climate change. There was no serious consideration to demanding emissions reduction obligations from developing states in the negotiation of the Kyoto Protocol, and the already existing Global Environment Facility was given the responsibility for funding the incremental costs incurred by developing states of meeting any obligations they had under the international agreements on climate change.

*Yeah but it did not matter USA?*

Conversely, developing countries have had a lower degree of international influence in negotiation on global issues that are less subtractable. One such issue is desertification, defined as "land degradation in arid, semi-arid and dry sub-humid areas resulting mainly from adverse human impact."[26] It is caused primarily by overgrazing, deforestation and erosion that can result either from poor forestry policy or from agriculture on marginal lands. These in turn are caused by a number of economic and other factors, and magnified by climate change. Though desertification is experienced in almost every country in the world, it is of particular concern to already arid developing countries with marginal croplands. International efforts to address this issue resulted in the negotiation of the Convention to Combat Desertification in 1994. Among the contentious North–South bargaining issues in this negotiation was whether the problem should be identified as "global." Industrialized countries feared that using a term would imply responsibility and obligations for them similar to those addressed in climate change and biodiversity; indeed this was the goal of the G-77 in pushing its use.[27] The industrialized countries therefore resisted the use of the term,[28] and were successful in this resistance.

Many developing countries, led by those in Africa, also called for the convention to address the socioeconomic causes of desertification, such as debt, exchange rate variation, and international trade regulations.[29] It is these types of issues, aside from climate change, that make desertification an international issue, but the industrialized countries successfully resisted this characterization. These issues are mentioned only in the preamble to the treaty.

*socio-economic causes of desertification*

The funding mechanism initially created by the agreement was weak as well. The "Global Mechanism" was created to "promote actions leading to the

*What makes desertification an international issue.*

mobilization and channeling of substantial financial resources, including for the transfer of technology" to developing countries.[30] The difference between this and even the vague commitments made in other international agreements negotiated at roughly the same time to provide new and additional funding is striking. This mechanism was created largely in the hope that such financial resources would be forthcoming, which for the most part they were not. And the industrialized countries participating in the negotiations were only willing to acknowledge the need to "rationalize and strengthen existing resources."[31] More recently, the Global Environment Facility has taken on desertification as one of its funding areas, but the issue of adequate funding for developing countries to address desertification persists.[32]

The desertification example shows the difficulties developing countries face gaining leverage on nonsubtractable issues. Developed countries that want to address the issue of desertification as it affects them will not be prevented from doing so if developing states do not participate. The participation of all states is not central to addressing the environmental problem, so rich or powerful states feel no need to make concessions to developing states to bring them in to international cooperative efforts. In desertification, developing countries have tried to work together despite the lack of subtractability of the issue – and have in fact tried to make it appear to be a global issue. But because the most proximate causes are local, and the effects are local, this solidarity has at times fallen apart, and has harmed the ability of developing countries to get even the modest assistance they might have been able to get.[33]

## Excludability and Solidarity

The other characteristic that can give states, including developing states, power in international environmental negotiation is excludability. Many environmental issues that are addressed on the international level are *not* excludable. In protection of the atmosphere, for example, states cannot be prevented from access to the advantages provided by the ozone layer. Ozone layer protection is a particularly good illustration of a *non*excludable resource, since the location of harm bears no relationship to the location of the activity that damages the ozone. But some environmental resources have a much greater degree of excludability. Species that do not migrate across borders are an example of an excludable resource, since states can deny to actors from other states access to those species.

The level of excludability changes the dynamics of the bargaining situation, by giving influence to states that can exclude others from their resources. Although it might seem that the ability to exclude other parties from benefits of resources located in your jurisdiction makes an issue a purely domestic one, excludable

*How are forests excludable.*

resources may nevertheless have important international elements, because of externalities. The clearest example is that of forests; they are physically located in only one place and can for all practical purposes be regulated as aspects of national policy. But because trees serve as a carbon sink – taking up carbon dioxide from the atmosphere when they are growing and releasing it into the atmosphere when they are cut – what is done with them in an individual country can affect global climate change and hence have impacts on other states. Similarly, biodiversity resources are often seen as the "common heritage" of the world, since they can provide potential benefits for the people of the world, and in that sense have externalities beyond the potentially excludable places where they are located.

This power to exclude is one that is not limited to developing countries, but may also be used more often by them, for two reasons. The first is that, by geographic chance, some of the most important excludable environmental resources are found in countries that happen to have a lower level of economic development than others. Tropical areas, which have a lower aggregate level of development than nontropical areas, have the most species diversity and ecosystem diversity of anywhere on earth.[34] The second is that the process of industrialization *forests* caused a level of environmental harm and resource extraction that decreased *bio-diver* the extent and quality of environmental resources present in the developed world. Much of the biodiversity and forests that might have once been present in North America and Europe has been destroyed. In terms of resources like biodiversity or forestry it is the developing countries that have, and therefore can exclude others from, many of the resources in question.  *← email.*

The power of exclusion has been used by developing states on issues such as biodiversity conservation, as discussed in chapter 8. Developing countries have had a mixed experience with this agreement. The effort for financial assistance showed some influence but not to the extent that developed countries sought. Developing countries won the guarantee of "new and additional financial resources" that will be used to "enable developing country Parties to meet the agreed full incremental costs to them of implementing measures which fulfill the obligations of this Convention."[35] They had less success on how that funding would be distributed, however, since the CBD adopted the modified GEF as its interim funding mechanism, over the objection of developing countries.[36]

But developing states unambiguously won the semantic battle of reaffirming states' "sovereign right to exploit their own resources pursuant to their own environmental policies."[37] Developing country parties to the CBD were also able to gain a stronger pledge for technology transfer than parties to other international agreements had accomplished. Article 16 addresses a wide variety of types of access to technology that are promised to developing countries, and indicates that transfer of technology is "essential … for the attainment of the objectives of this Convention." As one developing country negotiator said, "we have the biodiversity, they have the technology."[38] Most importantly, the biosafety protocol to the CBD was negotiated largely at the behest of developing countries, and is based fundamentally on their right – and ability – to determine what is allowed within their borders, refusing to import living modified organisms if they so choose.

Of particular note, within the issue of biodiversity conservation, are the private mechanisms, also discussed in chapter 8, made possible by the sovereign authority (and thus ability to exclude) that developing states have over their own biodiversity resources. The excludability of biodiversity resources also creates the opportunity for private deals to be made by those states with valued biodiversity within their borders. The variety of private agreements such as debt-for-nature swaps, bioprospecting agreements, and ecotourism, provide opportunities for biodiversity-rich countries to allow access on their own terms by others to their resources in return for compensation or profit. These private deals have resulted in greater benefits for the developing countries entering into them than alternate forms of biodiversity protection might have. Countries without important biodiversity (and in the case of debt-for-nature swaps, without available discounted debt) have been unable to benefit from these types of arrangements, however.

This latter dynamic suggests that excludability can influence a different aspect of developing country negotiations internationally: the extent to which we see developing country solidarity on an issue. For those environmental issues with a high degree of excludability, we should expect little meaningful effort by developing countries to work together for cooperative outcomes that appeal to all of them. But we should expect a higher degree of developing country solidarity in negotiations to address nonexcludable resources. The cohesion with which developing countries act on a given issue, not surprisingly, can influence their ability to achieve their goals. In addressing ozone depletion, developing countries generally acted as a unified block. China and India led the negotiations for funding for developing countries, but they resisted any efforts to make side deals and insisted that any agreement be global and generalizable. In an issue area like ozone depletion this strategy works well; no developing countries were especially fearful of the consequences of ozone depletion and as a group they could make a credible threat to continue their behavior.

Nonexcludability does not guarantee solidarity, however; what the preferences of states are on a given issue also influence the extent to which they are willing to work together in pursuit of a common goal. In some nonexcludable issue areas the preferences of developing countries are more varied. On climate change, for instance, some developing states would be particularly harmed by climate change and others would be particularly harmed by measures taken to prevent it. Developing countries have been less able to operate as a unified block, and that may harm their negotiating ability.

## Where and How Expensive?

Also important for determining developing country influence in negotiations over global environmental issues are the location of the causes and effects of the environmental harm in question. The more the developing world can credibly plan to ignore the problem, the greater the likelihood that developing states will be able to gain concessions for taking action. When addressing problems that are especially pressing for developing countries generally or for some countries particularly, it will be harder for these states to make a credible case of non-involvement in order to gain collective assistance. Similarly, the more concerned industrialized countries are about a given (subtractable) problem, whether from actual likelihood of harm or a mobilized domestic population, the more likely these states will be to give in to developing country demands, because they care about addressing a problem they cannot solve alone.

The costs of addressing these issues also play a role, but it is interesting that they alone do not determine the willingness of the industrialized countries to address developing country concerns. One of the reasons that climate change poses such a difficult problem for global agreement is not only that there are North–South disagreements, but that the costs that would need to be borne by developed countries to address the problem, apart from any financial aid, are likely to be so large; when funding incremental costs of changing developing country behavior are included the cost becomes almost unimaginable. But even if the cost were more modest and changing behavior more feasible, developing countries would run into greater difficulties negotiating about climate change than about ozone depletion, given that the negative effects of climate change are more widely distributed worldwide.

The desertification experience also provides evidence that cost is not the only factor preventing developing countries from realizing their goals. At the time of negotiation of the Convention to Combat Desertification, the United Nations Environment Programme determined that an effective twenty-year desertification program would cost around $10 billion annually.[39] While undertaking such a dramatic program is unlikely (and addressing the costs of programs foreseen by the desertification convention would require a fraction of that), its costs are modest compared to those of addressing climate change and within the range of costs undertaken to address ozone depletion. Low cost alone has clearly not made addressing this issue any more feasible.

Finally, we need to examine how costly and difficult measures to address the problem are; if the cost is too high, the North will be reluctant to take on obligations at all, much less help finance action by the South.

# Growing Influence of Developing Country Concerns

Despite this varied experience with the level of influence developing countries have been able to have in global environmental negotiations, there are some signs of cumulative effects of increased bargaining power, and the importance of precedent. The idea that developing countries should have a say in how the funding they are given should be allocated, and more specifically the use of double majority voting to carry that out, has become institutionalized. Even the Global Environment Facility, which originally gave less control to recipient countries than did the Montreal Protocol Multilateral Fund, was reformed as it was declared the interim funding mechanism for the FCCC and the CBD and now includes balanced representation and double majority voting.[40] It is no longer unusual to see such a funding mechanism for developing countries negotiated into international environmental agreements; in fact, its absence is now rare. Moreover, temporary experience with a funding shortfall in the Multilateral Fund[41] moved developing countries to include in the UNFCCC and other agreements the caveat that the obligations of developing country parties "will depend on the effective implementation by developed country Parties of their commitments under the Convention related to financial resources and transfer of technology."[42] The idea of "common but differentiated responsibilities"[43] of developed and developing countries in approaching global environmental agreements has been widely accepted. With some variation due to the characteristics of environmental problems, developing countries have become a powerful negotiating force in international environmental politics.

# Notes

1 Paul Steinberg, *Environmental Leadership in Developing Countries: Transnational Relations and Biodiversity Policy in Costa Rica and Bolivia* (Cambridge, Mass.: MIT Press, 2001).

2 See, for example, Marian A. L. Miller, *The Third World in Global Environmental Politics* (Boulder and London: Lynne Rienner, 1995).

3 Immanuel Wallerstein *The Capitalist World-Economy* (Cambridge: Cambridge University Press, 1979).

4 Timothy Doyle, *Environmental Movements in Minority and Majority Worlds* (New Brunswick, N.J.: Rutgers University Press, 2004).

5 Miller, 20.

6 Marc Williams "The Third World and Global Environmental Negotiations: Interests, Institutions, and Ideas," *Global Environmental Politics* 5(3) (August 2005): 48–69.

7 Adil Najam et al., "From Rio to Johannesburg: Progress and Prospects," *Environment* 44(7) (2002): 221–31.

8 Adil Najam, "The Collective South in Multinational Environmental Politics," in Stuart Nagel, ed., *Policymaking and Prosperity: A Multinational Anthology* (Lanham, Md.: Lexington Books, 2003), 197–240.

9 Adil Najam, "Dynamics of the Southern Collective: Developing Countries in Desertification Negotiations," *Global Environmental Politics* 4(3) (August 2003): 128–54.

10 International Development Research Centre, *For Earth's Sake: A Report from the Commission on Developing Countries and Global Change* (Ottawa: International Development Research Centre, 1992); Susan Feitelberg Jacobsen, "North–South Relations and Global Environmental Issues – A Review of the Literature," CDR Working Paper 96.3 Center for Development Research (Copenhagen), May 1996.

11 Uday Desai, "Environment, Economic Growth, and Government in Developing Countries," in Uday Desai, ed., *Ecological Policy and Politics in Developing Countries: Economic Growth, Democracy, and the Environment* (Albany: SUNY Press, 1998), 3.

12 Uday Desai, "Poverty, Government, and the Global Environment," in Uday Desai, ed., *Ecological Policy and Politics in Developing Countries* (Albany: SUNY Press, 1998), 295.

13 Steinberg, 41.

14 UNDP, *Human Development Report 1998* (Oxford: Oxford University Press, 1998), 66.

15 Michael Ross, *Timber Booms and Institutional Breakdown in Southeast Asia* (Cambridge: Cambridge University Press, 2001).

16 Williams, 56.

17 Rio Declaration on Environment and Development, 1992, Principle 3.

18 World Commission on Environment and Development, *Our Common Future* (Oxford: Oxford University Press, 1987), 8.

19 Hans Bruyninckx, "Sustainable Development: The Institutionalization of a Contested Policy Concept," in Michele M. Betsill, Kathryn Hochstetler, and Dimitris Stevis, eds., *Palgrave Advances in International Environmental Politics* (Basingstoke and New York: Palgrave Macmillan, 2006), 265–98.

20 Stacy D. VanDeveer and Ambuj D. Sagar, "Capacity Development for the Environment: North and South," in Elisabeth Corell, Angela Churie Kallhauge, and Gunnar Sjöstedt, eds., *Global Challenges: Furthering the Multilateral Process for Sustainable Development* (London: Greenleaf, 2005), 259–73.

21 Ambuj D. Sagar and Stacy D. VanDeveer, "Capacity Development for the Environment: Broadening the Scope," *Global Environmental Politics* 5(3) (August 2005): 14–22.

22 Frank Biermann, "Institutions for Scientific Advice: Global Environmental Assessments and Their Influence in Developing Countries," *Global Governance* 8 (2002): 195–219.

23 Sylvia Karlsson, "The North–South Knowledge Divide: Consequences for Global Environmental Governance," in Daniel C. Esty and Maria H. Ivanova, eds., *Global Environmental Governance: Options and Opportunities* (New Haven: Yale School of Forestry and Environmental Studies, 2002), 1–24.

24 Susan Sell, "North–South Environmental Bargaining; Ozone, Climate Change, and Biodiversity," *Global Governance* 2 (1996): 97–118.

25 Gregg Easterbrook, "Forget PCB's. Radon. Alar." *New York Times Magazine*, 11 September 1994, 60–63.

26 Giselle V. Steele, "Drowning in Sand; Environmental Effects of Desertification," *E* 8(1) (11 January 1997): 15.

27 "UN Convention to Combat Desertification," *M2 Presswire*, 9 January 1997, Lexis/Nexis.

28 International Institute for Sustainable Development, "A Brief Analysis of the Second Session of the INCD, 13–24 September 1993," *Earth Negotiations Bulletin* 4(22) http://www.iisd.ca/linkages/vol04/0422034e.html, 24 September 1993.

29 Pamela S. Chasek, David L. Downie, and Janet Welsh Brown, *Global Environmental Politics*, 4th edn. (Boulder, Colo.: Westview Press, 2006), 175–81.

30 Convention to Combat Desertification Article 21(4).

31 International Institute for Sustainable Development, "Summary of the Fourth Session of the INC for the Elaboration of An International Convention to Combat Desertification, 21–31 March 1994," *Earth Negotiations Bulletin* 4(44) http://www.iisd.ca/vol04/0444001e.html, 31 March 1994.

32 Chasek, Downie, and Brown, 180–81.

33 Pamela S. Chasek, "The Convention to Combat Desertification: Lessons Learned for Sustainable Development," *Journal of Environment and Development* 6 (June 1997): 156.

34 William P. Cunningham and Barbara Woodworth Saigo, *Environmental Science: A Global Concern* (Dubuque, Ia.: William C. Brown, 1997), 272.

35 Convention on Biological Diversity, Article 20(2).

36 David Fairman, "The Global Environment Facility: Haunted by the Shadow of the Future," in Robert O. Keohane and Marc A. Levy, eds., *Institutions for Environmental Aid* (Cambridge, Mass.: MIT Press, 1996), 76.

37 Convention on Biological Diversity, Article 3.

38 Kal Raustiala and David G. Victor, "Biodiversity Since Rio – The Future of the Convention on Biological Diversity," *Environment* 38(4) (1996): 19.

39 United Nations Environment Program, "Fact Sheet 8 – Financing Action to Combat Desertification," http://www.unep.ch/incd/fs8.html, 3 July 1997.

40 Fairman, 67.

41 Elizabeth R. DeSombre, "Compliance Implications of the Multilateral Fund," *International Conference On Ozone Protection Technologies*, Conference Proceedings, 21–23 October, 1996, Washington D.C., 910–19.

42 United Nations Framework Convention on Climate Change, Article 4(7).

43 See United Nations Framework Convention on Climate Change, Article 4(1).

# 5 The Role of Non-Governmental Actors

*NGOs appear to be key actors in moving societies away from current trends in environmental degradation and toward sustainable economies.*

Thomas Princen and Matthias Finger[1]

*The environment is not going to be saved by environmentalists. Environmentalists do not hold the levers of economic power.*

Maurice Strong, UNCED Secretary General[2]

International relations tends to be a state-centric endeavor; even the name of the field suggests that it is about relations among "nations." To the extent that non-governmental actors play a role, it is generally assumed that this role is subsumed within the actions of states; constituting, perhaps, the interests and actions of the states, but still fundamentally part of creating the process by which states interact with each other.[3] There are important advantages to examining international relations in this manner: much of the major action undertaken, even with international environmental politics, is done by, or mediated through, states. States, in governing themselves, create impacts on the international system. States are the actors that, through their representatives and political processes, negotiate international environmental agreements and then work domestically to implement them. Certainly they are central actors in examining what happens to the global environment.

Although it is states that actually agree to undertake international environmental commitments, there are a number of ways in which non-state actors influence this process, even within the state-centric view. Scientists (discussed further in chapter 3), international organizations, environmental non-governmental organizations (NGOs), and industry actors all contribute to the making and implementation of international environmental policy. Without their concern, often expressed first on the domestic level, international environmental policy would rarely get made, since one or more states must be interested enough in an environmental issue to attempt to create international cooperation to address it.

Environmental NGOs work to raise concern about environmental problems, both domestically and by sharing information across borders. Within one country, they can raise public awareness to the presence of an environmental problem. They can also lobby governmental actors to take action on international environmental policy issues, or lead consumer boycotts of products deemed harmful to the environment. Once an international organization exists to address a global environmental issue, NGOs may be invited to participate as observers, and may be allowed to participate in other ways.

Industry actors are also important players in environmental regulation on the international level. Often it is industrial activity of some sort that is implicated in the creation of a global environmental problem in the first place. So sometimes industry actors are active in resisting any costly regulations on their activities, and may call into question the scientific justification for acting. But occasionally it can be in the interests of industries to themselves undertake environmental regulations, and there are conditions under which businesses can benefit, comparatively at least, from international regulations. Industry actors within a state can sometimes be found, therefore, pushing for the creation of international environmental policy, or at least not hindering it.

From a theoretical perspective, however, it is also important to pay attention to the role that non-state actors play outside of the traditional view of state-centered politics. Examination of action by non-state actors, particularly within the literature on environmental policy, suggests that they help to create change in ways that subvert the traditional state-oriented approach to political analysis. Raised awareness may lead to citizen pressure to undertake environmental action with international consequences, even without national requirements to do so. Non-governmental organizations from within one country may work directly to influence citizens of another country to pressure their own governments, rather than doing so by influencing governments to negotiate with governments.

Multinational corporations may bring higher environmental standards than required to their foreign subsidiaries because of advantages to themselves to doing so, not because states have decreed that certain policies must be followed. Increasingly businesses are undertaking private regulations, neither required nor enforced by state structures. In other instances industries may pick up and move their operations to states with lower environmental regulations, influencing both the global environmental quality and the likelihood of states to resist higher standards for fear of losing revenue. In some circumstances, environmentalist and industry non-state actors may end up working together to influence the shape of international environmental policy, despite the general perception that the two groups are inherently at odds. To understand global environmental politics it is thus essential to examine the multiple pathways through which non-state actors influence behavior that impacts the natural environment.

## Environmental NGOs

The growth of environmental organizations addressing international problems has been dramatic over the last thirty-five years. While different in some ways from other non-governmental organizations, they share a number of characteristics with such organizations broadly, and it is useful to examine what is known generally about the role of non-governmental organizations addressing international issues. An initial question is what accounts for the development of citizen organizations, particularly transnationally. Have they become more prevalent on the international scene, and, if so, why? More importantly, what types of effects do they have? To what extent to they challenge, or support the roles of states?

Non-governmental actors, even those with a great deal of influence, have been around and even acting internationally for more than a century and a half, with religious and labor organizations among the first citizen groups to work for international goals.[4] One study suggests that conventional international NGOs numbered at about 1,000 in the 1950s, 2,000 by the 1970s, and had risen to nearly 5,000 by the mid-1990s.[5] The *Economist* estimates an increase in international NGOs from 6,000 to 26,000 during the decade of the 1990s.[6] Estimates that include local NGOs (which may nevertheless have international interests) put that number far higher,[7] and one of the important phenomena of the past thirty-five years is the growth in internationally interested indigenous non-governmental organizations in the developing world.[8] Environmental NGOs specifically have increased in number and have begun to focus more directly on international elements of the environment.

The first domestic environmental NGOs were created at the end of the nineteenth century in the United States and Britain. While these organizations began communicating across state borders early in their existence it was not really until the second half of the twentieth century that environmental issues were perceived as international in scope, so few organizations existed to address them in that form.[9] By the time of the United Nations Conference on the Human Environment in Stockholm in 1972, the parallel NGO meeting drew the participation of nearly 400 NGOs; the 1992 United Nations Conference on Environment and Development in Rio counted 7,000 participating NGOs.[10] The World Summit on Sustainable Development in Johannesburg in 2002 accredited 21,000 participants from NGOs to the conference itself, and an NGO conference operating in parallel to the summit had more than 40,000 participants.[11]

The phenomenon of NGO activity overall has thus grown, and certainly the presence of environmental activists, sometimes with different agendas and strategies than those in traditional NGOs, has been an important and growing phenomenon in the last half century. There are a variety of explanations for the growth of environmental NGOs, suggesting that there may be different contexts that lead to the formation or influence of different types of NGOs. Social movement theory, developed to explain activist organizations within national political systems, would seem an obvious place to look for explanations. Theories, such as those by Alain Touraine, suggest a cyclical process by which movements of underrepresented populations organize, fight for acceptance, and ultimately are co-opted into the system.[12] Traditionally these approaches would expect collective action to be triggered by some combination of relative deprivation, common interests, and economic or political conflicts. Matthias Finger supports the conventional wisdom that NGO participation is a political response to a lack of previous individual participation.[13] A related idea is that the inability of states to provide for their citizens creates a global civil society to demand what states are not providing.[14] Some see NGO responses to the ineffectiveness of states as a positive element, viewing social movements as efforts to politicize activity to help national political systems adapt, evolve, and learn.[15]

Certainly one explanation for the greater role of NGO involvement in international affairs is, as Peter Spiro calls it, the "dramatically heightened permeability of national borders" and the accompanying improvement in communications. It is simply easier for activists in dispersed locations to work together for a common goal than it used to be.[16] Increasing worldwide democratization contributes to this trend.[17] Paul Wapner suggests that NGOs, particularly those that have transnational impacts, emerge as part of a broader growth of "international civil society." He sees civil society, the realm

*Civil Society*

in which "people engage in spontaneous, customary, and nonlegalistic forms of association" for common goals as apart from, but interacting with, the state system.[18] The growth of the opportunity for people to work for common goals internationally both reflects and allows the growth of NGOs.

Additional external factors may account for the increasing prevalence of international NGOs more broadly. Steve Charnovitz argues that the influence of NGOs internationally coincides with periods of peace.[19] The end of the Cold War was also influential, as it changed the international arena in ways conducive to creation and influence of NGOs. Decreased security concerns (at least vis-à-vis other states) allowed for a lessening of the central importance of national allegiances, increasing the opportunities for coordinated action by people across borders.[20] Similarly, those who study the growth in human rights regimes, often seen in parallel to environmental organizations, suggest that the lessening of tensions between the former eastern and western blocs allowed for an international consensus to develop in favor of humanitarian action.[21] A related phenomenon is the lessening attention paid to developing countries that previously were courted with aid to keep them solidly in one bloc or another. Less funding from traditional donor states meant more unmet need.[22] This explanation fits into the privation explanation above, but with a post–Cold War twist: more non-governmental activity came about because the major powers no longer saw the political advantage in meeting the needs of people in developing countries. NGOs have been created, both domestically and internationally, to meet these needs.

The level of uncertainty present in environmental issues in particular is suggested as an additional reason that non-governmental actors are so involved in environmental policy-making.[23] Margaret Keck and Kathryn Sikkink note that what they call "transnational advocacy networks" arise most frequently in issues with high "informational uncertainty."[24] Barbara Bramble and Gareth Porter point to the rise in organizations during the 1970s and 1980s that collect and disseminate data and analysis.[25] Non-governmental actors may be particularly well placed to address transnational issues, which are less likely to be the focus of states, whose constituents are domestic.[26] While this kind of non-governmental actor exists within a number of different issue areas, the types of things about which there is uncertainty (as discussed in Chapter 3) are numerous in environmental issue areas, and non-governmental actors can help fill the information void.

## NGO Approaches

It is also important to examine how environmental organizations work to achieve their goals within global environmental policy. While the types of tasks they perform could be divided into almost infinite categories, it can be useful to think of them as fulfilling functions either within the state process or outside of it. Part of the reason this distinction can matter is that recent NGO activity, particularly by environmental organizations, challenges the traditional view of how non-state actors influence policy. Occasionally it can be difficult to categorize NGO actions even this simply; the variety of types of activities they undertake and pathways through which they attempt to influence the human impact on the natural environment are many. As Wapner points out, transnational NGOs are unconstrained by the idea of territoriality; "they focus and pursue aims free from the tasks of preserving and enhancing the welfare of a given, geographically situated population."[27]

The traditional view of how non-state actors influence international environmental politics generally begins with organizations that raise awareness of an environmental problem. They may be responsible for helping to create the awareness of the environmental problems in the first place, or helping create the will to do something to address them. This is the role these types of organizations are generally known for, but it is by no means the only role they play. They also work within the legislative process inside states, either to help elect candidates that are likely to support environmental causes, or by lobbying the legislature to pass environmental laws. On international issues, they can likewise work to pressure a state to adopt policies domestically that will ultimately help address international environmental problems, and they can put pressure on state actors to participate in, and take certain positions during, international environmental negotiations. Environmental organizations can be particularly effective within a political context in part because they do not share the time horizons of politicians, who think primarily of the next election. As Karen Litfin points out, "most environmental problems will outlast the policy makers charged with addressing them."[28] Similarly, transnational activists have a potentially global constituency, while politicians are elected locally or nationally. On the one hand both these factors make the work of activists more difficult; on the other hand, both make their work more necessary.

There are a number of ways NGOs can influence environmental action that do not involve lobbying their own state to take particular action. The increased number of organizations with membership or chapters in multiple countries creates opportunities for influence across state lines. A useful way to categorize these less-traditional forms of avenues for non-state actor influence is to look at those as acting within the state system but not through states, and those acting internationally in ways that circumvent the state system.

Environmental organizations can act within the state system without acting within states per se. Doing so may be as simple as working to raise awareness in a different state of an environmental issue in a way that inspires people to take action to get their own state to address the issue internationally. In addition, NGOs have come to play roles as critics or informants during the process of negotiation of international agreements. More and more frequently NGOs are allowed, if not to participate in, at least to observe, international negotiations. They are often allowed to speak in meetings when recognized by the chair, and interact with delegates in the hallways and coffeebreaks where some of the most important details of an impending agreement are discussed. Sometimes they help draft elements of what eventually becomes the treaty. In the negotiation of the Basel Convention on the Control of Transboundary Movements of Hazardous Wastes and their Disposal, for instance, both Greenpeace and the Center for Science and the Environment drafted some of the language that ultimately ended up in the text of the treaty.[29]

The participation of environmental organizations in the delegations of national representatives to international organizations may be considered part of the conventional activity of NGOs. In some contexts, however, environmental activists have taken this approach one step further, by essentially representing states in international fora. One clear example of this phenomenon is in the International Whaling Commission, where non-governmental organizations have brought a number of states into the agreement, by taking over the tasks normally required of a state in an international organization. The former IWC Secretary tells the story of the commissioner of an unnamed member state that simply signed over the check from an environmental organization to pay its dues. Similarly, a representative from a nonwhaling state that had recently joined the IWC showed up late for a meeting and had to ask directions to the non-governmental organization section to go get his briefing book from the organization that had prepared it for him.[30] A former Greenpeace consultant tells of a plan that added at least six new antiwhaling members in the period from 1978 to 1982 through the paying of annual dues, drafting of membership documents, and naming of commissioners to represent these countries, at an annual cost of more than $150,000.[31] Japan's representatives at the 47th IWC annual meeting in 1995 pointed out that "some individuals are listed as government delegates attending the preliminary meetings of working groups and sub-committees but registered as NGO observers in the plenary week."[32]

NGOs can play an essential role in monitoring compliance and reporting on other elements of state behavior on the international level after an environmental agreement is in place. While this role is often played informally, there are circumstances in which some NGOs are formally involved in the process of monitoring structured into the agreement itself. For instance, the International Bureau for Whaling Statistics in Norway has been the organization to which catch statistics are transmitted during the whaling season when commercial whaling is allowed; this organization is empowered to determine when overall quotas have been met and to end the whaling season.[33] The World Conservation Union (IUCN), which is an organization with both governmental and non-governmental members, acts as the secretariat for the Convention on International Trade in Endangered Species of Wild Fauna and Flora (CITES).[34] Even when NGOs are not formally involved in monitoring, they can play an invaluable role. The organization TRAFFIC tracks wildlife trade worldwide and has provided important evidence of smuggling of endangered species. Greenpeace has done an impressive job of publicizing the whaling activities of IWC members (even when those activities may be within the letter of the law), in a way that makes the general public more aware of state behavior than would otherwise be the case. The same is true for organizations such as Ozone Action, which first addressed issues of ozone depletion and has now moved on to address climate change, reporting especially on the behavior of member states relative to their obligations under international agreements. NGOs may also participate in the treaty implementation process by using advocacy or litigation to support international legal processes.[35]

Non-governmental organizations may also act internationally in a way that essentially subverts, rather than participates in, the state system, in a practice Wapner calls engaging in "world civic politics."[36] This type of action challenges most directly the traditional view of how non-governmental actors matter in international relations. While it is discussed most directly with respect to activist environmental organizations there are parallels as well within the discussion of industry influence on the global environment.

One way organizations can work around the state system is simply by attempting to change the actions of individuals, rather than working to change the regulations facing individuals. Greenpeace uses this tactic when its members place themselves between whales and whalers' harpoons. If whalers cease that particular whale hunt, it is not because environmental organizations have changed the law, or even changed their minds, but because the whalers have calculated that it would be damaging to their interests to harpoon Greenpeace members as would be portrayed in the international media.

At the same time, the international perception is created that these activists care so much for whales that they are willing to put their lives on the line, which is intended to influence public opinion worldwide. This is a second method of working around the state rather than through it. Wapner calls this strategy "bearing witness." This strategy is the most important one organizations like Greenpeace employ. While blockading the shipment of ozone-depleting CFCs from a DuPont plant by placing people literally on the railroad tracks by which the chemicals were shipped out, the organization made no noticeable dent in CFC production, but it did manage to raise awareness worldwide of the problem of ozone depletion and DuPont's role in it.[37]

There are other ways that non-state actors can work to change individual behavior, or lead to conservation, without working within a state regulatory structure. Organizations such as Conservation International literally buy tracts of land that they preserve,[38] rather than waiting for state or international agreements to provide protection. The non-governmental organizations involved in debt-for-nature swaps (discussed further in chapter 8) spend their own money to purchase from banks the commercial debt of highly indebted countries with rich biodiversity resources, and work out agreements to retire the debt in return for conservation activity on the part of the indebted states. More directly, organizations like the World Wide Fund for Nature (WWF; still called the "World Wildlife Fund" within the United States) work with local people in environmentally sensitive areas to help create a situation where they can protect their own local environment, whether required to by law or not.[39]

Collette Ridgeway calls this phenomenon "free-market environmentalism," and argues that it is a more effective method of protecting wilderness than state action provides.[40] It bears a resemblance to voluntary corporate environmentalism, discussed in the following section, in that individuals and organizations undertake to provide environmental protection, or raise awareness of environmental issues, when not compelled to by domestic or international regulation, and often without even the goal of creating such regulation. This type of activity, combined with the more "direct action" approaches of Greenpeace or Earth First!, suggests that much of what happens to influence the state of the global environment happens outside of the standard framework of the state, and suggests that non-governmental actors play a far more complex and nuanced role than traditional social movement theory would expect.

## Effectiveness of NGO Action

Assuming that NGOs have at least some impact on activity relating to the global environment, what determines how effective environmental NGOs will be at achieving their goals? There is some degree of uncertainty about the extent to which NGOs play a beneficial function in particular environmental issue areas,[41] but certainly there are conditions under which they are more or less likely to influence action on issues with which they are concerned. Although this question does not easily lend itself to categorization, the major factors examined here include choices of strategy (with whom one chooses to ally, whether to work within or against the system), and the context in which activist organizations are operating.

The question of international collaboration among NGOs is also an important strategic question. While some, such as Wapner, Princen and Finger, and Keck and Sikkink, point to examples of successful transnational collaboration, others suggest that when organizations from developed and developing countries work together the resulting power struggles and conflicts over ideals decrease the effectiveness of the organizations within the developing countries.[42] This could happen when the interests of northern NGOs are sufficiently threatening to governments in developing countries that they curtail NGO access to the policy process in the wake of collaboration with developed country NGOs. Additionally the added outside attention can cause developing country governments to put a gloss of "scenic and figurative environmentalism" on existing policies,[43] making true change less likely because progress appears to have been made. Alan Thomas concludes that, at least in African NGOs, outright opposition may be more likely to be successful than working on activities complementary to those of the state.[44] Nevertheless, most agree that collaboration between organizations from developed and developing countries on environmental issues does lead to additional information, financial resources, and expertise that might otherwise not have been present.[45]

On the issue of context, one question is the role that democracy plays in determining the effectiveness of non-governmental actors in global environmental politics. Though democratization may have led to an increase in NGOs overall, it is unclear whether NGOs hoping to influence policy in, or from within, a democracy have a greater degree of success than those working on issues in nondemocratic regimes. Conventional wisdom might expect greater success from NGOs acting within democracies because of more points of access into the political process, and because there are likely to be more non-governmental actors in general. Thomas's study, discussed above, supports this hypothesis broadly.[46] But there is at least some evidence that this expectation does not necessarily hold. One study comparing NGO success with policies on tropical deforestation within democratic India and nondemocratic Indonesia did not find the expected relationship.[47] It is also possible for NGO participation through democratic (or, more likely, democratizing) governments to create a backlash against the very openness that allowed participation. Thomas points out, however, that even when governments try to restrict previous NGO access to policy-making, they may nevertheless pluralize the political process by including additional institutions in the making of decisions.[48]

Related issues include other elements of state structure, including the extent to which the state that NGOs are trying to influence is "state" or "society" dominated. Ideas, as Thomas Risse-Kappan points out in an effort to persuade us to examine domestic structures, "do not float freely,"[49] but instead need to have a receptive state structure, for transnational organizations pushing them to be successful. Rodger Payne examines this model in the context of environmental NGO influence, and concludes that both the openness, or "society-dominated" nature of a state, and the centralization of that state, leave it more vulnerable to influence by nongovernmental actors.[50]

Another element of context that must be considered, although difficult to quantify, is the difficulty of the issue faced. As discussed in chapter 2, the difficulty of changing action surely depends on many factors unrelated to NGOs, including some about how difficult the goal they are pursuing is. Related is the issue of what other actors in the process desire. Although the logic seems somewhat tautological, some suggest that NGOs have the greatest influence internationally when their issues are backed by powerful countries.[51] In this logic, NGOs do not necessarily supplant or replace states, but become another way through which powerful states exert pressure.

While that view is perhaps overly pessimistic of the ability of environmental organizations to have an influence on international environmental politics, it does suggest that, while their role in working around or challenging the state is essential to remember and an important corrective to much of international relations theory, the role that they play acting within states, or that states play acting in concert with them, is also essential.

## Industry Actors

Businesses, whether local or international, can be some of the most important players in influencing global environmental policy. It is often actions, directly or indirectly, by industry actors that help create environmental problems in the first place.[52] In a number of circumstances, however, businesses are finding that it can pay to be "green," and are undertaking environmental measures not required of them. Ascertaining the conditions under which such corporate environmentalism is likely to be undertaken, or likely to benefit the environment, is essential in trying to understand the impact of industry on the global environment. Also important is examining the power of industry actors, particularly multinational corporations, relative to the state. To what extent can big polluters or those industries that rely on resource extraction influence policies of states, or be influenced by them? Related is the question of whether states lower their environmental policies to attract businesses that do not want to pay the added cost of environmental protection, or whether the increasing globalization instead results in higher industry standards worldwide. Finally, does environmental regulation increase or decrease the incentive for industry environmentalism?

All else being equal, there are costs, at least in the short run, to operating an environmentally friendly industry. Pollution is a problem precisely because it is an externality. It is an unintended and generally unpriced consequence of industrial activity and its effects are felt by those who do not create it. When environmental resources are not regulated by the government, a polluting factory shares with everyone the cost of decreased quality of the air or water, but alone bears the benefit of not having to clean its emissions. It therefore has little economic incentive to behave in an environmentally responsible manner.

Why, then (or, perhaps more usefully, under what conditions), do we see voluntary acts of corporate environmentalism? There are instances in which running an environmentally friendly business can be economically advantageous. 3M's slogan that "pollution prevention pays" can be true under certain conditions. Livio D. DeSimone and Frank Popoff of the World Business Council for Sustainable Development suggest many of the reasons that it may advantage industry to undertake environmental action. First, doing so may reduce current costs, under some circumstances. Second, future costs – or the possibility of future liability – may be reduced. Third, a "green image" may affect the company worth – to investors, consumers, or potential employees. Fourth, research into environmental alternatives or technology can open new markets for substitutes for environmentally harmful substances or technologies. Finally, adopting environmentalism before forced to by national or international regulation can lead to a long-term competitive advantage, despite potential short-term cost.[53]

The idea that pollution prevention actually does "pay," in its own terms, has spawned the field of industrial ecology. One definition of the concept notes that it is "a systems view, which seeks to optimize the total materials cycle from virgin material, to finished material, to component, to product, to obsolete product, and to ultimate disposal."[54] By taking this overall view of their operations, industries may be able to reduce costs by taking environmentally beneficial actions. Redesigning equipment can allow steam generated from one process to be used in another. Recovered waste products can be used as raw materials that would otherwise have to be purchased (or that can be sold to other manufacturers who need them). For example, 3M discovered that by making reusable shipping containers the company could simultaneously reduce the amount of waste generated and decrease the costs of procuring new shipping containers, with a yearly saving of more than $4 million. Industrias Fronterizas, a Mexican company that makes car engine manifolds, discovered that installing a filtration unit that separates waste products from clean water used in manufacturing saved the company more than $1 million annually by reducing overall waste and machine downtime.[55]

Another recent trend has been collective forms of voluntary industry certification, operating internationally. This phenomenon is part of what is increasingly referred to as "private environmental governance." Among the best-known of these efforts are the ISO 14000 environmental management standards. The international organization for standardization (ISO) is a non-governmental coordinating body based in Geneva. Its voluntary committees, about 80 per cent of whose delegates come from industry,[56] create standards that allow inter-operability across countries of physical things (such as the characteristics of an AA battery) as well as business practices more generally. The ISO has created a range of environmental management standards that companies are encouraged to adopt on such things as environmental communication, environmental design, and environmental performance evaluation. One set of these standards, ISO 14001, allows businesses to seek certification for meeting a set of requirements. To gain certification a company must comply with environmental laws in the jurisdiction in which it operates, ensure that it lives up to its own environmental policy statement, and commit to prevent pollution and to improve its environmental management continually, among other things. As of 2005 there were more than 90,000 firms that had received certification under this system, in 127 different states.[57] Firms publicize their certification as a way to trumpet their environmentalism. The effect of these standards on environmental behavior is not clear, however. Participants in the committee that creates the standards overwhelmingly believe that the environmental behavior of firms implementing ISO 14001 has improved.[58] But others suggest that the goals are less strict than they should be, and are especially unlikely to increase the access to environmental technology in developing states or decrease the generation of hazardous waste.[59] In addition, because of its focus on management rather than on performance, there is no clear indication that certified industries will have a lower environmental impact.[60]

Pollution prevention, or environmentalism more generally, will not be equally beneficial to all industry actors. Stuart Hart and Gautam Ahuja, for instance, find that the economic advantage of environmentalism is greatest for slower, more inefficient firms they call "high polluters."[61] Not surprisingly, these are the ones for which making environmental improvements are the least costly. The closer a firm comes to zero pollution, the greater the costs of innovating more environmentally sound production techniques increased.

## Voluntary Environmentalism in the Shadow of Regulation

The idea of national or international regulation is often lurking in the background, unacknowledged, in discussions of whether voluntary environmental action by industries will be economically beneficial. As Frances Cairncross notes, "Most companies will only be as green as governments make them."[62] It is thus important to examine the intersection between voluntary and mandatory environmental protection by industries. First, one of the reasons that pollution prevention may pay comes when governments or consumers force industries to internalize the costs of externalities. It pays to diminish the waste stream in manufacturing when regulations prohibit dumping waste into the water, or when local dumps charge increasing amounts for accepting waste or limit the amount or types of waste they will accept. The use of substitutes for environmentally damaging substances may become cost effective only when the harmful chemicals they replace become more costly. Nonrenewable natural resources (such as oil) provide that incentive on their own; as they become depleted they become more costly and it pays to develop ways to use them more efficiently or to find substitutes. But the same incentive can be created by governmental regulation.

Second, the anticipation of regulation is often behind the actions of firms to address environmental problems, hoping to prevent regulation by their voluntary behavior. A study by the World Resources Institute in the 1980s suggests that self-regulation by industry could stall the imposition of national or international environmental rules.[63] Similarly, there are advantages to industries of working to increase environmentalism on the local level, where they can find compromises with people whose economic lives are tied to the industry, before the need to regulate at the national or international level becomes an issue.[64] This incentive operates similarly for firms hoping to avoid liability; they may adopt environmental practices not specifically required by law because they operate in a system in which they can be held responsible for accidents or other environmental problems.[65] ISO 14001 certification is often sought by firms hoping to persuade their governments that additional regulation is therefore unnecessary, and some countries have been willing to accept ISO certification as evidence of positive environmental behavior in their monitoring and enforcement processes.[66]

In addition, the advantage gained through making the technology used in environmental clean-up, or substitutes for environmentally damaging substitutes, comes primarily when other industries undertake environmental action, most frequently because they are required to domestically or internationally. The "first mover" advantage is only advantageous if others move eventually as well, and technology made to counter pollution or clean up environmental damage is only valuable if states have decided to do so.

## Industry-Driven Regulation

There are also, surprisingly enough, situations in which industries may *want* to be regulated, either nationally or internationally. Sheldon Kamieniecki found that when U.S. industries take on proposed Congressional legislation for environmental protection they support it more often than they oppose it.[67] This phenomenon comes despite the possibility of costs to an industry from environmental regulation, either from increased costs for pollution abatement or higher prices for more environmentally friendly inputs. Several studies of pollution regulation in the United States suggest that they do decrease industry productivity,[68] certainly in the short run. Why, then, would industries accept, or even push for, environmental regulation? There are a number of circumstances under which regulation may be advantageous to industries.

First, and perhaps least convincing, is the argument that environmental regulation on its own actually helps industries compete. Counterarguments to the studies mentioned above, by those such as Michael Porter, suggest that "tough standards trigger innovation and upgrading." Moreover, Porter argues that states with the strictest environmental requirements generally are leaders in exports, even of the regulated product.[69] While there are certainly alternate explanations for such a correlation – the possibility, perhaps, that states with higher wealth from competitive industries are concurrently likely to have a greater degree of environmental regulation – at the very least it suggests that regulation will not be harmful for the economy as a whole, and may not even harm individual industries in the long run. One way this relationship could work is if environmental regulations result in the use of resource-efficient advanced technologies that could lead to lower production costs.[70] There are reasons to be dubious of this logic – after all, if new technology would lead to cost savings, could it not be adopted even without regulations? Nevertheless, the existence of standard operating procedures, and the investment of time required to develop potential new ways of doing business, may hinder useful innovation unless required by regulation.

Second, regulation, particularly at the international level, can help standardize obligations that industries must meet when operating across countries. A World

Resources Institute study suggests that multinational corporations "can thrive in a planned and regulated climate if the rules are explicit and predictable," and that consistent national and international regulation actually facilitates corporate planning.[71]

Similarly, industry can play an important role in moving international environmental regulation forward, in several different ways. If a state that is a leader on environmental protection domestically has already regulated its industries, these industries may prefer international regulation. This preference can come from several different sources. Perhaps the industry fears that future domestic regulation is likely to be more severe than international regulation will be. More importantly, since environmental regulation generally bears a cost, if the regulated industry competes internationally with industry in another state that is not regulated, the regulated industry will suffer a competitive disadvantage because its production process will be more costly. It would therefore prefer, if it is going to be regulated anyway, that these regulations apply worldwide. Second, if a certain industry has developed substitute products or processes to address the environmental problem in question, it would prefer that as many actors as possible be bound by regulations on this issue, so that the market for its substitutes will increase.

## Industry Influence

The question of whether or how to regulate industry leads to a broader, and temporally earlier, discussion of the influence of industry on the creation of policy, particularly the role of multinational (or transnational) corporations vis-à-vis the state. Industry in general tends to have a disproportionate level of influence within politics, for several understandable reasons. Building on Mancur Olson's "logic of collective action," many theorists have pointed out that public or collective goods tend to be underprovided,[72] because of the problem of free riders. David Vogel, for instance, points out that groups with diffuse interests, such as those desiring environmental protection, can be less successful than industry actors at having their interests represented in the political process.[73] This phenomenon occurs because a given industry fighting environmental regulation cares most intensely about this particular issue and gains specific benefits from avoiding a regulation. For the population at large it may be one of many issues people care about and those who care are more likely to be geographically and ideologically dispersed and therefore harder to organize to work for a specific goal.

What is the impact of different levels of environmental regulation on industry? One concern on the international level is that, if there are different levels of environmental regulation, industries are likely to want to locate in areas where they have the lowest regulatory burden. That would be of concern for states that lose economic advantages because they have chosen to impose tough environmental standards. The logical extension of this hypothesis is the concern that some states will decide to competitively deregulate, creating what have come to be known as "pollution havens" in order to attract industry.

H. Jeffrey Leonard suggests, in support of the pollution haven hypothesis, that there is more to the question of location of industry than naturally existing comparative advantage and that, in particular, "artificial factor endowments [such as low levels of regulation] created by governments have become at least as important as natural factor endowments" for states that want to attract industries.[74] On the whole the evidence for the existence of individual states lowering environmental standards to attract industry is mixed. Leonard's study showed that Ireland, Spain, Mexico, and Romania in the 1970s all took steps consistent with the pollution haven hypothesis. The states that Leonard examined, however, all eventually reversed or moderated some of their laxity.[75]

Some argue that empirically the evidence is in, and that "the literature as whole presents fairly compelling evidence across a broad range of industries, time-periods, and econometric specifications, that regulations do not matter to site choice."[76] There are several reasons that, even if competitive lowering (or avoidance) of environmental standards existed, firms might not move to take advantage of them. One would be if the firm has already adapted to the regulatory costs. Particularly in the case of environmental controls that require investing in equipment or altering production processes, there is little to be gained from going back to a form of production that does not control pollution. When the cost of relocating and the other disadvantages (such as a lower quality labor force) that may accompany a move to a pollution haven are added in, there may be little incentive for an industry to take advantage of low regulations in a new location.

Yet evidence, both anecdotal and statistical, suggests that industries sometimes will move to take advantage of low environmental regulations. An examination of level of environmental regulation and industry location choices in OECD states does find a relationship between environmental regulations and level and patterns of exports.[77] As David Wheeler points out, even those who do not find clear evidence of industries moving to areas of lower environmental standards should exercise caution, because "there is no theoretical reason why industries with exceptionally high pollution control costs should ignore regulatory concerns."[78] The jury appears to be out on the extent to which pollution havens will come to exist and to draw industry to them.

Moreover, there is evidence that even industries that make initial decisions based on trying to avoid regulatory standards may ultimately be able to be held to them regardless of their decision about where to locate. A good example is the phenomenon of "flags of convenience." Some states have, as the pollution haven hypothesis would suggest, tried to attract ship registrations by removing the traditional rules by which ship owners need to abide in order to register a ship in a given location. These rules have generally included restrictions on the nationality of the crew (so that a large percentage would need to be from the state in which the ship is registered), and certain environmental, safety, and labor requirements, both national and international. Ship owners have increasingly chosen to register their ships in flag-of-convenience states, in order to circumvent these restrictions. Since 1993, more ships have been registered in Panama, as measured both by number of ships and by gross tonnage, than anywhere else in the world. Second in both categories is Liberia.

Recent trends in international environmental standards as they pertain to ocean vessels, however, suggest that while the phenomenon of flag-of-convenience registration is growing, its ability to decrease international environmental standards is less clear. That these open registries exist as pollution havens is clear. That they have forced a lowering of overall global standards is less so. More importantly, there is evidence that ships flying flags of convenience have been persuaded themselves to undertake higher standards than would be required by their flag states, and have sometimes been able to convince their flag states to join international agreements or require higher levels of environmental regulation than they initially did.[79]

There are also circumstances under which industries operating across borders may export environmentalism[80] such that subsidiary or related plants take on higher environmental standards than they would otherwise be required to do. Ronie Garcia-Johnson concludes that multinational chemical firms operating in Brazil and Mexico took on greater environment protection measures than they would have had they not been pressured by U.S. parent companies. Even so, a variety of factors influenced the degree to which corporations were willing to upgrade their environmental practices when pressured. In particular, a high level of dependence on trade with the U.S., previous adoption of neo-liberal policies by the government, nationalist sentiment, and economic uncertainty all increase the likelihood that industries within a state will import the environmentalism of their parent companies.[81] Moreover, she provides evidence that this process can, under these conditions, lead to greater adoption of environmental standards than domestic or international regulation would induce, and to square the circle of industry influence presented here, that adoption of these higher standards can pay off in terms of competitive advantage.[82]

In assessing the overall role of industry in international environment, it is likely that cases of corporate "Greenwash," in which industries disguise business as usual as environmental, exist.[83] And certainly it is not true that industry action will always raise environmental standards. But it is clear that industry is an influential non-state actor that needs to be considered when examining global environmental policy. In addition, once policy has been created on the international level, industry actors often remain involved, as advisors, consultants, and in industry organizations present at international meetings to ensure that their interests are considered. It is, after all, those who have created a particular manufacturing process that may best know how to retrofit it with new technology, or the manufacturer of substitute chemicals that knows in what circumstances they can be used. While the presence of industry actors within the international system can lead to a situation of chemical solutions to chemical problems rather than a complete rethinking of the way industrial activities are carried out, it is hard to imagine, given their influence within states, a realistic system on the international level that would not include industry actors as important players.

## Assessing the Roles of Non-State Actors

The discussion of the role of non-state actors in international environmental politics leads to important conclusions about the roles of industry actors and environmental organizations separately. But it also suggests some broader observations about the types of roles that actors who are not governments can play in a realm that otherwise appears dominated by states. Few expect the state-based international system to disappear any time in the near future, but many attribute the rise in importance of all types of non-state actors to a dissatisfaction with the institutions of state-run civil society. The extent to which, and ways in which, these types of actors challenge the state system is an important question more broadly. It is also essential to examine the means by which these non-state actors gain influence on international environmental issues, either directly, or mediated through or across states. Finally, both types of groups present concerns about accountability. On the one hand, non-governmental actors tend to undertake action because of a concern that their interests, whatever they may be, are not adequately represented by the state apparatus, and NGOs in particular are often applauded for the grassroots support they represent. But a reasonable argument can be made that they are fundamentally as undemocratic as industry organizations. Finally, the relationship among these groups is important to examine, particularly in light of how it relates to the other themes.

The dominant view of the role of non-governmental actors is that they challenge the state-centric view, for better or for worse, in their effect on the environment. Non-governmental actors may increase environmental destruction by escaping the regulatory confines of state structures, or may improve the ability of the world to address environmental problems that states would otherwise overlook or not be able to mitigate. Concerns about the abilities of multinational corporations to circumvent or prevent the creation of national or international environmental regulations abound.[84] Similar stories about the ability of international industries to bring environmentalism to areas where states have failed to do so, or of environmental activists fulfilling roles that states cannot, suggest that non-state actors have supplanted some of the functions of states in addressing the global environment. Charnovitz states that "participation by NGOs does not mesh well with a state-centric view of global governance."[85]

Many, however, argue that these actors actually reinforce the role of states, or are (or should be) at least subsidiary to it. States are susceptible to the influence of both environmental organizations and business actors, but that may serve to make state action more effective. Wapner's view of NGOs as challenging the state nevertheless implies that there is a necessary and desirable role for the state overall.[86] Charnovitz, despite his comments on the incompatibility of state-centric approaches and NGO activities, suggests that NGO participation is directly related to the needs of the government, with NGOs stepping in to take over certain roles when states lack capacity.[87] Helmut Breitmeier and Volker Rittberger suggest that the international activities of environment NGOs have the effect of preserving the power between the state and civil society, rather than weakening the state.[88] The role that states play in actually negotiating and signing international agreements ensures their continuing centrality, even when NGOs may influence the process.[89] Kal Raustiala even argues that NGO participation enhances the ability of states to regulate through the treaty process, as evidenced by the greater roles states grant to these non-governmental organizations over time.[90]

This debate is particularly strong in discussion of the role of industry, especially trans- or multinational corporations (MNCs). Much of the concern about these actors has been in the power they wield, particularly vis-à-vis impoverished developing countries. Many point to the ability of these transnational corporations to replace the role of states in making – or preventing – regulatory decisions. It has been noted that the bargaining power of MNCs engaged in extracting natural resources, relative to their host countries, shifts over time in favor of host-country control, as part of an obsolescing bargain. But Steven Kobrin finds that this transfer of bargaining power is less true in manufacturing sectors,[91] and thus pollution-producing industries do not lose their influence on policy matters in their host countries. Matthias Finger and James Kilcoyne argue that MNCs have used the guise of sustainable development and their influence over governments to "subvert the efforts by the United Nations to prevent the further degradation of the natural environment."[92] Jennifer Clapp points out that voluntary environmentalism on the part of multinational corporations may result in decreased state oversight when it is not yet clear that industry will choose the most environmentally beneficial options for its activity.[93]

Others, however, note that even with respect to industries operating across borders, the state either does retain ultimate control or should. These are quite different arguments; the first empirical and the second exhortatory. Those who argue the latter make the argument that voluntary corporate environmentalism can only accomplish certain things, and even those most frequently come about within the context of a governmental regulatory structure.[94] Others, however, make the case that despite the importance of companies as international actors, they are vulnerable to state regulation, particularly when combined with the ability of non-governmental organizations to influence state behavior. Moreover, industries rely on states and the state system more broadly to create the framework within which they do business.[95] Nazli Choucri points out that international environmental agreements force MNCs to evaluate the environmental impacts of their actions in order to stay competitive.[96]

The increasing role of private governance is also a testament to the importance of non-state actors.[97] In addition to ISO, important private environmental governance processes include the Responsible Care program, developed by U.S. and Canadian chemical manufacturers and more widely adopted since, and the Forest Stewardship Council that promulgates standards for sustainable forestry that are used to designate forest products as coming from a well-managed operation.[98] As these examples suggest, industry actors are central in developing and implementing these forms of private governance, but non-governmental organizations are also involved, in providing pressure for firms to change their behavior and specifically to adopt, and fully implement, environmental standards. Some see this phenomenon of private governance as evidence of the declining power of the state,[99] but most forms of private governance operate in a state-centric context, and gain legitimacy through recognition and acceptance by states that would not be possible without state proceses.[100] Some states, for instance, have adopted ISO 14000 standards as their own, and the World Trade Organization has recognized the standards as acceptable under WTO rules.[101]

How do non-state actors gain the influence they seem to have? In part by their ability to frame issues. Both industry actors and non-governmental organizations seek to gain leverage by framing issues into a form that appeals to the desire of a society that is increasingly concerned with environmental degradation. Business actors are particularly astute at framing their efforts. The World Business Council on Sustainable Development supports free trade and business growth as a solution to the problem of environmental degradation, arguing that ending poverty will improve the state of the environment.[102] Voluntary corporate environmentalism, and the public relations campaigns that usually accompany it, are aimed at gaining the support of consumers and often leverage in specific debates about form, content, or existence of regulation. In some instances the frame may be all there is; examples include industry organizations that give themselves "environmental" sounding names in order to work against environmental regulations. The Information Council on the Environment (with the chilly acronym ICE) was the creation of a group of utility and coal companies that embarked on a public relations campaign to call climate change into question.[103] The Global Climate Coalition, comprised of major coal, oil, and automobile companies (some of which have now left), was created to cast doubt on the idea that human activity, particularly the burning of fossil fuels, causes global warming.[104]

Non-governmental organizations frame their appeals as well. Organizations concerned about protecting biodiversity more broadly frame their appeals with posters of endangered elephants and giant pandas, charismatic megafauna that will move the general public to contribute, even if the goals of the organizations may be broader and the resources used to protect species that don't look as cute on calendars. NGOs may present their work as relevant to a wide range of interests, such as sustainable development, indigenous rights and multiple specific environmental problems, as a way to appeal to a wide variety of interests and sources of funding.[105] Keck and Sikkink argue that successfully framing an issue is central to the activities of transnational activists, suggesting that they can "transform the terms and nature of the debate." Such framing of issues can help intended audiences understand the message, or fit the issues to the mandate of the institutional structures within which they are working.[106] Keck and Sikkink see this as a particularly important role in addressing environmental issues, which have less of an immediate emotional pull than issues like human rights, and cannot rely on existing "rights." They point to the creation of the issue of "tropical deforestation" as an important way that environmental organizations chose to frame issues such as land conflict, development, or difficulties facing indigenous people.[107] The way organizations choose to frame issues can have important impacts later on activity in that issue area, as certain issues, such as tropical deforestation, come to have resonance with the public and others are successfully fitted within the frames already created.

Non-governmental actors also gain greater effectiveness by the alliances they make. Groups of ideologically-opposed NGOs working together on a particular issue may have a greater influence because of their increased constituencies.[108] Often alliances are made internationally, with organizations (business or environmental) working elsewhere for similar goals. In the wake of Montreal Protocol–mandated reduction in the use of ozone-depleting substances, producer industries across countries cooperated to test toxicity of substitute chemicals, and to jointly run recycling processes.[109]

Importantly, some of these alliances may be across different types of organizations, with industry and environmentalist actors working either explicitly together or at the same time for compatible goals. Kenneth Oye and James Maxwell note that "general environmental concerns are often advanced through the particularistic pursuit of rents or subsidies," and argue that environmental regulations are the most successful when they benefit those actors that are regulated. They argue that when a coalition of self-interested profit-seekers and environmentalists joins together in favor of profit-generating environmental regulation, the coalition is more likely to achieve its goals than either coalition partner acting alone would be able to.[110] Insights from the study of public policy more broadly support these observations. Randall Ripley and Grace Franklin report that industry actors may accept inevitable regulation but "pursue other options designed to make the regulation as light as possible or to acquire governmentally conferred benefits simultaneously as a form of compensation for being regulated."[111] In this context, working with those that are the source of the regulation is one option for doing so. Other observations have been made that states are most likely to push domestic environmental regulations internationally when supported by both industry and environmentalist actors.[112]

The issue of accountability is an important one. Non-governmental actors can bring people into the process of global environmental politics whose voices would never have been heard without the activities of such groups. Wapner argues that NGOs are a positive challenge to statism because they increase accountability vis-à-vis underrepresented sectors of society and also help increase accountability outside of their borders.[113] Per Lindström argues that "NGOs can be the voice of the people when [g]overnments prevent the people from speaking."[114] Some go as far as to suggest that NGOs are essential aspects of the development of a political democracy. They can represent minority aspects of a society, whereas a democratically elected legislature may only represent majority interests.[115] A study in former Soviet bloc countries suggests that environmental NGOs can be the vehicle through which people express views they would otherwise be afraid to express to officials in authority, resulting in both greater public participation and a better environmental outcome.[116] While this study specifically examined postcommunist governments, the representational aspect of NGO participation would likely be even more true in nondemocratic societies. Ultimately, then, many see NGOs as bringing the voices of the otherwise underrepresented into the political process.

But NGOs are not representative in the sense that most people mean when they think about representative democracy. NGOs are in essence self-appointed political actors who are not generally elected to represent specific interests. When they are then given consultative status in international organizations or negotiations it may give the impression that they speak for the population, but there is no guarantee that they do. As Marie Price points out, NGOs "are accountable only to their supporters. It is therefore difficult to know how well these organizations represent popular concerns."[117] John Clark points to this lack of accountability as a reason that NGOs are so easy to form; they are not accountable to any constituency other than their funders.[118] They are really special interest groups influencing elected governments; should they be considered as any more accountable to society at large than any other special interest group? Moreover, they may become even less responsive to the needs of those they arose to serve as they grow in size and influence.[119]

When NGOs operate across borders accountability may be even more elusive. Organizations operating internationally may be out of touch with the people whose interests they supposedly represent. Rusli bin Mohd and Jan Laarman argue that in the case of forestry policy, for example, U.S.-based NGOs rarely consult with the forest-dwellers in the countries whose forests they aim to protect.[120] Accountability across groups of NGOs working jointly on issues may be lacking as well. Jonathan Fox and David Brown point out that many NGOs working on international issues are intermediary organizations, that may not always fully represent the interests of the grassroots organizations with whom they are supposed to be in coalition.[121] Philosophical differences between environmental organizations in industrialized countries and those in the developing world may prevent one from adequately representing the interests of the other,[122] and some have called relations between the two "emerging colonialism."[123]

NGOs may face difficulties of representation in other ways as well. Many operate on a shoestring budget and can thus become beholden to their donors.[124] And as NGOs become more integrated into the state or international decision-making process they may lose some of their representational advantages, becoming part of the system rather than bringing otherwise unheard voices to the table.[125]

Regardless, it is clear that the policies and practices pertaining to the global environment are not made by states alone, nor even by non-state actors acting solely within state borders. Action taken by industry actors and by non-governmental environmental organizations influences the existence, character, and success of international environmental regulations, and does so in ways that challenge the state-centric view of international relations.

## Notes

1   Thomas Princen and Matthias Finger, "Introduction," in Thomas Princen and Matthias Finger, *Environmental NGOs in World Politics: Linking the Local and the Global* (New York: Routledge, 1994), 11.

2   Quoted in Kenny Bruno, "The Corporate Capture of the Earth Summit," *Multinational Monitor* 13 (July/August 1992): 18.

3   Kenneth N. Waltz, *Man, the State, and War* (New York: Columbia University Press, 1959); Hans J. Morgenthau, *Politics Among Nations: The Struggle for Power and Peace* (Boston: McGraw Hill, 1978).

4   Peter J. Spiro, "New Global Communities: Nongovernmental Organizations in International Decision-Making Institutions," *The Washington Quarterly* 18(1) (1994): 45–56.

5   Peter Willetts, ed., "Introduction," in *The Conscience of the World: The Influence of Non-Governmental Organisations in the U.N. System* (Washington D.C.: Brookings Institution, 1996), 9.

6   "Citizens' Groups: The Non-Governmental Order – Will NGOs Democratise, or Merely Disrupt, Global Governance?" *Economist*, 11 December 1999, 20.

7   *The Yearbook of International Organizations*, published by the Union of International Associations, lists more than 20,000. *1993–4*, vol. 1 (Munich: K.S. Saur, June 1993), cited in Willetts, 9. Others, such as the World Watch Institute, count the number of local NGOs in the millions. See "Citizens' Groups," *Economist*, 11 December 1999, 20.

8   Willetts, 10.

9   John McCormick, "The Role of Environmental NGOs in International Regimes," in Norman J. Vig and Regina S. Axelrod, *The Global Environment: Institutions, Law, and Policy* (Washington D.C.: CQ Press, 1999), 57.

10   Elizabeth R. DeSombre, "United Nations Conference on the Human Environment," and "United Nations Conference on Environment and Development," in Andrew Goudie,

ed., *Oxford Encyclopedia of Global Change* (New York and Oxford: Oxford University Press, 2000).

11  Pablo Gutman, "What Did WSSD Accomplish? An NGO Perspective," *Environment* 45(2) (March 2003): 22.

12  See, for examples, Alan Touraine, *Return of the Actor: Social Theory in Postindustrial Society* (Minneapolis: University of Minnesota Press, 1988).

13  Matthias Finger, "NGOs and Transformation: Beyond Social Movement Theory," in Princen and Finger, *Environmental NGOs in World Politics*, 48–65.

14  Miguel Darcy de Oliveira and Rajesh Tandon, "An Emerging Global Civil Society," in Miguel Darcy de Oliveira and Rajesh Tandon, eds., *Citizens: Strengthening Global Civil Society* (Washington D.C.: Civitas: World Alliance for Citizen Participation, 1994).

15  Claus Offe, *Contradictions of the Welfare State* (edited by John Keane; Cambridge, Mass.: MIT Press, 1984); Princen and Finger, *Environmental NGOs in World Politics*.

16  Spiro, 47.

17  Ruben Cesar Fernandes, "Threads of Planetary Citizenship," in De Oliveira and Tandon, eds., 319–46.

18  Paul Wapner, *Environmental Activism and World Civic Politics* (Albany: SUNY Press, 1996): 1–6.

19  Steve Charnovitz, "Two Centuries of Participation: NGOs and International Governance," *Michigan Journal of International Law* 18 (Winter 1997): 270.

20  Spiro, 48.

21  Shirin Sinnar, "Mixed Blessing: The Growing Influence of NGOs," *Harvard International Review* (Winter 1995–96): 54–57, 79.

22  Sinnar, 55.

23  See, for example, Tanja Bruhh, "NGOs and Formation of International Environmental Regimes: Explaining their Inclusion," paper presented at the Third Pan-European International Relations Conference, September 1998, Vienna, Austria; Sheila Jasanoff, "NGOs and the Environment: From Knowledge to Action," *Third World Quarterly* 18(3) (1997): 579–94.

24  Margaret E. Keck and Kathryn Sikkink, *Activists Beyond Borders: Advocacy Networks in International Politics* (Ithaca and London: Cornell University Press, 1998), 2.

25  Barbara J. Bramble and Gareth Porter, "Non-Governmental Organizations and the Making of U.S. International Policy," in Andrew Hurrell and Benedict Kingsbury, eds., *The International Politics of the Environment* (Oxford: Clarendon Press, 1992), 313–53.

26  McCormick, "The Role of Environmental NGOs in International Regimes," 52–71.

27  Paul Wapner, "Reorienting State Sovereignty: Rights and Responsibilities in the Environmental Age," in Karen T. Litfin, ed., *The Greening of Sovereignty in World Politics* (Cambridge, Mass.: MIT Press, 1998), 284.

28 Karen Litfin, "Ecoregimes: Playing Tug of War with the Nation-State," in Ronnie Lipschutz and Ken Conca, eds., *The State and Social Power in Global Environmental Politics* (New York: Columbia University Press, 1993), 100.

29 Wapner, "Reorienting State Sovereignty," 285.

30 Interview with Ray Gambell, IWC Secretary, 3 June 1997, Histon, UK.

31 Leslie Spencer with Jan Bollwerk and Richard C. Morais, "The Not So Peaceful World of Greenpeace," *Forbes*, 11 November 1991, 174ff. (Lexis/Nexis).

32 International Whaling Commission, "Chairman's Report of the 47th Annual Meeting," 1996, 41.

33 International Convention for the Regulation of Whaling (1946), Article VII.

34 Wapner, "Reorienting State Sovereignty," 286.

35 P. J. Sands, "The Role of Non-Governmental Organizations in Enforcing International Environmental Law," in W. E. Butler, ed., *Control over Compliance with International Law* (Dordrecht: Martinus Nijhoff, 1991), 61–68.

36 Paul Wapner, "Politics Beyond the State: Environmental Activism and World Civic Politics," *World Politics* 47(3) (April 1995): 311.

37 Wapner, *Environmental Activism and World Civic Politics*, 53.

38 See, for example, Alex Chadwick, "The Treasured Islands of Palmyra," *National Geographic* (March 2001): 46–56.

39 Wapner, *Environmental Activism and World Civil Politics*, 15.

40 Collette Ridgeway, "Privately Protected Places," *Cato Policy Report* (March/April 1996), http://www.cato.org/pubs/policy_report/pr-xviii2-ridgeway.html.

41 See David Potter, ed., *NGOs and Environmental Policies: Asia and Africa* (Portland: Frank Cass, 1996).

42 Bernard Eccleston, "Does North–South Collaboration Enhance NGO Influence on Deforestation Policies in Malaysia and Indonesia?" in Potter, ed., 66–89; see also Charnovitz, 275–76.

43 Ricardo Arnt, "The Inside Out, the Outside In: Pros and Cons of Foreign Influence on Brazilian Environmentalism," in Helga Ole Bergesen, Magnar Nordergaug, and Georg Parmann, eds., *Green Globe Yearbook 1992* (Oxford: Oxford University Press, 1993), 22.

44 Alan Thomas, "NGO Advocacy, Democracy, and Policy Development," in David Potter, ed., *NGOs and Environmental Policies: Asia and Africa* (Portland: Frank Cass, 1996), 38–65.

45 Eccleston, 67.

46 Thomas, 61.

47 David Potter, "Democratisation and the Environment: NGOs and Deforestation Policies in India (Karnataka) and Indonesia (North Sumatra)," in Potter, ed., 9–38.

48 Thomas, 62.

49 Thomas Risse-Kappan, "Ideas Do Not Float Freely: Transnational Coalitions, Domestic Structures, and the End of the Cold War," *International Organization* 48(2) (Spring 1994): 185–214.

50 Rodger A. Payne, "Nonprofit Environmental Organizations in World Politics: Domestic Structure and Transnational Relations," *Policy Studies Review* 4(1) (Spring/Summer 1995): 171–82.

51 Sinnar, 55.

52 David L. Levy and Peter J. Newell, "Introduction: The Business of Global Environmental Governance," in David L. Levy and Peter J. Newell, eds., *The Business of Global Environmental Governance* (Cambridge, Mass.: MIT Press, 2004), 1–16.

53 Livio D. DeSimone and Frank Popoff with the World Business Council for Sustainable Development, *Eco-Efficiency: The Business Link to Sustainable Development* (Cambridge, Mass.: MIT Press, 1997).

54 T. E. Graedel and B. R. Allenby, *Industrial Ecology* (Upper Saddle River, N.J.: Prentice-Hall, 1995), as quoted in Braden R. Allenby, *Industrial Ecology: Policy Framework and Implementation* (Upper Saddle River, N.J.: Prentice-Hall, 1999), 40.

55 DeSimone and Popoff, 31, 39–40.

56 Susan Summers Raines, "Perceptions of Legitimacy in International Environmental Management Standards: The Impact of the Participation Gap," *Global Environmental Politics* 3(3) (August 2003): 49.

57 International Organization for Standardization, *The ISO Survey of Certifications 2004* 14th edn. (Geneva: ISO, 2005).

58 Raines, 66.

59 Clapp, "The Privatization of Global Environmental Governance," 241.

60 Gareth Porter, "Little Effect on Environmental Performance," *Environmental Forum* 12(6) (November–December 1995): 43–44.

61 Stuart L. Hart and Guatam Ahuja, "Does it Pay to be Green? An Empirical Examination of the Relationship Between Emission Reduction and Firm Performance," *Business Strategy and Environment* 5 (1996): 30–37.

62 Cairncross, "Cleaning up."

63 Charles S. Pearson, *Down to Business: Multinational Corporations, the Environment, and Development* (Washington D.C.: World Resources Institute, 1985).

64 Bruce Smart, *Beyond Compliance* (Washington D.C.: World Resources Institute, 1992), 250.

65 Michael S. Baram, "Multinational Corporations, Private Codes, and Technology Transfer for Sustainable Development," *Environmental Law* 24(1) (1994): 33–66.

66 Jennifer Clapp and Peter Dauvergne, *Paths to a Green World: The Political Economy of the Global Environment* (Cambridge, Mass.: MIT Press, 2005), 176.

67 Sheldon Kamieniecki, *Corporate America and Environmental Policy: How Often Does Business Get Its Way?* (Stanford: Stanford University Press, 2006).

68 Anthony J. Barbera and Virginia D. McConell, "The Impact of Environmental Regulations on Industry Productivity: Direct and Indirect Effects," *Journal of Environmental Economics and Management* 18 (1990): 56–65; Gary W. Yohe, "The Backward Incidence of Pollution Control – Some Comparative Statics in General Equilibrium," *Journal of Environmental Economics and Management* 6 (1979): 187–98.

69 Michael E. Porter, "America's Green Strategy," *Scientific American* (April 1991), 168; Michael E. Porter, *The Competitive Advantage of Nations* (London: Macmillan, 1990), 647–49.

70 OECD, *Environmental Policy and Technical Change* (Paris: Organization for Economic Cooperation and Development, 1985).

71 Pearson, 70.

72 Mancur Olson Jr., *The Logic of Collective Action: Public Goods and the Theory of Groups* (Cambridge, Mass.: Harvard University Press, 1977).

73 David Vogel, "Representing Diffuse Interests in Environmental Policymaking," in David Vogel, *Do Institutions Matter?: Government Capabilities in the United States and Abroad* (Washington D.C.: Brookings Institution, 1993). Vogel examines what types of institutional structures best represent these diffuse interests.

74 H. Jeffrey Leonard, *Pollution and the Struggle for World Product: Multinational Corporations, Environment, and International Comparative Advantage* (Cambridge: Cambridge University Press, 1988), 6.

75 Ibid., 7.

76 Arik Levinson, "Environmental Regulations and Industry Location: International and Domestic Evidence," in Jagdish Bhagwati and Robert E. Hudec, *Fair Trade and Harmonization: Prerequisites for Free Trade?* vol. I: *Economic Analysis* (Cambridge, Mass. and London: MIT Press, 1996), 450.

77 Cees van Beers and J. C. J. M. van der Bergh, "An Empirical Multi-Country Analysis of the Impact of Environmental Regulations on Foreign Trade Flows," *Kyklos* 50(1) (1999): 29–46.

78 David Wheeler, "Beyond Pollution Havens," *Global Environmental Politics* 2(2) (2002): 6.

79 Elizabeth R. DeSombre, *Flagging Standards: Globalization and Environmental, Safety, and Labor Regulations at Sea* (Cambridge, Mass.: MIT Press, 2006).

80 In the phrase of Ronie Garcia-Johnson, *Exporting Environmentalism: U.S. Multinational Chemical Corporations in Brazil and Mexico* (Cambridge, Mass: MIT Press, 2000).

81 Ibid.

82 Ibid.

83 Kenny Bruno and Jed Greer, *Greenwash: The Reality Behind Corporate Environmentalism* (Penang: Third World Network/Apex Press, 1997).

84 See, for example, Charles S. Pearson, *Down to Business: Multinational Corporations, the Environment, and Development* (Washington D.C.: World Resources Institute, 1985).

85  Charnovitz, 277.

86  Wapner, *Environmental Activism and World Civic Politics.*

87  Charnovitz, 269.

88  Helmut Breitmeier and Volker Rittberger, "Environmental NGOs in an Emerging Global Civil Society," Centre for International Relations/Peace and Conflict Studies, Institute for Political Science, University of Tübingen, Nr. 32.

89  Eccleston, 71–74.

90  Kal Raustiala, "States, NGOs, and International Environmental Institutions," *International Studies Quarterly* 41 (1997): 719–40.

91  Steven J. Kobrin, "Testing the Bargaining Hypothesis in the Manufacturing Sector in Developing Countries," *International Organization* 41(4) (Autumn 1987): 609–38.

92  Matthias Finger and James Kilcoyne, "Why Transnational Corporations are Organizing to 'Save the Environment,'" *The Ecologist* 27(4) (August 1997): 142.

93  Jennifer Clapp, "Multinational Corporations and Environmental Hazards in the Asia-Pacific Region," paper prepared for the International Studies Association Annual Meeting, San Diego, April 1996.

94  Frances Cairncross "Cleaning up," *Economist*, 8 September 1990, S1ff.; Frances Cairncross *Costing the Earth* (Boston: Harvard Business School Press, 1991).

95  Nick Butler, "Companies in International Relations," *Survival* 21(1) (Spring 2000): 149–64.

96  Nazli Choucri, "The Global Environment and Multinational Corporations," *Technology Review* 94(3) (April 1991): 52–60.

97  A. Claire Cutler, Virginia Haufler, and Tony Porter, eds., *Private Authority and International Affairs* (Albany: SUNY Press, 1999).

98  Benjamin Cashore, Graeme Auld, and Deanna Newsom, *Governing Through Markets: Forest Certification and the Emergence of Non-State Authority* (New Haven: Yale University Press, 2004).

99  Susan Strange, *The Retreat of the State: The Diffusion of Power in the World Economy* (Cambridge: Cambridge University Press, 1996).

100 Robert Falkner, "Private Environmental Governance and International Relations: Exploring the Links," *Global Environmental Politics* 3(2) (May 2003): 72–87; Jennifer Clapp, "The Privatization of Global Environmental Governance: ISO 14000 and the Developing World," *Global Governance* 4(3) (1998): 295–316.

101 Virginia Haufler, *A Public Role for the Private Sector: Industry Self-Regulation in a Global Economy* (Washington D.C.: Carnegie Endowment for International Peace, 2001), 37.

102 Interestingly, both the WBCSD and its critics agree with this assessment. Jed Greer and Kenny Bruno, *Greenwash: The Reality Behind Corporate Environmentalism* (Penang, Malaysia: Third World Network, 1996), 14; Stephan Schmidheiny and Federico Zorroquín Livio with the World Business Council for Sustainable Development, *Financing Change:*

Ed we had aligned double and triple note numbers on the decimal and retained the standard indent. Please advise what you require specifically for notes into triple figures. Thanks.

*The Financial Community, Eco-Efficiency, and Sustainable Development* (Cambridge, Mass.: MIT Press, 1996).

103 Ross Gelbspan, *The Heat Is On* (Reading, Mass.: Addison-Wesley, 1997), 34.

104 Ibid., 85. See chapter 6 for more details.

105 Marie Price, "Ecopolitics and Environmental Nongovernmental Organizations in Latin America," *The Geographical Review* 84(1) (January 1994): 55.

106 Keck and Sikkink, 2–3.

107 Ibid., 121, 133–35, 155–56. They argue that the idea of tropical deforestation as an issue area did not even exist in the early 1970s, but was framed as an issue by environmental organizations in response to specific problems.

108 Bramble and Porter, 321–22.

109 Cairncross, "Cleaning Up," S1.

110 Kenneth A. Oye and James H. Maxwell, "Self-Interest and Environmental Management," in Robert O. Keohane and Elinor Ostrom, eds., *Local Commons and Global Interdependence: Heterogeneity and Cooperation in Two Domains* (Newbury Park, Calif.: Sage, 1995), 191–221.

111 Randall B. Ripley and Grace A. Franklin, *Congress, The Bureaucracy, and Public Policy*, rev. edn. (Homewood, Ill.: The Dorsey Press, 1980), 123.

112 Elizabeth R. DeSombre, *Domestic Sources of International Environmental Policy: Industry, Environmentalists, and U.S. Power* (Cambridge, Mass.: MIT Press, 2000).

113 Wapner, *Environmental Activism and World Civic Politics*, 120; see also Charnovitz, 274.

114 Per Lindström, "The Role of NGOs as Seen by the United Nations and its Member States," in Jürgen Schramm, ed., *The Role of Non-Governmental Organizations in the New European Order* (Baden-Baden: Nomos Verlagsgesellschaft, 1995), 46.

115 Erik Hundewadt, "The Role of Voluntary Associations (NGOs) in a Democratic Society," in Schramm, ed., 7–12.

116 Tim Richardson, Jiri Dusik, and Pavla Jidrova, "Parallel Public Participation: An Answer to Inertia in Decision-Making," *Environmental Impact Assessment Review* 18 (1998): 201–16.

117 Price, 57.

118 John Clark, *Democratizing Development: The Role of Voluntary Organizations* (West Hartford, Conn: Kumarian Press, 1990).

119 De Oliveira and Tandon.

120 Rusli bin Mohd and Jan G. Laarman, "The Struggle for Influence: U.S. Nongovernmental Organizations and Tropical Forests," *Journal of Forestry* 92(6) (June 1994): 35.

121 Jonathan A. Fox and L. David Brown, "Introduction," in Jonathan A. Fox and L. David Brown, eds., *The Struggle for Accountability: The World Bank, NGOs, and Grassroots Movements* (Cambridge, Mass.: MIT Press, 1998), 3.

122 McCormick, "The Role of Environmental NGOs in International Regimes," 60.

123 George Aditjondro, "A Reflection about a Decade of International Advocacy Efforts on Indonesian Environmental Issues," paper presented at the International NGO Group on Indonesia Conference, Bonn, Germany, April 1990, 16; quoted in L. David Brown and Jonathan A. Fox, "Accountability within Transnational Coalitions," in Fox and Brown, eds., 441.

124 Sinnar.

125 Hundewalt, 11.

# 6 Ozone Depletion and Climate Change

The atmosphere is central to the functioning of life on earth. A thin layer of ozone in the stratosphere, approximately twelve to twenty-five kilometers above the earth, protects the surface of the earth from ultraviolet-B (UV-B) radiation. Human activities have caused the destruction of some of this ozone, faster than it can be replenished. As this layer grows thinner, increased UV-B radiation reaches the earth's surface, where it damages DNA. This damage increases the likelihood of skin cancers in mammals, causes immune system disruption in humans and other animal species and harms crops and other plant species.[1] Carbon dioxide and other greenhouse gases in the atmosphere make life on earth possible by retaining some of the sun's energy in the lower atmosphere. As human activity increases the amount of greenhouse gases additional energy is retained, with potentially serious consequences: dramatic sea level rise that would inundate low-lying areas, increased storms in some areas and droughts in others, a change in disease vectors, and impacts on ecosystems. Strong evidence exists that this human-induced climate change is already underway.[2]

It is fitting to begin an examination of cases in international environmental policy with an examination of problems of the atmosphere. Atmospheric issues are among the most global of problems, in which the effects of the harm has almost no relationship to the location of the activity that contributes to the environmental problem. This chapter examines one of the true success stories in international environmental cooperation, and one seemingly similar case that has met with much greater resistance.

Ozone depletion and climate change are different environmental problems with important structural similarities that have influenced the way they have been addressed. Both are common pool resource problems: states that do not participate in addressing the problem can still benefit from the actions undertaken by others to protect the atmosphere, and those that do not participate can damage the resource in a way that undermines the ability of others to protect it. In this case, emissions of harmful substances from anywhere in the world have an impact on the atmosphere that is not dependent on the location of emissions. It is thus essential to involve all states engaged in activities that produce the substances responsible for these threats in efforts to address them if the environmental problems are to be prevented or mitigated.

Both ozone depletion and climate change involved initially highly uncertain science and international processes that responded to potential future threats to the global atmosphere before the impacts of these problems were manifest. Regulation on both of these issues was likely to have significant impacts on industrial processes, and the preferences of industrial actors (along with environmental non-governmental organizations) strongly influenced the process of international negotiations to address the problems. The concerns of developing countries and their role shaping the eventual obligations states take on is also important in addressing both environmental problems. Moreover, precedents set in the earlier negotiations to protect the ozone layer have carried over to influence the negotiations on climate change.

There are nevertheless important differences between the two issues. The types of activities that cause the harm to the ozone layer are largely the result of industrial process, and the substances in question are almost entirely human-made. At the time the potential problem was discovered, activities that harmed the ozone layer were carried out primarily by the industrialized world. It was also the industrialized world that cared most about the possibility of ozone depletion. While it is certainly also true that developed countries bear the greatest responsibility for the increase in the emission of greenhouse gases over the course of history, many of the types of activities responsible for the emission of greenhouse gases take place in developing countries as well; these countries are the fastest growing source of these substances.

There are also many types of activities that contribute to the level of emissions of greenhouse gases. Some emissions come from processes of industrialization, but some come from land use and agriculture. Most greenhouse gases occur naturally though their extent is dramatically augmented by human activity. Likewise, the impact of the environmental damage caused by these global problems is differently distributed in these two issues. While there are a few states near the Antarctic ozone hole that have thus far felt the greatest impact from harm to the ozone layer, and there are others who depend more on activities likely to be disrupted by ozone depletion, the harm in general is likely to be globally distributed. The variation across states in terms of the likely harm to result from climate change is much broader. In particular, it does not divide neatly into developed vs. developing states.

To make things even more complicated, while the environmental issues themselves are largely unconnected, there are some substances (chlorofluorocarbons, for instance) that contribute to both environmental problems. And the regulatory processes, though run almost entirely separately, have some impacts on each other, even apart from the precedents adopted. Some of the substitute chemicals used in place of those that deplete the ozone layer are themselves greenhouse gases, contributing to climate change. These points of connection bring up the broader question of whether the regulation of different environmental issues by different treaties and organizations is an appropriate way to address environmental issues that turn out to connect to each other in various ways. Might it be better to create a global "law of the atmosphere" rather than continue to regulate atmospheric issues in separate institutional processes? Would such an effort be possible?

## Ozone Depletion

Ozone depletion is caused by the interaction of various industrial chemicals with ozone molecules in the stratosphere. The chemicals in question (the most common of which are chlorofluorocarbons (CFCs) and halons) have been used primarily for refrigeration and air conditioning, cleaning of electronic parts, as aerosol propellants, and in fire suppression.[3] These substances are stable and therefore do not decompose until they reach the upper atmosphere, where in the presence of sunlight they break down into chlorine or bromine free radicals that attach themselves to ozone molecules, causing a chain reaction that destroys large numbers of ozone molecules at a time. A depleted ozone layer allows increased levels of ultraviolet radiation to get through to earth. The potential effects of depletion of the ozone layer include increases in skin cancer, immune disorders and cataracts in humans, crop damage, and similar harm to other species.[4] Although there was uncertainty about this process when first hypothesized (and when early negotiations to address it were taking place) there is now strong scientific evidence that these substances cause ozone depletion and that such depletion has already occurred. Early evidence of effects from the damaged ozone layer is becoming apparent.

## Climate Change

Climate change, more commonly known as global warming, is caused by increasing levels of greenhouse gases in the atmosphere. These gases include carbon dioxide, methane, chlorofluorocarbons, ozone, and nitrous oxides. These substances are primarily naturally occurring, but are produced by human activities in larger quantities than occurred preindustrialization. The activities most responsible for production of greenhouse gases include the burning of fossil fuel, agriculture (particularly cattle ranching and rice cultivation), deforestation, and other industrial processes. The increased greenhouse gases in the atmosphere essentially absorb radiation from the sun that would otherwise be released, increasing the average global temperature. More important than the possibility that the average temperature will become higher are the associated weather effects; storms are expected to increase in frequency and severity, rainfall patterns in general will likely change, polar ice caps are expected to melt, and sea level is expected to rise.[5] Recently concerns have emerged that climate change will impact ocean currents, which could have dramatic and sudden effects on temperature, making some areas in the Northern Hemisphere much colder than they currently are.[6] It is because of the variety of predicted effects that most scholars refer to the phenomenon as climate change, rather than global warming.

# International Cooperation

International cooperation to address ozone depletion and climate change has followed a number of similar patterns. International scientific efforts to begin cooperation on research with an eye toward building a regulatory regime began for both issues in the 1970s, with the climate discussions beginning somewhat earlier, even though international regulations were created much more quickly and, so far, effectively, to address ozone depletion. They both began under conditions of great uncertainty, and the process and form of international cooperation reflects that.

## Ozone Depletion

Research on understanding the science of ozone depletion began in the early 1970s. Two U.S. scientists – F. Sherwood Rowland and Mario Molina – hypothesized in 1974 that CFCs could, because of their stability, last long enough to reach the stratosphere. There, interaction with sunlight would cause them eventually to break down into chlorine free radicals, which could destroy ozone.[7] It was quickly realized that international scientific efforts would be needed to determine whether this hypothesized reaction was taking place, and what impact it would have on the earth's environment.

International cooperation started with a conference of experts from thirty-two countries, convened by the United Nations Environment Programme (UNEP) in 1977. This conference adopted a World Plan of Action and established a Coordinating Committee to continue to address the issue. By May 1981 the UNEP Governing Council authorized negotiations to attempt to create a binding treaty on measures to protect the ozone layer. This negotiation process resulted in 1985 in the Vienna Convention for the Protection of the Ozone Layer. This treaty creates a framework in which states agree to take "appropriate" (but unspecified) measures to protect the ozone layer, cooperate in scientific research and exchange information.[8] The 1985 Convention was followed by the negotiation in 1987 of the Montreal Protocol on Substances that Deplete the Ozone Layer, which required specific abatement measures for ozone-depleting substances. As laid out in the Vienna Convention, amendments to the Protocol can be made with a two-thirds majority vote and are then subject to ratification by the Parties.[9] Only those that ratify the Amendments are bound by them, although states that ratify the Protocol are bound by any Amendments in force at the time of ratification. Amendments have so far been agreed to in London in 1990, Copenhagen in 1992, Montreal in 1997, and Beijing in 1999.

The Convention/Protocol process resulted in a more robust agreement, at an earlier point, than would have occurred if negotiations had only begun once serious abatement measures could have been agreed upon. The Protocol added specific abatement measures and the amendments added new regulated substances and new regulatory processes. The London amendments added regulations for carbon tetrachloride, methyl chloroform, and fully halogenated CFCs, as well as introducing the funding mechanism to provide assistance to developing countries.[10] The Copenhagen Amendments added HCFCs, hydrobromide fluorocarbons, and methyl bromide to the list of controlled substances, and made the funding mechanism permanent.[11] The Montreal Amendments adjusted the timetable for phase-out of some substances, and modified trade restrictions, including the creation of a licensing system to attempt to decrease the black market in ozone-depleting substances,[12] and the Beijing Amendments also set and advanced timelines for control of various ozone-depleting substances. An agreement that would have addressed all these issues could certainly not have been negotiated in 1985 or even 1987, and it can be argued that it was only because of the incremental action that further regulations were made possible within an existing framework.

In addition, the Montreal Protocol makes use of a system of adjustments that sets it apart from both major approaches to creation of environmental law.[13] It neither empowers a commission to make rules that states are allowed to opt out of, nor requires that all changes be ratified by all parties before they take effect. Unusual among treaties that follow the convention/protocol approach, the Montreal Protocol allows for adjustments within the agreement. Adjustments require the consent of two-thirds of the Parties, representing a majority of both developed and developing countries (the latter part an addition of the London Amendments). They become binding on all Parties six months after the Parties are formally notified about them, even those states that did not vote in favor of them.[14]

Adjustments have taken place at meetings of the parties and other negotiations, and have generally addressed faster phase-out of certain chemicals. Many of the most dramatic changes in the phase-out schedule for various ozone-depleting substances have come through adjustments rather than Amendments.[15] For example, the original Montreal Protocol called for a freeze at 1986 levels for the main halons by 1993 for developed countries. That was first adjusted in 1990 to a freeze in 1992 and a complete phase-out by 2000. In 1992 it was adjusted to consumption by 1994 at 25 per cent of 1989 levels and a complete phase-out by 1996. Similarly, the initial Montreal Protocol requirement that developed countries cut their use of the major CFCs to 50 per cent of 1986 levels by 1999 was ultimately adjusted to a complete phase-out by 1996. Similar adjustments were made for developing country parties.

# Climate Change

Scientific exploration of the earth's climate has taken place for centuries, but modern climate science can be traced to Jean Baptiste Joseph Fourier, who in 1827 postulated that the atmosphere influenced the temperature of the earth's surface. He described what is now known as the greenhouse effect, by which certain gases of the atmosphere prevent the sun's radiation from escaping and keep the earth warmer than it would otherwise be. Throughout the nineteenth and the beginning of the twentieth centuries this understanding was further refined, and international scientific cooperation undertaken to monitor the atmosphere. Swedish scientist Svante Arrhenius even explored, at the turn of the twentieth century, the idea that a doubling of carbon in the atmosphere, made possible by human activities, would increase the temperature of the earth. These observations, however, went largely unexplored until after World War II, when interest in meteorological data increased, due to better technology and to air travel.[16] The designation by the International Council of Scientific Unions of the International Geophysical Year (IGY) from 1957 to 1958 increased the focus on the relationship between carbon and climate, and resulted in the first permanent station to monitor $CO_2$ emissions. Regular measurements taken initially at this station indicated that emissions of carbon dioxide are not all absorbed by the ocean, as was previously believed, but also taken up in the atmosphere.[17] After the IGY even more scientific cooperation emerged on issues of climate and weather, including the creation of the World Weather Watch and the Global Atmospheric Research Programme.[18]

International cooperation on climate science thus has a long history, and it is difficult to pinpoint when international efforts to address human impacts on the climate began. An important early step to integrate scientific study with political concern came in 1971, with an international meeting of scientists in Wijk, Sweden, to discuss issues of long-term climate change. The United Nations Conference on the Human Environment in 1972 also helped raise the profile of the climate issue, although no specific action on climate change was taken there. The World Meteorological Organization (WMO) sponsored a symposium on the topic in 1975, at the same time that the U.S. National Academy of Sciences published a report suggesting the need to improve climate science. WMO convened the First World Climate Conference in Geneva in 1979, with a number of other international conferences following in the subsequent years.[19]

One of the most significant developments nearly a decade later was the creation, by WMO and UNEP, of the Intergovernmental Panel on Climate Change (IPCC) in 1988. This group consists of the world's most eminent climatologists and other relevant researchers, appointed by their own governments. It is not a standard international organization, in that the scientists do not represent their states but rather serve in their own capacity. They are charged with investigating climate science and issuing a report on the status of the science and recommending options. The IPCC functions via three working groups that investigate the scientific, socioeconomic, and mitigation aspects of climate change. It also has a Task Force on National Greenhouse Gas Inventories, to assist in the calculation of national emissions.[20]

In the same year as the creation of the IPCC an international conference in Toronto called for 20 per cent cuts in emissions of carbon dioxide by 2005, and the United Nations General Assembly passed a resolution calling for "protection of the global climate for present and future generations."[21] In 1989, the UNEP Governing Council requested that UNEP and WMO begin negotiations for a framework convention to address issues of climate change. The first IPCC report the following year, as well as the Second World Climate Conference, agreed on the necessity for negotiation for a global climate treaty.

These negotiations led to the first international agreement to address issues of climate change: the United Nations Framework Convention on Climate Change (UNFCCC), signed in 1992 at Rio. As suggested by its title, it is a framework convention, requiring no actual abatement measures but instead committing states to working to achieve "stabilization of greenhouse gas concentrations in the atmosphere at a level that would prevent dangerous anthropogenic interference with the climate system." Parties commit themselves to undertake national inventories of greenhouse gas emissions, and cooperate in the process of studying and controlling greenhouse gas emissions, among other important, but quite general, obligations.[22]

The Kyoto Protocol to the UNFCCC, signed at the end of 1997, requires actual reductions in emissions of greenhouse gases of varying amounts for developed countries, with an average of a 5 per cent reduction from 1990 emissions by the period 2008 to 2012. The Protocol includes three instruments to introduce flexibility into how states meet their goals. First, states with reduction obligations can trade among themselves, so if a state reduces more than it is required to it can sell the excess amount to another state to use for its own reduction obligations. Second a Clean Development Mechanism permits developed country states to receive emissions reductions credits for projects undertaken to reduce carbon emissions in developing countries. Third is what has come to be known as Joint Implementation, which allows developed country parties to receive credit for emissions reductions for projects done in other developed country parties. In addition, the agreement allows states to count the removal of carbon from the atmosphere by what are called "sinks" (resources such as forests that remove carbon from the atmosphere) toward their goals.[23] All these measures have been controversial and subject to negotiation on how they will be implemented.

The Kyoto Protocol entered into force in 2005 but without the participation of the United States. The United States is the largest emitter of greenhouse gases and the ability of the Protocol to protect the global climate without its participation is severely limited. In addition, the effort to bring the Kyoto Protocol into force without U.S. participation weakened it considerably. Article 25 of the Protocol requires that fifty-five states, representing 55 per cent of developed country emissions of greenhouse gases as of 1990, ratify the Protocol for it to enter into force. Since the United States accounted for more than 36 per cent of 1990 GHG emissions by the group of regulated states,[24] the participation of almost all other developed states was necessary. Ultimately, the refusal of the United States to ratify the agreement gave additional bargaining power to the other developed state countries, primarily Russia, Canada, Japan, and Australia, in negotiations on how to implement Kyoto. Because their participation became essential if the protocol were to go forward without the United States, they were able to bargain for interpretations of the agreement, such as rules on how carbon sinks would be counted, that required less action from them, and significantly weakened the agreement.[25]

# The Role of Science

Both ozone depletion and global climate change challenged the conventional approach to the role of science in regulation of international environmental agreements, in several ways. In the first place, unlike an issue like transboundary acid rain in which an effect was first noticed and a search undertaken for the cause, regulation began for ozone depletion (and, to a lesser extent, climate change) when there was no clear evidence of an actual environmental problem.

The Vienna Convention on the Protection of the Ozone Layer (or, more realistically, the Montreal Protocol, which required actual abatement measures) is seen as the first global environmental treaty to address an environmental problem that was considered to be only theoretical at the time it was negotiated. The idea that halogenated compounds could destroy ozone had been demonstrated in the laboratory, and Roland and Molina had theorized that human-created CFCs could migrate into the stratosphere where the ozone layer protected the earth from harmful ultraviolet rays. But no one had seen the destruction of the ozone layer by these chemicals and, more importantly, no one had witnessed actual environmental damage resulting from this potential problem. Even initial evidence of a seasonal thinning (known as the ozone "hole") over Antarctica was initially disregarded by scientific instruments designed to discard information so far from expected measurements.[26] Once this hole had been clearly observed in 1986, there was no immediate evidence linking it clearly to human activities.[27] Conclusive evidence was offered by the NASA-sponsored Ozone Trends Panel, which reported in 1988 (after the Montreal Protocol had already been negotiated) that ozone depletion was occurring and that it had human-induced causes.[28] The timing suggests, as Karen Litfin points out, that scientific knowledge was necessary but not sufficient in the process of negotiating the Montreal Protocol, and that the combination of politics with science is essential in understanding the willingness of states to agree to change their behavior before the mechanisms or extent of ozone depletion were clearly understood.[29]

The Montreal Protocol process made scientific inquiry an integral part of the regulatory process. Some of this happened outside the treaty organization but in response to it. The WMO/NASA Assessment from 1986 that helped provide the basis for the Montreal Protocol, for example, was an explicit response to the call under the Vienna Convention for international cooperation to provide a better understanding of ozone depletion.[30] The Conference of the Parties to the Protocol created assessment processes shortly after the negotiation of the Protocol. Currently the Technology and Economic Assessment panel evaluates progress toward the phase-out of ozone-depleting substances. It has technical options committees that assess the economic and technological appropriateness of substitute chemicals and processes within different sectors.[31] Findings and recommendations from these committees and other research brought about by the existence of the international agreement were essential in the amendments and adjustments to obligations under the agreement.

Science in international negotiations to prevent climate change has likewise been uncertain and controversial. Unlike with ozone depletion, new research has tended to create as many new uncertainties as it resolves. On the one hand, there is now a strong consensus from the international scientific community that humans have impacted the global climate system. The latest IPCC assessment indicates that "there is new and stronger evidence that most of the warming observed over the last 50 years is attributable to human activities."[32] The IPCC in 2001 also indicated its increasing confidence in climate models to predict climate in the future.[33] But there is a lot that is still not known about climate science, and that uncertainty has been used for political ends by those who would prefer not to take action to mitigate global climate change.

One interesting difference between the case of ozone depletion and climate change was the existence of a broadly international scientific body, the IPCC, before the climate negotiations. In 1990 its first report indicated that "emissions resulting from human activities are substantially increasing the concentration of greenhouse gases" and that these "increases will enhance the greenhouse effect, resulting on average in an additional warming of the Earth's surface."[34] So while the Framework Convention on Climate Change required cataloging of greenhouse gas emissions by states and called for international scientific cooperation, most of it has been carried out through the IPCC, a group independent from the agreement, as well as the also pre-existing WMO. Findings from the second IPCC Assessment Report in 1995, augmenting its 1990 report, were influential in the willingness of states to negotiate the Kyoto Protocol.

Much remains uncertain about climate change, however. Estimates of the magnitude of expected average temperature change have varied over even the last decade, with IPCC estimates of the amount of average warming increasing (from a 1995 estimate of a 3.5 degrees Celsius increase by 2100 to a predicted 5.8 degree increase in the 2001 assessment). But the range of uncertainty increased as well, particularly in describing the extent of warming that has already taken place.[35]

The roles of other factors in climate change bring new uncertainties. Aerosols, which come from burning of all sorts (including of fossil fuels), play some sort of role in atmospheric response to solar radiation, but in a way that is unclear. They may, if bright, reflect energy back to space, which would moderate the effects of greenhouse gases, or they may, if dark, absorb even more energy and increase the greenhouse effect. As climate modeler Jeffrey Kiehl of the National Center for Atmospheric Research explains, "the more we learn [about aerosols], the less we know."[36] Clouds, which may be more abundant with increasing water vapor likely from higher temperatures (as well as independently from aerosols), are subject to similar uncertainties. Clouds could increase from warming, but then in turn block solar radiation from entering the atmosphere leading to cooling, or clouds may decrease or form in a different part of the atmosphere, and thus increase warming.[37] The role played by oceans is also complicated and not sufficiently understood. Climate research from a century ago already knew that much of the human-created carbon dioxide is taken up by the oceans, but what it will do there, or how the warming of the oceans affects broader climatic patterns, is still unknown.[38]

The feedback mechanisms from any parts of the climate system could have major impacts in ways that are currently not well understood. For instance, there are suggestions that at high enough temperatures, or during droughts, plants may switch from being net sinks for carbon dioxide to being net sources.[39] Since these conditions may themselves result from climate change, plant behavior could accelerate the changes. Other feedback mechanisms could come from changed albedo. As ice on the earth melts with warming, the earth's surface becomes less reflective and therefore takes in even more sunlight and warmth, leading to increased warming. Most of these mechanisms could work in either direction, increasing the uncertainty about what magnitude of changes, and on what timescale, should be expected from the climate system.

Potential mechanisms for abatement of anthropogenic carbon are also untested, and new large-scale ideas, if attempted, could have a big impact on how much carbon is released into the atmosphere. Recent suggestions have included seeding the ocean with iron or nitrogen to increase the growth of plankton or other aquatic plants that would serve as a carbon sink, burying carbon dioxide in abandoned mines, oil wells, underground rock formations, or at the bottom of the ocean, or even using large scale reflective material to reflect excess sunlight away from the earth's surface.[40] Any such schemes could have a huge impact on human ability to mitigate climate change, but they create even greater uncertainties about long-run impacts of these types of policies.

The biggest uncertainty is, as Dale Jamieson suggests in other contexts, social.[41] Jerry Mahlman, former director of the U.S. National Oceanic and Atmospheric Administration's Geophysic Fluid Dynamics Laboratory, agrees that social uncertainty is both important and difficult to resolve: "we don't have a clue how people are going to react 30 years from now."[42] There are too many types of activities, practiced by too many sectors of very different countries, to realistically predict human behavior with respect to greenhouse gas emission or abatement in the near future. This level of uncertainty, both scientific and social, cannot help but impact the ability to make political decisions about how to address climate change.

# Non-Governmental Actors

## Industry

In both issue areas industry actors have played a significant role, though a somewhat different one. In particular, the industry involved in ozone depletion is much smaller and more uniform than in the case of climate change. While the substances that depleted the ozone layer are important to industrial development, they are less integrated throughout the fabric of daily life than are those activities that contribute to climate change. Industry's action on ozone depletion was thus much more unified than has been the case with climate change. It is also important to note the relationship between industry action and domestic and international regulation. In both cases, industry resisted initial attempts at regulation. In ozone depletion consumer demand combined with U.S. regulation gave ozone-depleting substance (ODS) manufacturers an incentive to create the substitutes that would be used for their products, push for international regulation, and thus benefit from being among the first to change their behavior.

The experience with ozone depletion may suggest some of the reasons that industry has been much more successful in resisting regulation in climate change. Lack of consumer demand and little domestic regulation has given industries a weaker incentive to change their behavior absent international regulation. This dynamic is particularly apparent in the United States, which has almost no national regulation to give its industries an incentive to decrease their greenhouse gas emissions. As a result the United States has been reluctant to act internationally, because its domestic industries would suffer from international regulation.[43] This situation creates a catch-22 in which states resist regulating their industries because the industries resist regulation, yet they will see few advantages to changing their behavior until regulated.

Fortunately, some consumer pressure combined with an acceptance of the inevitability of action on climate change is convincing multinational industries in particular to begin changing their activities, even before they are required to do so. The Chicago Climate Exchange is a group of companies and other entities (including cities and universities) in North America that have agreed to take on voluntary but legally-binding annual reductions in greenhouse gas emissions, and have formed an emissions trading network to allow them to trade emissions obligations.[44] Other industries in the United States where reductions are not required are pledging to reduce their greenhouse gas emissions,[45] for the recognition they can receive by trumpeting their environmentalism, and perhaps out of a belief that such action will eventually be required.

Industry's main role in addressing ozone depletion was the eventual creation of substitute chemicals to use as international regulations required the phase-out of ozone-depleting substances. It is often mistakenly assumed that there were readily available substitutes for ozone-depleting substances at the time of the Montreal Protocol, and that the existence of these substitutes made the negotiation process simpler.[46] That perception is incorrect. DuPont, the primary manufacturer of CFCs, after introducing non-CFC propellants for use in aerosol spray cans due to U.S. consumer pressure in the 1970s, had ceased research into other CFC substitutes at the beginning of the 1980s. It began research again in 1986, only after the Vienna Convention was signed and negotiations for the Montreal Protocol underway.[47] The realization that international regulation was likely (and, in the United States, that domestic regulation was inevitable), jump-started the search for alternatives.

In the intervening years, in an effort to stave off regulations, industry downplayed the possibility that substitutes or recycling would be cost effective or viable. The Alliance for Responsible CFC Policy, an industry organization, indicated that "all promising compounds identified have one or more limitations ... consequently, we conclude that fully satisfactory fluorocarbon alternatives will not become available in the foreseeable future."[48]

It is all the more remarkable to note, then, how quickly substitutes became available and widely adopted after the negotiation of the Protocol. In 1988 several traditional CFC producers such as AT&T and DuPont announced the availability of competitively priced CFC substitutes for use in electronics, food packaging and other applications.[49] Other substitutes followed in the early 1990s. Ultimately most OECD countries phased out their use of ozone-depleting substances faster than was required under the Protocol.[50] While meeting obligations ahead of time could be seen as evidence that the obligations were not onerous or that the changes did not happen because of the treaty process,[51] in this case the fundamental shift in industrial processes is evident and would have been inconceivable without international regulation. Several factors, both from the Protocol itself, and from the ways that individual states chose to implement it, contributed to this profound industrial transformation.

The mere existence of the Vienna Convention, which promised abatement measures, followed by the negotiation of the Montreal Protocol which required them, put industry on notice that it would not be able to continue profiting from ozone-depleting substances to the extent it previously had. In the same way that DuPont found substitute propellants for aerosol spray cans in anticipation of certain U.S. regulation (and with the support of consumer demand), the ODS industry responded to the inevitability of international regulations.

More importantly, the same industries that several years previously had reasonably concluded that substitutes would not be cost-effective had reason to change their calculations. In addition to adding the element of necessity, international regulations provided additional incentives for the creation of viable substitutes to ozone-depleting substances. Alan Miller argues that "the competitive incentive brought forth by a recognition that those companies who develop the best alternatives will capture a multi-billion dollar world market" created a sufficient incentive for innovation.[52] Investment in research could pay off with the promise of a huge set of potential consumers required to use non–ozone-depleting chemicals,[53] in a way that it might not for a purely domestic market.

The other major hurdle for the development of substitutes, their likely cost, was surmounted both by the existence of the Protocol itself and by the way states chose to regulate under it. Many substitutes were projected to, and in fact did, sell for five to ten times the price of the CFCs they would replace. Only the presence of an assured market of consumers that would be required to use them, despite the increased cost, would make them reasonable to develop.[54]

For instance, when substitute chemicals were first introduced by DuPont and AT&T for ozone-depleting substances they were prohibitively expensive. It was only the U.S. implementation of an excise tax on ozone-depleting substances, adopted in the context of the Montreal Protocol on Substances that Deplete the Ozone Layer, that made ozone depleting substances increasingly expensive relative to their substitutes. Substitute chemicals that might have been more expensive than ozone-depleting substances before the Montreal Protocol and domestic regulation suddenly became the most cost effective option. Even when industries were still allowed to use ozone-depleting substances, they chose the more environmentally friendly option of not doing so, because it was more cost effective. It was therefore a regulatory tool that made taking the environmentally beneficial action cost effective. The excise tax in Europe was smaller, but still significant enough to lower the relative cost of alternatives. Some, in fact, attribute the success in phase-out of ozone-depleting substances overall more to the tax than to the regulations themselves,[55] although of course domestic taxes, particularly in the United States, would have been unlikely to exist had it not been for the international regulations.

Other ways in which industry has been involved in the Montreal Protocol process has added to its willingness to work within the regulatory system. For example, much of the funding from the Multilateral Fund, discussed below, goes to purchase equipment, chemicals, or expertise from developed country industries, thereby disseminating technology and increasing the advantages of the overall regulatory process to the main ODS industries. In addition, the role of industry actors within the committees discussed above may contribute to the implementation of regulations. Owen Green suggests that the participation of industry actors on the Technology and Economic Assessments Panel increases the likelihood that new ozone-friendly technologies are adopted within the industries represented. He gives the example of oil and gas industry representatives who, after serving on panels discussing the options for phasing out the use of halons, were able to change the way fire fighting was conducted within their own companies and then in the industry as a whole.[56] In short, the Montreal Protocol process has found a way to give industry actors incentives to create and use the substitute chemicals and processes required to implement the agreement.

Industry's role in climate change has been as varied as the industries and countries involved in creating greenhouse gases. Traditionally, the economic health of a country has been attributable largely to its reliance on fossil fuels. Ian Rowlands suggests that the willingness of a state to take action on climate change can be ascertained from the extent to which it has been able to de-link its gross domestic product from pollution generating industries.[57]

In the United States, the largest emitter of greenhouse gases and the most resistant developed country participant in international measures to mitigate climate change, the fossil fuel industry has been particularly active in leading the opposition to global (or national) action. A group of utility and coal companies created an industry group, the Information Council on the Environment, and in the run-up to the FCCC negotiations hired a public relations firm to increase publicity to "reposition global warming as theory rather than fact" and increase the visibility of scientists skeptical of some of the hypotheses about climate change.[58]

The international industry organization, with the intentionally misleading name of The Global Climate Coalition, initially included the major fossil fuel industries worldwide, and lobbied strongly against the Kyoto Protocol, out of concern that reduced greenhouse gas emissions would hurt their profitability. More recently many of the main companies involved, including Royal Dutch Shell, BP Amoco, Dow Chemical, Ford, and Texaco have withdrawn from membership. Moreover, the group has recently toned down its message, questioning the magnitude of climate change rather than its existence or causes.[59]

Additionally, former members of the coalition have been moving into alternative energy operations: Texaco, for instance, bought a large stake in an energy conversion company whose main focus is energy from hydrogen.[60] BP recently created a new unit, BP alternative energy, and dramatically increased its investment in renewable energy.[61] Some remain resistant, however. ExxonMobil stated at the end of 2005 that it would not invest in alternative energy.[62]

The sector that has taken the lead in pushing for regulation on greenhouse gases has been the insurance industry. Insurers face the biggest potential for losses from dramatic weather events and rising sea level predicted from climate change, and they have been involved in addressing the situation, both privately and in urging international action. In 1995 fourteen of the world's largest insurance firms signed a Statement of Environmental Commitment pledging to incorporate climate considerations into their future assessments; the first U.S. insurer signed on the following year.[63] In addition, other industries, including those involved with the use of fossil fuels, are themselves taking out insurance to hedge against the possibility that their profits will go down if people consume less greenhouse gas producing substances.[64]

While many industry groups have publicly opposed any action on climate change, most are preparing for what they see as approaching obligations. This is particularly true of automobile manufacturers, which are working toward increased fuel efficiency and towards alternatives to the internal combustion engine.[65] Other fossil fuel intensive industries, such as most oil companies, realize the inevitability, even if some of their governments do not, of international regulation to restrict greenhouse gas emissions.

## Other Non-State Actors

Environmental and consumer groups created pressure for behavior change on both ozone depletion and climate change long before government action was taken. It is their pressure, in combination with increased understanding of these global problems, that influenced industry actors to change their behavior even before required to do so by national or international regulation. In the United States, the first state to restrict use of ozone-depleting substances, consumer pressure created markets for goods made without ODS.

In addition to activists lying down across rail distribution lines for ozone-depleting substances or blocking coal shipments in Australia to protest that country's lack of participation in international climate change efforts,[66] traditional methods for gaining media attention, organizations have started to gain influence at other levels in addressing these two issues. Non-governmental organizations have been increasingly active participants in pushing for negotiations on both these issues and have generally been present at the negotiations and at subsequent meetings of the parties.

An interesting strategy used by environmental activists on both these issues involved getting commitments from subnational governmental (or quasi-governmental) entities to address the environmental problems, acting either sooner or more thoroughly than states or international organizations have been willing to. In the case of ozone depletion, Berkeley, California, declared itself to be "styrofoam free" as a way of indicating its support for protection of the ozone layer. The environmental organization Friends of the Earth convinced twenty-four other cities to undertake similar pledges, going further in the immediate wake of the Montreal Protocol than they were required to.[67] The more explicitly international "Cities for Climate Protection" project, led by the International Council for Local Environmental Initiatives, has done the same for climate change policies, with nearly 475 participant cities worldwide by 2006[68] agreeing to undertake climate protection greater than that legally required. A similar initiative operates on the university level. The organization Clean Air-Cool Planet attempts to persuade universities to undertake pledges to reduce their contribution to climate change. Tufts University, for instance, has pledged to meet Kyoto obligations on its own, though obviously not required to.[69] This organization also works to get voluntary commitments from businesses and cities to take action to reduce their greenhouse gas emissions.

Other substate governmental actors have undertaken action on climate change. In 2001 the states of New England and the provinces of Eastern Canada agreed that they would reduce their greenhouse gas emissions by 12 per cent by 2010.[70] Massachusetts requires the six power plants that produce the greatest greenhouse gas emissions to reduce emissions with limits becoming increasingly strict over time.[71] Seven states in the northeastern United States created a Regional Greenhouse Gas Initiative at the end of 2005 that limits greenhouse gas emissions and allows companies to trade emissions allocations.[72]

This type of action, sometime intended to have a demonstration effect, may in fact show governments both the concern of the population and the feasibility of climate protection measures. On the other hand, it presents an irony, to the extent that it is largely the unwillingness of people in developed countries to undertake lifestyle changes that precludes serious governmental action to address the issue.

# The Role of Developing Countries

Developing countries have played a powerful role in the politics of both ozone depletion and climate change. Their participation in efforts to address the problems are necessary, given the common pool resource nature of the environmental issues. Historically they have contributed little to the creation of these problems, and have for the most part given low national priority to the potential environmental damage. These factors, in combination with their growing emissions of ozone-depleting substances and greenhouse gases, has given them extensive bargaining power in the negotiation of international arrangements to address these issues. But in the case of climate change where the international incentive structures are murkier than in ozone depletion, this increased bargaining power has been insufficient to gain strong international action on climate issues that are likely to affect some developing states.

The participation of developing countries was essential if the Montreal Protocol process was to work. Although at the time the Protocol was signed the per capita consumption of ozone-depleting substances by developing countries was miniscule and production in most of these countries negligible, these figures were likely to grow significantly. Chlorofluorocarbons had been essential in the process of industrialization for the countries of the North, and others at early stages of development were likely to use these cheap, safe chemicals in their process of industrialization as well. It was estimated at the time that India and China alone would account for one-third of the world's consumption of CFCs by 2008.[73] Moreover, the problem had clearly been created by Northern industries, and the concern about the environmental problem was most prevalent in the industrialized world. Absent sufficient incentives to join the agreement, developing countries showed every sign of remaining outside the regulatory system. By the time of the London negotiations in 1989 the only major CFC-using developing countries that had joined the agreement were Mexico, Nigeria, and Venezuela.[74]

The initial efforts to bring developing countries into the agreement revolved around a grace-period (initially ten years, though it has been renegotiated for a variety of different ODS) during which developing countries would not have to meet the obligations of the Protocol. This measure allowed member developing countries whose annual consumption of ODS was less than 0.3 kilograms per capita to continue and even increase their use of these substances. The Protocol acknowledged that these countries had special needs for financial and technical assistance to meet their obligations, but without specifying the way in which these needs would be met, the lag-time was insufficient to convince most developing countries to join.

Second was a trade incentive: states that are party to the agreement can only trade in controlled substances with those that are in the agreement.[75] For states that did not produce ozone-depleting substances but hoped to use them, joining the agreement was the obvious way to guarantee their access to these chemicals. The scenario would only work, however, if the developing countries capable of producing ozone-depleting substances were brought into the agreement as well. Otherwise a separate trading bloc could emerge outside of the agreement that could undermine, rather than encourage, participation. Mexico was the only developing country producer of ODS that initially signed the Protocol.[76] The reluctance of other producer states such as China and India to join the Montreal Protocol initially indicated that the trade sanctions would be insufficient to bring developing countries into the agreement. These states, potentially unaffected by the sanctions, would have to be convinced to join.

The most innovative and essential element in bringing these states into the agreement was the elaboration of a financial transfer mechanism. The Multilateral Fund, as the mechanism was ultimately named, was the factor that allowed for universal participation in the agreement, and facilitated the process of moving away from ozone-depleting substances in developing countries. It is a generally well-designed instrument for bringing developing states into the Montreal Protocol and helping their implementation of the agreement.

The creation of this fund can be attributed to the power that a CPR issue gives to those states whose participation is essential to addressing the environmental problem but for whom it is not a priority. A number of states explicitly tied their participation in the treaty process to the creation of a funding mechanism. India and China, whose participation in the agreement was essential due to their large and growing populations, rapid industrialization, and ability to produce ozone-depleting substances, refused to join the agreement unless an aid package with which they were satisfied was created.[77] The resulting funding mechanism is specified in Article 10 of the protocol (as amended), and involves funding from developed countries based on the United Nations scale of assessments, put into a multilateral fund overseen by a committee composed both of donors and recipients.[78]

The creation of the Fund had the intended effect. China joined the Protocol immediately, followed by India and Brazil in 1992 and eventually by almost all developing countries. Importantly, the operation of the Fund has gone a long way toward helping some developing countries avoid ozone-depleting substances or change over their use of ODS to ozone-safe chemicals or processes. By the end of 2005 the fund had allocated more $2 billion, and the Executive Committee had approved nearly 5,000 projects in 139 developing countries. These projects are expected to result in the phase-out of more than 204,843 tonnes of ozone-depleting substances, as measured by their ozone depletion potential (ODP).[79]

Developing countries have been wary of taking on obligations to prevent or mitigate climate change, and this reluctance is reflected in the international agreements on climate change. Following shortly after the specification of a funding mechanism under the London Amendments to the Montreal Protocol, developing country negotiators of the UNFCCC were insistent that aid be included in the agreement as a quid pro quo for signing.[80] In a victory for the developing countries, the idea that there would be funding (and that it would be new and additional) was essentially taken as a given; it was the format for it that was more contentious.

In this case, a mechanism had already been created outside of the UNFCCC framework. The Global Environment Facility (GEF), run largely by the World Bank (with assistance from UN agencies), had been set up to provide multilateral funding to address four initial global environmental issues: ozone depletion, climate change, biodiversity, and international waters. Industrialized countries wanted to use the GEF as the funding mechanism for climate change because they had a larger degree of influence over funding through that organization than they thought they would over a new mechanism; developing countries opposed the use of the GEF for precisely the same reason.[81] Developed countries refused to provide serious levels of aid if the GEF were not chosen as the interim funding mechanism for the convention, and they were successful. But developing countries did make a credible threat to reject the agreement if the GEF were not at least restructured to give them more influence over its activities; the restructuring that resulted made the decision processes in the GEF similar to those in the Multilateral Fund.[82]

The UNFCCC requires that developed country parties provide "new and additional financial resources to meet the agreed full costs incurred by developing country Parties" in meeting their obligations under the convention.[83] Within that agreement the obligations pertain to gathering and communicating information about the sources and sinks of greenhouse gases, but it is likely that any new obligations will be undertaken only with the financial assistance to meet them. The funding obligation outlined in the UNFCCC goes further in some ways than that under the Montreal Protocol. The convention specifies that "the extent to which developing country Parties will effectively implement their commitments … will depend on the effective implementation by developed country Parties of their commitments … related to financial resources."[84]

The Kyoto Protocol indicates further commitments for transfer of financial resources and technology.[85] Most importantly, developing countries have no emissions reductions obligations under the first commitment period of the Kyoto Protocol. There were never any serious efforts in the negotiation process to craft abatement obligations for developing countries, itself a testament to the political power of developing states, who refused to even consider taking on abatement obligations until developed states acted first. But their lack of reduction commitments has been controversial. In even the medium term, action by developing states will be necessary for any progress on slowing climate change. Although these states have played little role in the historical increase in greenhouse gas emissions, their current emissions increases are dramatic. Indonesia's increased by 21.2 per cent between 1990 and 1994. Many smaller countries are increasing even more dramatically, albeit from a lower starting point: Paraguay's greenhouse gas emissions increased 115 per cent during that same period.[86] Of particular concern are the largest of the developing countries. India's greenhouse gas emissions are estimated to have risen 50 per cent during the 1990s.[87] China is currently the second largest emitter of greenhouse gases, and is expected to surpass the United States in emissions by 2020.[88]

The interests of developing countries on climate change are not uniform. Some large developing states care primarily about avoiding restrictions on the processes they can use for industrialization. Many of the major oil-producing states are developing countries, and they are concerned that their major export will be impacted by any restrictions on fossil fuel combustion that may result from efforts to prevent climate change. These states have gone so far as to attempt to gain special consideration in climate change for their status. The Organization of the Petroleum Exporting Countries (OPEC) asked in negotiations over the implementation of the Kyoto Protocol for economic aid if a switch to renewable energy causes their income from oil producing to drop.[89]

Other developing states are particularly vulnerable to the effects of climate change. Low-lying states with extensive coastlines will be harmed by sea-level rise and could be negatively impacted if the severity and frequency of storms increases. The Alliance of Small Island States (AOSIS) has been an important player in international negotiations on climate change. Though its members have little power in the traditional international relations sense, and also do not have the "power to destroy" that gives big states like China and India the ability to influence international negotiations, AOSIS and states in similar dire situations have some degree of moral suasion. Vanuatu claims to have the first "climate change refugees," as residents of a coastal village were resettled, with the help of the United Nations Environment Programme and funding from the Canadian government, on higher ground further inland. Funding from the Global Environment Facility has gone to developing National Adaptation Programmes for Action for developing states to address how to adapt to the extent of climate change that is already seen as inevitable.[90] The Kyoto Protocol explicitly states the need "to assist developing country Parties that are particularly vulnerable to the adverse effects of climate change to meet the costs of adaptation."[91] The lack of a single developing country negotiation position has, however, made it more difficult for some of the less powerful developing states – such as the most vulnerable states who want strong action on climate change – to accomplish their goals.

# International Environmental Cooperation

## Implementation and Effectiveness

It is realistic to begin to examine the effectiveness of the Montreal Protocol because the process of cooperation has been fairly complete. Nearly all states have joined the agreement. Developed countries have almost entirely phased out their use of the initially regulated ozone-depleting substances and decreased their use of newly regulated ones; developing countries have begun the process of lowering their consumption of regulated substances and have phased out some substances entirely. While the ozone layer has not yet recovered and will not for some time, a process has been started that, if it continues, will eventually fully address the problem. There is evidence of non-compliance both on the state level and in a black market in regulated substances, but both these aspects are minor and temporary compared to the overall accomplishments of the treaty and its likely eventual effectiveness.

In the case of climate change, it is too soon to tell, but signs are not yet promising. The Kyoto Protocol only entered into force in 2005, without the participation of the largest greenhouse gas emitter. Developing countries do not have abatement obligations under the agreement, which limits the extent to which even the modest cuts required by the agreement, if implemented, will impact the environment. Yet there are signs that individually states and non-state actors are changing their behavior in a way that might ultimately have an impact on the ability of the world to implement Kyoto and the necessary measures beyond it, to address the problem of climate change. The initial obligations under Kyoto were only intended to be a preliminary step. It remains to be seen whether they will move the world in the right direction.

## Participation

Because both ozone depletion and climate change are problems of the global commons, participation by all major states is necessary for the agreements to have a meaningful impact. Negotiators for both agreements chose to address the issue of participation by giving developing countries aid to meet any obligations they undertake, and by giving them extra time before they would have to meet any emissions reductions deadlines taken on by developed countries.

The Montreal Protocol is a model for widespread global participation. Once the concerns of developing countries were met with the creation of the Multilateral Fund, they were willing to participate in the agreement that most of the world's developed states had already joined. As of 2006, 189 states have ratified the Montreal Protocol. Not quite that many have ratified the amendments (180 have ratified London, 170 Copenhagen, 141 Montreal, and 105 Beijing),[92] leading to a situation in which not all parties to the Montreal Protocol have the same obligations. But overall participation is widespread, and the states that have not taken on the later amendments to the protocol are not major producers or consumers of ozone-depleting substances.

To increase the likelihood that states would be willing to join the Kyoto Protocol, the agreement as negotiated included a number of flexibility mechanisms, described above, giving states with emissions reductions options for how to meet them.

In addition, the agreement differentiates not only between the obligations of developed and developing states, but also within developed states. Former Communist countries with economies in transition were given a choice of base year from which to calculate reductions. The agreement also takes the relatively unusual step of differentiating levels of developed country abatement obligations under the Protocol. The "Qualified Emission Limitation or Reduction Commitments" for developed country parties varies from 92 per cent of 1990 emissions to 110 per cent.[93] And although the Convention indicates the need to take into account "specific national and regional development priorities, objectives, and circumstances," there is no specific formula for arriving at the differentiated commitments of the parties. Instead, commitments agreed to were those that were politically feasible, as much as each individual party was willing to commit to. In order to reach an agreement that had a chance of including the major developed country parties, negotiators agreed to targets that states were more or less willing to accept.

By 2006, 162 states had signed and ratified the Kyoto Protocol. The lack of participation by the United States is worrying, however. In 1990 it was responsible for 36 per cent of greenhouse gas emissions by developed countries,[94] and U.S. emissions have risen dramatically since then. Australia, responsible for 2 per cent of developed country greenhouse gas emissions in 1990, has also as of 2006 refused to ratify Kyoto and increased its emissions since then. And while many developing countries have ratified the protocol, they have not yet agreed to take on emissions reductions obligations. They are legally participating in the agreement, but are not contributing to a reduction in greenhouse gas emissions.

## Compliance and Implementation

Measures to protect the ozone layer require extensive action. While there are instances of non-compliance, they are almost the exception that proves the rule: states have fundamentally changed the way their industries operate in order to live up to a set of ever tightening international agreements to protect the ozone layer.

There have been two types of non-compliance with the Montreal Protocol that have taken place. The first is state-level non-compliance with specific deadlines for reducing the use of ozone-depleting substances. Initially such non-compliance happened as former Soviet bloc states found their economies in disarray at the time that they were supposed to be phasing out their use of many ozone-depleting substances. Due to an accident of timing, under the agreement they are considered developed countries, but the fall of communism in this region in the late 1980s and early 1990s left them in economic and political situations that were more similar to those of developing countries. In particular, Belarus, Bulgaria, Poland, Russia, and Ukraine were not able to meet the 1996 deadline for complete phase-out of a set of ozone-depleting substances. These states were persuaded by the treaty secretariat to turn themselves in to the non-compliance procedure developed under the Montreal Protocol. This process allowed for increased funding and flexibility in the phase-out dates to be negotiated for the states that went through this process.[95]

Since then, some developing states, as their reduction obligations have begun, have not met their deadlines. For instance, at the end of 2005 Azerbaijan, Bangladesh, Chile, China, Ecuador, Micronesia, Fiji, Honduras, Kazakhstan, Kyrgyzstan, Libya, Sierra Leone, and Uruguay were all singled out by the Ozone Secretariat as not fully meeting their substantive obligations under the agreement.[96] In all these cases their non-compliance was identified through self-reported data, so they were clearly not attempting to hide their lack of implementation of their obligations. The way the Montreal Protocol compliance process is structured requires these states to create a plan of action for compliance, at which point the Implementation Committee will help gain the financial or technical assistance they need for compliance. This type of non-compliance has so far been minor and temporary, and the overall level of compliance with the fairly onerous obligations of the agreement has been high.

Also important is the black market that emerged in ozone-depleting substances. This problem initially appeared in developed countries as the requirements to phase out the use of CFCs took effect. CFCs were smuggled into the United States, Europe, and other developed countries where CFC manufacturing for domestic consumption was no longer allowed. High excise taxes (particularly in the United States) made legal purchase of these substances too costly even before the total developed country phase-out, and some who wanted cheap access to these chemicals were been willing to skirt the law to obtain them.

The extent of the black market, although unknown, has been significant. In some U.S. ports CFC smuggling was at points second only in value to the smuggling of narcotics.[97] Industry estimates suggest that up to 20 per cent of CFCs in use in developed countries in the 1990s may have been purchased on the black market.[98] The black market in developed countries has declined recently because new technology is made in ways that does not use CFCs. As older machinery (such as air conditioners, one of the major destinations of black market CFCs) is replaced, the demand for CFCs decreases. The major concern at this point is whether an analogous black market will emerge in developing countries as they phase down their use of CFCs. So far the evidence is inconclusive.

Predictions of when the ozone layer will recover have been based on consumption numbers that assume complete compliance with Montreal Protocol requirements, and the increase in CFC use that is made possible by the black market is certain to delay the environmental recovery foreseen by the treaty process. Jerry Mahlman, then of the U.S. National Oceanic and Atmospheric Administration, suggests that a "cheating rate of only 10% can keep stratospheric CFC levels from declining."[99] The effect of the black market on the ozone layer can be seen in the fact that of the two main types of CFCs, the concentration of one in the atmosphere changed not at all during the 1990s, and the other increased during that period.[100] In addition, the Montreal Protocol regulatory system as a whole depends on the adoption of substitute chemicals and processes in a way that reinforces the phase-out process and is undermined when CFC smuggling becomes prominent.[101]

As suggested by the low level of non-compliance, the Montreal Protocol has had an impressive impact on state behavior overall. All developed states have now, with small exceptions for essential use, phased out their consumption and production of CFCs, halons, carbon tetrachloride, and methyl chloroform.[102] There are some concerns that states are filing greater numbers of petitions for "essential use" of substances – especially methyl bromide – than was anticipated, but for the most part developed country behavior has changed dramatically. Developing states have begun their process of freezing and then phasing out ozone-depleting substances, with some states doing so dramatically ahead of schedule.

All evidence suggests that this phase-out activity is due almost entirely to the existence of the agreement. Realistic substitutes for ozone-depleting substances were largely unavailable before the Montreal Protocol process and those that became available were initially prohibitively expensive. It was only in a worldwide regulatory context that a market was created, and technological processes fundamentally shifted, to favor approaches that did not harm the ozone layer. The scientific processes within the Montreal Protocol that provided increasing evidence for human-caused destruction of the ozone layer and evaluated potential substitute processes, along with the Multilateral Fund that made transition possible for developing countries, persuaded states to fundamentally change their industrial practices to address an environmental problem.

There is, as yet, no substantive non-compliance with the Kyoto Protocol, because the date of required emissions reductions has not yet arrived. An examination of the implementation of commitments thus far gives an indication that some states are on target to implement their Kyoto commitments and that some are unlikely to succeed. The extent to which decreasing greenhouse gas emissions can be attributed to the existence of the Kyoto Protocol varies as well.

There are some optimistic implementation trends. Between the 1990 base year and 2003, greenhouse gas emissions collectively for parties with abatement obligations decreased by 5.9 per cent (or 6.5 per cent including activities that take up carbon, such as land use and forestry). But individual emissions trajectories vary considerably, from an increase of 57.5 per cent by Canada to a decrease of 77.5 per cent by Lithuania.[103] Some European states, like Italy and Spain, are not likely to meet their targets, while others, like Britain, France, and Germany, are.[104]

If an agreement is to have an impact, it is not enough that states undertake action that is (mostly) congruent with its obligations, but rather that it must be the cause of that action. Otherwise there is no way to know that stricter obligations will be implemented. In the case of climate change, many of the emissions reductions undertaken to date are most likely not caused by the existence of the Kyoto Protocol. The first set of states to which this assessment applies are the Eastern European and former Soviet states. These states exhibit the most dramatic decrease in greenhouse gas emissions. These are mostly attributable to the change away from heavy industry that happened at the end of communism, and the enormous economic disruption that resulted from the transition to capitalism. The enthusiasm by these states for the Kyoto Protocol comes mainly because they will be able to sell their "excess" emissions reductions and thereby gain financially.

Changes in emissions in other states may also not be due to international regulation. Some European states have changed away from high greenhouse gas emitting energy production (such as coal), to less climate-harmful sources (such as gas, nuclear, or even renewable energy) for reasons other than climate change concerns. The European Union is, nevertheless, working hard on changes in industrial and transportation policy that take Kyoto obligations into account, so future efforts may be Kyoto-driven.

## Effectiveness

The Montreal Protocol has had an impressive impact on state behavior, which is beginning to translate into a noticeable environmental effect. Because the most common ozone-depleting substances have atmospheric lifetimes of 100 years or longer, it will take a long time for the ozone layer to recover. At this point, the concentrations of ozone-depleting substances in the stratosphere are no longer increasing and some are beginning to decline. Because of these existing concentrations the thinning of the ozone layer has not yet decreased; the seasonal thinning of ozone over Antarctica, commonly known as the "ozone hole," in December 2005 was the among largest recorded.[105] But it is likely that the peak of depleted ozone is nearing. Current estimates suggest that, even taking into consideration the black market in ozone-depleting substances, the ozone layer over Antarctica will recover by 2065.[106] It is generally agreed that the process has done as much to combat the environmental problem, in a relatively quick time frame, as any other international environmental agreement.

The effectiveness of the UNFCCC and the Kyoto Protocol is so far relatively low. Though many member states are taking action consistent with their obligations, the impact of the agreement on the environmental problem of climate change is minimal. In part this lack of effectiveness is due to the dramatically increasing emissions of the largest greenhouse gas emitting states, which have not agreed to abatement obligations. The United States, not bound by the Kyoto Protocol and therefore without a clear legal requirement to reduce its emission of greenhouse gases, increased its emissions by 20.2 per cent from 1990 to 2003[107]; its emissions have been increasing even more dramatically since then.[108] Developing countries, the largest of which are among the main current sources of greenhouse gas emissions, are not required under the Kyoto Protocol to reduce their emissions, and they are consequently increasing. The worldwide increase in GHG emissions suggests that the problem of climate change is nowhere close to being ameliorated. Moreover, the emissions cuts required under the Kyoto Protocol, even with United States participation, are minimal compared to what will be required to reverse centuries of human-led increases in greenhouse gas emissions. The U.S. Energy Information Agency estimated in 2006 that greenhouse gas emissions worldwide will increase by 75 per cent between 2003 and 2030.[109] Indeed, the IPCC acknowledges that many of the impacts of climate change are inevitable at this point.[110]

The important question is what happens next. The Conference of the Parties to the UNFCCC began negotiation in December 2005 for action to be taken beyond 2012. Others doubt that action to address climate change will or even should be undertaken within the UNFCCC process. But it is clear that there will be changes by states and non-state actors to reflect an increasingly accepted understanding that climate change is happening.

# Notes

1   Ozone Secretariat, "2002 Environmental Effects Assessment," http://ozone.unep.org/Public_Information/4D_PublicInfo_FAQ.asp.

2   IPCC, *Climate Change 2001: The Scientific Basis* (Cambridge: Cambridge University Press, 2001).

3 Arun Makhijani and Kevin R. Gurney, *Mending the Ozone Hole: Science, Technology, and Policy* (Cambridge, Mass., and London: MIT Press, 1995), 93–114.

4 Ibid., 51–90.

5 Irving M. Mintzer and J. Amber Leonard, eds., *Negotiating Climate Change* (Cambridge: Cambridge University Press, 1994).

6 Robert B. Gagosian, *Abrupt Climate Change: Should We Be Worried* (Woods Hole, Mass: Woods Hole Oceanographic Institution, 2003).

7 M. J. Molina and F. S. Rowland, "Stratospheric Sink for Chlorofluoromethanes: Chlorine Atom-Catalyzed Destruction of Ozone," *Nature* 249 (1974): 810–12.

8 Vienna Convention for the Protection of the Ozone Layer (1985), Article 2.

9 Vienna Convention, Article 9(4).

10 London Amendments to the Montreal Protocol (1990).

11 Copenhagen Amendments to the Montreal Protocol (1992).

12 Montreal Amendments to the Montreal Protocol (1997).

13 Geoffrey Palmer, "New Ways to Make International Environmental Law," *American Journal of International Law* 86 (April 1992): 274–76.

14 Montreal Protocol (as amended), Article 2(9).

15 For a comparison, see Edith Brown Weiss, "The Five International Treaties: A Living History," in Edith Brown Weiss and Harold K. Jacobson, *Engaging Countries: Strengthening Compliance with International Environmental Accords* (Cambridge, Mass.: MIT Press, 1998), 140–44.

16 Discussed in Matthew Paterson, *Global Warming and Global Politics* (London and New York: Routledge, 1996), 17–21.

17 Ibid., 22–23.

18 Marvin S. Soroos, "The Atmosphere as an International Common Property Resource," in S.S. Nagel, ed., *Global Policy Studies* (London: Macmillan, 1991), 201.

19 See Ian H. Rowlands, *The Politics of Global Atmospheric Change* (Manchester and London: Manchester University Press, 1995), 68–72.

20 Intergovernmental Panel on Climate Change, "About IPCC," n.d., http://www.ipcc.ch/about/about.htm.

21 UN General Assembly Resolution A/RES/43/53, 6 December 1988.

22 Framework Convention on Climate Change, 1992, Articles 2 and 4.

23 Kyoto Protocol to the Framework Convention on Climate Change, 1997.

24 Framework Convention on Climate Change, Conference of the Parties, "Actions Taken by the Conference of the Parties," 4th Session, Annex 60, FCCC/CP/1997/7/Add.1, 1997.

25 W. M. McKibben and P. J. Wilcoxen, "Estimates of the Costs of Kyoto: Marrakesh versus the McKibben-Wilcoxen Blueprint," *Energy Policy* 32(4) (2004): 467–79.

26  Rowlands, 55.

27  Richard A. Kerr, "Antarctic Ozone Hole is Still Deepening," *Science* 232 (27 June 1986): 1602.

28  Robert T. Watson, F. Sherwood Rowland, and John Gille, *Ozone Trends Panel: Executive Summary* (Washington D.C.: NASA, 1988).

29  Karen T. Litfin, *Ozone Discourses: Science and Politics in Global Environmental Cooperation* (New York: Columbia University Press, 1994); see especially ch. 4.

30  Ibid., 82.

31  Edward A. Parson, *Protecting the Ozone Layer: Science and Strategy* (Oxford: Oxford University Press, 2003), 212–14.

32  Intergovernmental Panel on Climate Change, "Summary for Policymakers: A Report of Working Group I of the Intergovernmental Panel on Climate Change," 2001, 10.

33  Intergovernmental Panel on Climate Change, "Summary for Policymakers," 9.

34  Quoted in Rowlands, 78.

35  Richard A. Kerr, "Rising Global Temperature, Rising Uncertainty," *Science* 292 (13 April 2001): 192–94.

36  Quoted in Kerr, "Rising Global Temperature," 194.

37  Jason Webb, "Scientists Clearing Up Clouds' Effects on Climate," *Reuters News Service*, 10 November 1998.

38  Patricia Reaney, "Deep Ocean Current Linked to Global Climate Change," *Reuters New Service*, 3 August 2000; Global Commons Institute, "Draft Proposals for a Climate Change Protocol Based on Contraction and Convergence," Section 2.14, September 1996, http://www.gci.org.uk/contconv/protweb.html [date visited: 26 June 2001].

39  D. A. Clark, S. C. Piper, C. D. Keeling, and D. B. Clark, "Tropical Rain Forest Tree Growth and Atmospheric Carbon Dynamics Linked to Interannual Temperature Variation During 1984–2000," *PNAS* 100(10) (13 May 2003): 5852–56; Dennis Baldocchi, "The Carbon Cycle Under Stress," *Nature* 437(22) (2005): 483–84.

40  Fred Pearce, "A Cool Trick," *New Scientist* (8 April 2000): 18; "Sinking $CO_2$" *Environment* 43(2) (March 2001): 6; Rober H. Socolow, "Can We Bury Global Warming?" *Scientific American* (July 2005): 49–55.

41  Dale Jamieson, "Scientific Uncertainty and the Political Process," *Annals of the American Academy of Political and Social Sciences* 545 (May 1996): 35–43.

42  Quoted in Kerr, "Rising Global Temperature," 194.

43  Elizabeth R. DeSombre, "Understanding United States Unilateralism: Domestic Sources of U.S. International Environmental Policy," in Regina S. Axelrod, David Leonard Downie, and Norman J. Vig, eds., *The Global Environment* (Washington D.C.: CQ Press, 2005), 181–99.

44  CCX, "About CCX," http://www.chicagoclimatex.com/about/.

45 EPA Press Release, "Progress to Reduce Greenhouse Gas Emissions Achieved by Climate Leaders Partnership – Voluntary Partnership Expands; Greater Emission Reductions Will Be Achieved," 11 June 2003.

46 Alan S. Miller, "Incentives for CFC Substitutes: Lessons for Other Greenhouse Gases," in John C. Topping, ed., *Coping with Climate Change: Proceedings of the Second North American Conference on Preparing for Climate Change* (Washington D.C.: Climate Institute, 1989), 547. Miller does not himself make this argument, but mentions others who do. For others who follow this logic implicitly, see Detlef Sprinz and Tapani Vaahtoranta, "The Interest-Based Explanation of International Environmental Policy," *International Organization* 48(1) (1994): 93–94; James K. Sebenius, "Challenging Conventional Explanations of International Cooperation: Negotiation Analysis and the Case of Epistemic Communities," *International Organization* 46(1) (1992): 358.

47 Richard Elliot Benedick, *Ozone Diplomacy: New Directions in Safeguarding the Planet*, enlarged edition (Cambridge, Mass.: Harvard University Press, 1998), 31, 33.

48 Alliance for Responsible CFC Policy, *A Search for Alternatives to the Current Commercial Fluorocarbons*, 24 February 1986, as quoted in Miller, "Incentives for CFC Substitutes," 549.

49 Ibid., 547.

50 David Victor, "The Montreal Protocol's Non-Compliance Procedure," in David G. Victor, Kal Raustiala, and Eugene B. Skolnikoff, *The Implementation and Effectiveness of International Environmental Commitments* (Cambridge, Mass.: MIT Press, 1998), 147.

51 This explanation is considered and discarded by Edward A. Parson, "Protecting the Ozone Layer," in Peter M. Haas, Robert O. Keohane, and Marc A. Levy, eds., *Institutions for the Earth: Sources of Effective International Environmental Protection* (Cambridge, Mass.: MIT Press, 1993), 66.

52 Miller, 550.

53 Elizabeth DeSombre and Joanne Kauffman, "The Montreal Protocol Multilateral Fund: Partial Success Story," in Robert O. Keohane and Marc A. Levy, eds., *Institutions for Environmental Aid* (Cambridge, Mass.: MIT Press, 1996), 95.

54 Kenneth Oye and James H. Maxwell, "Self-Interest and Environmental Management," in Robert O. Keohane and Elinor Ostrom, eds., *Local Commons and Global Interdependence: Heterogeneity and Cooperation in Two Domains* (Newbury Park, Calif.: Sage, 1995), 198.

55 John C. Dernbach, "Sustainable Development as a Framework for National Governance," *Case Western Reserve Law Review* 49(1) (Fall 1998): 93.

56 Owen Greene, "The System for Implementation Review in the Ozone Regime," in Victor, Raustiala, and Skolnikoff, eds., 97–98.

57 Rowlands, 126–50.

58 Ross Gelbspan, *The Heat Is On: The High Stakes Battle over Earth's Threatened Climate* (Reading, Mass.: Addison-Wesley, 1997), 34.

59 Timothy Gardner, "Global Warming Business Group Cools Its Message," *Reuters News Service*, 9 November 2000; Patrick Connole, "Ford Exits Anti-Kyoto Climate Change Group," *Reuters News Service*, 7 December 1999; "Texaco Quits Anti-Kyoto Climate Change Group," *Reuters News Service*, 2 March 2001.

60 Lee Daniels, "Texaco Buys 20% Stake In Energy Conversion Company," *Reuters News Service*, 7 June 2000.

61 Thomas Catan and Fiona Harvey, "BP Earmarks 8bn for Green Investment," *The Financial Times*, 29 November 2005, 22.

62 James R. Healey, "Alternative Energy not in the Cards at ExxonMobil," *USA Today*, 28 October 2005, 5B.

63 Gelbspan, 88–89.

64 Greg Schneider, "Taking No Chances: Disaster-Conscious Firms Treat Global Warming as a Reality," *Washington Post*, 26 June 2001, E01.

65 Jeffrey Ball, "Ford to Study How Steps to Curb Global Warming Might Affect It," *Wall Street Journal*, 31 March 2005, 7D.

66 Anthony Marx, "Greenpeace Coal Export Protesters Held," *The Courier Mail*, 28 July 2005, 29.

67 Paul Wapner, *Environmental Activism and World Civic Politics* (Albany: SUNY Press, 1996), 127.

68 Cities for Climate Protection, "Members," http://www.iclei.org/index.php?id=642.

69 Tufts Climate Initiative, "Who We Are," http://www.tufts.edu/tie/tci/WhoWeAre.html.

70 Beth Daley, "Region Struggles on Greenhouse Emissions Goals," *Boston Globe*, 15 March 2004, A1.

71 Beth Daley, "Big Gaps in State's Plans for Emissions," *Boston Globe*, 17 January 2006, A1.

72 Mark Clayton, "One Region's Bid to Slow Global Warming," *Christian Science Monitor*, 22 December 2005, 2.

73 Friends of the Earth, *Funding Change: Developing Countries and the Montreal Protocol*, 1990.

74 Richard Benedick, *Ozone Diplomacy: New Directions in Safeguarding the Planet* (Cambridge, Mass.: Harvard University Press, 1991), 151.

75 Montreal Protocol, Article 4.

76 DeSombre and Kauffman, 96.

77 Benedick, ch. 13.

78 Montreal Protocol Article 10; see also Elizabeth R. DeSombre and Joanne Kauffman, "The Montreal Protocol Multilateral Fund: Partial Success Story," in Robert O. Keohane and Marc A. Levy, eds., *Institutions for Environmental Aid* (Cambridge, Mass.: MIT Press, 1996), 89–126.

79 Multilateral Fund, *Creating a Real Change for the Environment* (Montreal: Multilateral Fund Secretariat, 2005), 2–7; Multilateral Fund for the Implementation of the Montreal Protocol, http://www.multilateralfund.org/.

80 Chandrashekhar Dasgupta, "The Climate Change Negotiations," in Irving Mintzer and J. A. Leonard, eds., *Negotiating Climate Change* (Cambridge: Cambridge University Press, 1994), 138–39; see also Michael Grubb et al., *The Earth Summit Agreements: A Guide and Assessment* (London: Earthscan, 1993).

81 Paterson, 66.

82 David Fairman, "The Global Environmental Facility: Haunted by the Shadow of the Future," in Robert O. Keohane and Marc A. Levy, eds., *Institutions for Environmental Aid: Pitfalls and Promise* (Cambridge, Mass., and London: MIT Press, 1996), 55–87.

83 UNFCCC, Article 4(3).

84 UNFCCC, Article 4(7).

85 Kyoto Protocol, Article 11.

86 UNFCCC, Key GHG Data: Greenhouse Gas Emissions Data for 1990–2003 Submitted to the United Nations Framework Convention on Climate Change (Bonn: UNFCCC, November 2005).

87 "Climate Change: The Big Emitters," BBC Online, 4 July 2005, http://news.bbc.co.uk/1/hi/sci/tech/3143798.stm.

88 Jia Hepeng, "China is Second Biggest Greenhouse Gas Emitter," SciDeiv.net, 24 November 2004, http://www.scidev.net/news/index.cfm?fuseaction=readnews&itemid=1761&language=1.

89 IISD, "Summary of the Ninth Conference of the Parties to the United Nations Framework Convention on Climate Change 1–12 December 2003," *Earth Negotiations Bulletin* 12(231) (15 December 2003): 16.

90 "Peter Gorrie, "U.S. Rejects Bids for Post-Kyoto Talks," *Toronto Star*, 7 December 2005, A4.

91 Kyoto Protocol to the United Nations Framework Convention on Climate Change (1997), Article 12(8).

92 Ozone Secretariat, "Table: Status of Ratification as at 28.2.2006," http://ozone.unep.org/Treaties_and_Ratification/2C_ratificationTable.asp?choices=MP&submit2=Submit.

93 Kyoto Protocol, Annex B.

94 UNFCCC, "Kyoto Protocol, Status of Ratification," http://unfccc.int/files/essential_background/kyoto_protocol/application/pdf/kpstats.pdf.

95 Brown Weiss, 154–55.

96 UNEP, "Report of the Seventh Meeting of the Parties to the Vienna Convention for the Protection of the Ozone Layer and the Seventeenth Meeting of the Parties to the

Montreal Protocol on Substances that Deplete the Ozone Layer," 16 December 2005, 58–69.

97  Saleem S. Saab, "Move Over Drugs, There's Something Cooler on the Black Market – Freon," *Dickenson Journal of International Law* 16 (Spring 1998): 634.

98  "Chemical Production: Holed Up," *Economist*, 9 December 1995, 63.

99  Better Hileman, "Ozone Treaty: Successful but Pitfalls Remain," *Chemical and Engineering News*, 15 September 1997, 24.

100 S. A. Montzka, J. H. Butler, J. W. Elkins, T. M. Thompson, A. D. Clarke, and L. T. Locke, "Present and Future Trends in the Atmospheric Burden of Ozone-Depleting Halogens," *Nature* 398 (22 April 1999): 690–93.

101 Frederick Pool Landers Jr., "The Black Market Trade in Chlorofluorocarbons: The Montreal Protocol Makes Banned Refrigerants a Hot Commodity," *Georgia Journal of International and Comparative Law* 26 (Spring 1997): 478–79.

102 UNEP, "Backgrounder: Basic Facts and Data on the Science and Politics of Ozone Protection," August 2003, http:// hq.unep.org/ozone/pdf/Press-Backgrounder.pdf.

103 UNFCCC Secretariat, "Greenhouse Gas Emissions Data for 1990–2003," http://unfccc.int/essential_background/background_publications_htmlpdf/items/3604.php

104 "EU Industry Must Cut CO2 to Meet Kyoto Targets," *Planet Ark* (Reuters Environmental News Service), 11 January 2006.

105 British Antarctic Survey Bulletin, 19 December 2005, http://www.theozonehole.com/ozonehole2005.htm.

106 Alexandra Witze, "Antarctic Ozone Hole Set to Take 60 More Years to Recover," *Nature News* (online), 8 December 2005, http://www.nature.com/news/2005/051205/full/051205-9.html.

107 UNFCCC, *Key GHG Data*, 20.

108 Energy Information Administration, "Emissions of Greenhouse Gases in the United States 2004 – Executive Summary," Report DOE/EIA-0573(2004/es), March 2006.

109 Timothy Gardner, "World $CO_2$ Emissions to Rise 75 Pct by 2030 – EIA," *Planet Ark Reuters Environmental News Service*, 21 June 2006.

110 IPCC, "16 Years of Scientific Assessment in Support of the Climate Convention," December 2004.

# 7 Whaling and Whale Conservation

## Chapter Outline

Early Whaling History
International Regulation of Whaling
The Role of Science
The Role of Non-Governmental Actors
Developing Countries
International Cooperation
The Future of Whaling and Whale Conservation?

*When the whale gets strike*
*And the line runs o'er*
*And the whale makes a plunder with her tail*
*And the boat capsized, and four men were drowned*
*And we never caught that whale, brave boys*
*We never caught that whale*

Greenland Whale Fisheries, traditional folk song

Commercial whaling has taken place since at least 1100 C.E. and has captured the imaginations of folklorists, the economies of nations, and, eventually, so many of the great whales that they nearly became extinct. Whales have served as important natural resources and symbols for the environmental movement. Whaling is a complex issue to address in examining environmental protection, involving problems of management of a shared natural resource, the difficulty caused by uncertainty, and ultimately the role of ethics. It has a longer history of international regulation than the other issues examined here and a more controversial one as well.

The effort to regulate whaling brings up important issues for the protection of the environment. Like ozone depletion and climate change, conservation of whales is a global issue that involves a global common pool resource – the oceans. Technology plays a role in this issue as in others. With the invention of factory whaling ships that could travel long distances, stay out for months, and process and preserve their catches on board, previously abundant whale stocks quickly became depleted. Catches of tens of thousands of whales per year in the Antarctic alone for much of the twentieth century meant that by the 1960s there were so few whales in the oceans that states could not fulfill the quotas they were allowed.[1]

There are aspects of whaling that should make it easier to regulate than some other international environmental issues. In the first place, the same actors who create the problem (whalers) are the ones who suffer from it. Whale depletion is not a standard externality in which an unrelated industry is causing harm to an entirely different set of actors.[2] The universe of actors is not only circumscribed and known but potentially self-interested. The preamble to the International Convention for the Regulation of Whaling explains that "whale stocks are susceptible of natural increases if whaling is properly regulated and that increases in the size of whale stocks will permit increases in the number of whales which may be captured without endangering the natural resource."[3] If whalers can sufficiently self-regulate, they will ultimately help themselves. Nevertheless, conservation of whales presents the potential for exactly the sort of "tragedy of the commons" that Garrett Hardin identified,[4] and there are several aspects of whaling that make it even more complicated to regulate than herders on Hardin's cow pasture would be.

Regulation of whaling is difficult in part because of the uncertainty involved in regulating a resource that you cannot directly measure. It has been uncertain at any given time how many whales were in the oceans and how many of them could be taken sustainably. When scientists themselves disagreed about how depleted a particular whale stock was, what incentive did whalers have to undertake sacrifices to protect a stock that might not even be depleted? Early regulatory efforts, intended to protect the whaling stocks from overharvesting, met with difficulty as whalers were wary of individual sacrifice for collective gain or certain limits in the present for the uncertain prospect of future benefits. More importantly, because of concern that whaling states would pull out of the International Whaling Commission (IWC) (the international regulatory body that regulates whaling internationally) rather than adhere to a quota considered to be too restrictive, the quotas were set consistently higher than the organization's own Scientific Committee recommended.[5]

Non-state actors have been central to the politics of whaling. Whaling is conducted by whaling companies whose incentives to protect the stock on which they depend can be undermined by the CPR nature of the oceans, the difficulty of ensuring the long-term health of the resource, and a short-run profit motive.

Environmental activists have played an important role in this process as well, first in publicizing the depletion of the ocean's great mammals. "Save the whales!" became the rallying cry of environmentalists in the 1970s. The actions of non-governmental organizations, both within their countries and across borders, changed the attitudes of some whaling states and ultimately the composition of the international body charged with the regulation of whaling. Eventually some non-governmental organizations attempted to shift the terms of the debate about the regulation of whaling. They argued that whales should not be seen as a resource to be exploited, but should be protected as individuals. These organizations convinced nonwhaling states to join the IWC, which is open to membership regardless of whaling activity, with the goal of restricting – or ending – commercial whaling. Occasionally, they even paid the dues of these antiwhaling states they convinced to join.[6] These organizations raised awareness of the issue of whaling, and ultimately an alliance between those opposed to whaling on moral grounds and those who supported a ban on whaling in order to replenish the stocks was sufficient to support a moratorium on commercial whaling. As some whale stocks have replenished, this coalition is breaking down and providing the focal point for the debate over the future of commercial whaling.

Power politics has also played a role in the whaling debate in its recent history. The United States used threats of economic sanctions to persuade states whaling outside of the agreement to join and to submit to the regulations passed by the organization. Pro-whaling states have also tried to influence the members of the IWC through promises of aid or threats of its removal depending on a state's participation in the commission. Developing states have been particularly vulnerable to these threats and promises. The politics of whaling have featured developing states joining the organization, and taking positions, for reasons that have little to do with their concern for whales or whaling.

As the international whaling regime matured and began to impose strict limits on whaling, individual whalers, or even entire whaling fleets, found ways – both legal and illegal – around international regulations, and thus contributed further to the depletion of the whales on which their livelihoods depended. Some whaling ships registered in states not belonging to the IWC.[7] Some long-time whaling states chose initially not to join the agreement. Whaling states within the organization took advantage of the ability to opt out of quotas that would have hurt the livelihood of their whalers, or resorted to using "scientific" whaling to allow whale fleets to persist, and to meet local demand for whale products, when commercial whaling was restricted.

Compliance, difficult to monitor for most environmental issues, is even harder when addressing obligations involving ocean resources. The ocean is huge, and few states want to submit to either searches or an international observer program (although the latter was ultimately implemented in a limited way for whaling in the Antarctic). Such searches or monitoring programs are also likely to be costly. It is up to individual whalers or states to report their catches. Since information is self-reported and the IWC only has the power to ask the individual states to investigate and punish infractions, it is difficult to determine non-compliance, but there has been consistent evidence throughout the history of the IWC that some states or ships were not living up to their obligations. The most dramatic example was widespread non-compliance by the former Soviet Union, well-hidden from the IWC until later revealed. This non-compliance contributed to scientific uncertainty because misreported catches were used to make stock estimates. In this case the non-compliance was sufficient to undermine scientific models of whale populations. Moreover, the recent evidence of past non-compliance with whaling regulations demonstrates the ever-present possibility of non-compliance with international obligations more broadly, and the need to find ways to detect or prevent it.

The most serious regulatory step taken by the IWC was a moratorium on commercial whaling which began in 1986. By this point it was clear that all stocks were seriously depleted, and scientists and NGOs lobbied hard for the protection of whales. The moratorium was initially supposed to last ten years, but it has not yet been removed, despite the fact that some stocks have recovered substantially. Some states have withdrawn from the organization and/or recommenced commercial whaling, which they believe can be done sustainably. The issue for many at this point seems to be a possible conflict between the issue of sustainable harvest and the issue of whether (as some environmentalists believe) there are some species that for moral reasons should not be subject to harvesting at all.

Currently the future of whaling is in doubt. Iceland, which withdrew from the IWC in order to protect its rights to catch whales commercially, has rejoined and is conducting scientific whaling. Norway is engaging in commercial whaling while still in the organization, legally accepted because of its objection to the commercial whaling moratorium. Japan is engaging in increasingly extensive scientific whaling and trying to expand the definition of aboriginal subsistence whaling to allow whaling to be done by whalers in coastal communities. The future both of whaling, and of the international efforts to regulate it, are in doubt.

# Early Whaling History

The first large-scale whalers were probably the Basques and the Vikings, although human interaction with whales has been recorded from the time of Alexander the Great.[8] The first important resource whales provided was oil, used for lamps and as a lubricant, an ingredient for soap, paint, and medicine. Whale bones and baleen (the flexible strips of bone in the mouths of nontoothed whales) were used in the construction of corset stays, umbrellas, and a wide variety of other products. Whale products also became an important source of protein for much of the world.[9]

Initially whalers hunted those whales close to their shores, faced them from small boats and towed dead whales back to shore for processing. By the mid-fifteenth century, however, Basque whalers were already venturing far from home in search of whales. Doing so necessitated the construction of larger vessels that could travel across the oceans and bring back the barrels of oil gained from whales off the eastern coast of Canada. Whalers from other regions joined the hunt, and by the beginning of the seventeenth century whale ships from a number of countries were hunting for whales in the Arctic, and coming into conflict with each other as each vied for use of the best whaling grounds.[10] As the intensity of the whale hunts increased, so too did the level of technology to allow the whalers to hunt more efficiently. Whaling companies established permanent whaling stations in the Arctic so they could leave their equipment year-round, rather than having to transport it and assemble it for each whaling season. They then began to hunt whales further out to sea, and created processing facilities for boiling the blubber into oil on the ships themselves so whales would not have to be towed to shore for processing. Other whales, such as the sperm whale whose head contains a waxlike substance useful for making bright-burning, nearly smokeless candles (and whose intestines sometimes contained ambergris, which fetched a high price as an ingredient in perfume), could be found further from shore, and provided new targets for the whaling industry. England and the United States became the predominant whaling countries, and their vessels spanned most of the globe. By the mid-nineteenth century the American whaling industry reached its peak with 735 whaling vessels, accounting for approximately 80 per cent of the world's whaling fleet.[11]

It was not until the middle of the nineteenth century that human impact on the world's population of whales became apparent. The response of whalers, however, was to improve technology so as to be able to find and hunt whales more efficiently. Steam was introduced to power whaling vessels, and the handheld harpoons were replaced by lances shot from vessels and designed to explode once in the whale.[12] Improvements in processing techniques ultimately resulted in "industrial whalers" – ships powered by steam, equipped with harpoon cannons, and capable of processing and storing oil on board, and pioneered by the Norwegian whaling fleet. Other innovations, such as the electric lance, invented initially by German whalers, allowed for easier (and, some argued, increasingly humane) killing of whales. The addition in the twentieth century of refrigeration increased the parts of the whale that could be taken and the length of time such vessels could remain at sea. The whalers had the tools with which to capture whales, but there were fewer and fewer whales to hunt.

# International Regulation of Whaling

Concern by the whaling industry about possible depletion of the whales on which they depended for their livelihood led to early domestic and international efforts to regulate whaling. Norway passed legislation beginning in 1904 to limit whaling in its coastal waters and in 1929 to limit whaling on the high seas of depleted species such as right whales, as well as all whale calves.[13] The first international agreement, The Geneva Convention for the Regulation of Whaling, was negotiated under the auspices of the League of Nations in 1931. It contained rules similar to the Norwegian restrictions, but several of the important whaling states, most notably Japan, Germany, and the Soviet Union, did not sign it. The first two of these countries used whale products to support their international political ambitions (Nazi Germany to reduce its dependence on edible oil from abroad and Japan for export of whale oil to fund its activities in China and Manchuria), and maintained whaling vessels for strategic uses.[14] Without several of the most important whaling states (accounting for up to 30 per cent of whaling at the time), the agreement was incapable of effectively regulating whaling.

In the absence of effective international whaling regulation, individual whaling companies attempted cartel-like agreements through an organization called the

International Association of Whaling Companies.[15] These whaling companies attempted to stabilize world whale oil prices by limiting total production of whale oil and dividing it into individual quotas for each company. But this effort went the way of most cartels: voluntary agreements were routinely ignored when they hurt competition, were subject to free riding, and could not survive the increased market importance of those – such as Japan – that refused to go along with agreements.[16] An additional effort was made by whaling states to gain cooperation in limiting whale catches in 1937, with the negotiation of the International Agreement for the Regulation of Whaling. This agreement set catch size limits and designated a whaling season, but neither was sufficiently stringent, especially in the absence of actual catch limits, to have an effect on protecting whale stocks.[17]

Further negotiations on protocols followed annually with some progress, but the greatest effect on protecting whale stocks came during the near cessation of commercial whaling that came during World War II, suggesting the advantage of warfare for the recovery of at least some species. One agreement was reached in 1944 in anticipation of the need for whale oil that would emerge at the war's conclusion, regulating whaling by categorizing whales by how much oil they contained and then restricting catches based on those units of measure. A blue whale was the standard unit of measure and the other species of whales were expressed in "Blue Whale Units," (BWU) or how many whales of different species contained the amount of whale oil in a blue whale. One BWU, for example, was equal to two fin whales, two and a half humpbacks, or six seis.[18] Whale quotas would then be set in terms of how many BWUs could be caught.

The end of the war provided the best opportunity yet to finally gain true international regulation of whaling. Japan's whaling fleet, used as wartime vessels, was in ruins, and Germany's whaling industry was sufficiently destroyed that the country decided not to rebuild. In addition, the war years gave whaling stocks sufficient time to recover that when whaling states began negotiations at the end of the war on how to prevent overharvesting of whales they could set realistic catch limits that could (at least potentially) allow both for the protection of whales and for the survival of the industry. The agreement still governing most commercial whaling in the world, the International Convention for the Regulation of Whaling, was signed on 2 December 1946. The objective of the Convention is the "proper and effective conservation and development of whale stocks" in order to enable "the orderly development of the whaling industry."[19]

The states negotiating the agreement attempted to remedy some of the problems of the earlier whaling agreements while at the same time unquestioningly adopting some of their structures in ways that caused later difficulties.

One important goal was to create an agreement that would not have to be renegotiated and reratified every year, and could nevertheless allow whaling restrictions to be changed from year-to-year, responding to information on the health of whale stocks. To do so, the Convention created the International Whaling Commission. The IWC is global; it has regulatory control over all whales caught wherever whaling takes place, even within coastal seas claimed by adjacent nations.

The convention established three committees for the IWC: Scientific, Technical, and Finance and Administration. These committees meet and make recommendations to the IWC as a whole. The Scientific Committee (SC) was instructed by the original Rules of Procedure to "keep under review the statistical, biological, and other technical information ... and to make recommendations thereon."[20] The Scientific Committee reports on and analyzes research results achieved from scientific studies conducted within individual states, but does not carry out research itself. The Committee was reorganized in 1977, to include advisors from the United Nations Environment Program and Food and Agriculture Organization and the (then) International Union for the Conservation of Nature (IUCN), and its meetings were opened to NGO observers. The Technical Committee (TC), under the Rules of Procedure of the IWC, was constituted to "review regulations, consider questions involving time, manner, and intensity of whaling operations, [investigate] infractions reports," among other things; and to make recommendations. It was charged with including nonscientific factors in consideration of proposed regulations.[21] Its role was changed in 1978 to include screening the business for the Plenary sessions, in order to speed up the work of the IWC meetings.[22] Both the Scientific Committee and the Technical Committee can consider and report on proposed changes to whaling regulations. The Finance and Administration Committee advises the IWC on issues of contributions, budgets and other related matters.

Importantly, the IWC creates regulations through a "schedule," passed each year, which denotes how many of which types of whales may be caught in which areas. Passage of the schedule requires an affirmative vote of three-quarters of the IWC members and then becomes binding on all members. But international law cannot bind those who choose not to participate and states would hesitate to hand over control of whaling regulation to a commission that might consistently pass rules they oppose. The IWC therefore contains a procedure by which states can opt out of any of the provisions of the schedule with which they do not agree. To do so a state lodges an "objection" to any amendment to the schedule within ninety days after it has passed, and it is thereby not bound by the regulation.[23] Under the agreement, the IWC is not allowed to limit the number of ships engaged in whaling, nor may it pass national quotas.[24]

## IWC Regulation in Practice

There have been several different management approaches in the history of the Commission. Initially, quotas were not placed on specific whale species. The Commission instead continued the pre-IWC practice of expressing catch limits in terms of numbers of Blue Whale Units (BWU) that could be taken, rather than regulating stocks separately. In 1972 the IWC divided stocks into individual species regulated separately, with quotas even occasionally used for subspecies. This type of regulation was codified and further developed in a "new management procedure."[25] Stocks were divided into "initial management stocks," "sustained management stocks," and "protected stocks," for the basis of regulation.[26] The catching of some species was banned altogether. The current system, a moratorium on commercial whaling, was actually created under the normal regulatory process, by reducing the quotas to zero beginning with the 1986 whaling season. There is current pressure to lift the moratorium for some species, but the IWC has not yet taken that step. In preparation for such a time a "revised management procedure" has been created.

Quotas during the periods of whaling were global and not allocated among specific states, which would have been prohibited by the convention. But the race for whales in the region and the uncertainty for each whaling company of what that year's catch might be created economic difficulties for the industry, and contributed to the depletion of whale stocks. Whalers had to compete with each other in what came to be known as the "Whaling Olympic," as each industrial whaling ship worked around the clock to catch as many whales as possible before the season was declared to be over. This scramble led to overcapitalization, as whaling ships had to be better prepared to beat others to the catch. In the five-year period from 1946 to 1951 the number of days in the whaling season fell from 112 to only 64, as ships grew more and more efficient at catching whales. The cost of building a whale fleet concomitantly doubled by 1960.[27]

Britain proposed in 1958 that the states engaged in open ocean whaling in the Antarctic consult outside the auspices of the organization and divide up the allocated catch into national quotas. The states were able to agree initially on a scheme that limited the number of factory whaling ships a state could have in the region and to allocate 20 per cent of the total catch in the region to the Soviet Union. Difficulty agreeing on the division of the rest of the catch, however, almost led to the collapse of the organization, as the Netherlands, Norway, and Japan threatened to withdraw from the IWC because of lack of agreement on national quotas in the Antarctic and the suspicion that the USSR was not abiding by the quota it had been given. These states gave official notices of withdrawal but intimated that they would reconsider if quotas were allocated. The withdrawal of the first two states actually took effect, and actual quotas were not assessed during the time they were not members of the commission. The two rejoined and the issue of national quotas was finally resolved in 1962.[28]

## The Commercial Whaling Moratorium

By the early 1970s, whale stocks were clearly depleted and it seemed likely that only drastic measures could remedy the situation. A number of scientists and other organizations began to recommend a temporary suspension of commercial whaling to allow stocks to recover. The 1972 United Nations Conference on the Human Environment in Stockholm criticized IWC practices and recommended that the IWC implement a ten-year commercial moratorium.[29] The United States re-proposed the idea at IWC meetings in subsequent years.

Several elements had to come together before such a radical change in whaling policy could be adopted by the International Whaling Commission. The increasing evidence that whaling stocks were depleted, while never quite convincing the diehard whaling states that a moratorium was necessary, did at least serve to persuade some states that the cause of whaling could best be served by allowing whale stocks to recover. The conversion of some states within the IWC from whaling states to nonwhaling states because of the decreasing economic viability of the industry meant that the universe of states whose behavior had to change decreased. The transformation of an increasing number of these former whaling states into vehement antiwhaling states, as their domestic populations came to believe that the whales must be saved, was brought about largely by the conviction and activities of activist organizations. That one of these states was the United States, willing to put economic threats behind its antiwhaling stance, could only help the move in this direction. At the same time, the sufficient conviction of other nonwhaling states, some of it aided in a number of ways by activist organizations, that commercial whaling must be at least temporarily stopped eventually resulted in a nonwhaling supermajority in the IWC. It was not until 1982, ten years after the original Stockholm Conference proposal, that agreement was reached within the IWC for a temporary halt to commercial whaling, for the purpose of allowing stocks to recover. Even then, the moratorium was not to take effect until the 1986 whaling season, to allow whaling industries time to adjust. Actual commercial whaling ceased later than that, as it took several years longer to convince all whaling states to participate.

## After the Moratorium?

The commercial whaling moratorium was supposed to last, at most, a decade. The status of whale stocks was to be evaluated in 1990, with a view toward considering the resumption of commercial whaling. Instead, while many estimates suggest that some species of whale – particularly minke – could be harvested sustainably, the moratorium remains. The number of states – many of them new IWC members – in the organization in favor of removing the moratorium is increasing, however. In 2006 pro-whaling states gained the majority in the organization for the first time, passing a resolution that called for repealing the moratorium, by a vote of thirty-three to thirty-two.[30] But agreement of three-quarters of IWC members is required to remove the moratorium, and many member states have refused to change their position. Both the debate and the activities of whaling states have changed somewhat in the years since the moratorium.

Three of the four primary whaling states that went along with the moratorium only reluctantly have indicated a renewed interest in whaling. (The fourth, the former Soviet Union, ceased an interest in commercial whaling in the wake of the other political and economic changes it faced during the decade of the 1990s, although it has suggested the possibility of renewed whaling eventually.) Iceland pulled out of the International Whaling Commission in 1992 to preserve its right to catch whales (although it rejoined in 2001, hoping to influence the organization from the inside to allow whaling),[31] and has begun to catch minke whales for scientific research. Norway, which maintained its objection to the moratorium and therefore is not legally bound to uphold it, resumed commercial whaling in 1993. It catches only minke whales, for which it sets its own quota annually. It has caught more than 6,000 minke whales since it restarted commercial whaling.[32] Japan continues to hunt whales for "scientific" purposes, as allowed – and not regulated – by the IWC, and has increased the types of whales it catches, seeking not only minkes but also fin and humpback whales. Japan has also labored within the IWC, thus far unsuccessfully, to redefine its coastal whaling as allowable under international regulatory processes. Japan periodically threatens to withdraw from the organization and create an organization of whaling states that would allow and regulate commercial whaling.[33]

# The Role of Science

Decisions of the IWC with respect to restrictions on whaling are to be "based on scientific findings."[34] In practice, however, this instruction has been contentious and subject to abuse in a number of different ways. It has been suggested that the IWC history through 1970 "is one of almost constant failure to set the … quotas at levels commensurate with scientific advice."[35] The postmoratorium time period has also been filled with allegations that the organization is neglecting its obligation to base decisions about quotas on science, continuing the moratorium when scientific consensus is high that some species of whales have reached population levels that would allow them to be harvested sustainably. On the other hand, continued scientific uncertainty is invoked by those who do not want a return to commercial whaling.[36] Because of the IWC's requirement that decisions be based on science, all sides in the whaling debate have couched their arguments in the guise of science and uncertainty, whether or not it actually provided the reasons for the positions taken.

There has legitimately been a consistently high degree of uncertainty about whale populations. The Scientific Committee of the IWC, charged with resolving the uncertainty and making catch recommendations, faced a number of problems in doing so. Scientists on the committee often held different opinions about the number of whales that could be sustainably caught, with some of the highest estimates from scientists from whaling states. Japan, the Netherlands, and the Soviet Union (three of the major whaling states), for example, often had higher estimates of the stocks than did scientists from other countries.[37] Even the meaning of the different assessments is hard to interpret: did traditional whaling states have better informed whale specialists, or were Scientific Committee members from major whaling states influenced by the short-term desire of the whaling industries in their states for higher catch levels?

The composition of the committee compounds this uncertainty. It is supposed to be composed of "qualified experts," but there is no requirement of scientific qualifications and the members are often representatives and sometimes employees of the whaling industries within their countries. In some instances states appoint committee members who are not scientists, and some members of the committee "are under instructions to argue in support of a position adopted by their government for reasons other than science alone."[38]

The way that decisions about quotas are made has always been contentious, and clearly based on more than scientific recommendations. Because of initial concern that whaling states would pull out of the IWC rather than adhere to too small a quota, the quotas were set consistently higher than even the Scientific Committee or other scientists recommended.[39] Any scientific errors or misjudgments by the Scientific Committee were likely compounded when its recommendations were debated in the Technical Committee and then in the IWC as a whole, both of which take economic and social interests of member states into consideration, along with the health of the whale populations.[40]

This self-interested action in the face of genuine uncertainty is exactly what one would predict. When it is unclear what the optimal solution is, individual actors should be expected to "pick and choose from the existing often diverging scientific reports or opinions" in the calculation of advantage.[41] But this calculation ultimately led to the creation of unrealistic quotas. For most of the 1960s and the early 1970s the quotas set were never reached, a clear indication that quotas were set too high: despite the efforts of the whalers they could not catch as many whales as they were allowed to. Moreover, the concomitant decline in whale stocks (suggested in part by the annual lowering of whaling quotas) supports the assertion that quotas were set far above those that would protect the resource.

The stock evaluations and the understanding of the level of sustainable harvest were clearly flawed, as the population levels of most species plunged. It is necessary to differentiate, however, between the assessments of the members of the Scientific Committee and the quotas set by the IWC. Although quotas suggested by the Scientific Committee were probably too high, the Commission as a whole often did not heed even those suggestions and set the quotas still higher. A notable example came in the late 1970s: for two years in a row the Scientific Committee recommended that the catch limit for sperm whales in the North Pacific be set at 763; the IWC chose instead to set a quota of 6,444 in 1977 and 6,344 in 1978 for the region, almost ten times higher than the scientific recommendation.[42]

The IWC also failed to heed other advice given to it by its Scientific Committee. One major example is the continued use of the BWU as a tool for regulation longer than any scientific advice supported its use. When whales were regulated only in terms of the proportion of BWUs they represented, individual threatened species could not be specifically protected. When individual species, including the blue whale itself, were threatened with possible extinction, a collective quota could not protect them, nor could it prevent other whale species from facing the same problems in the future. Outside organizations even joined the effort to convince the IWC of the wisdom of changing its regulatory unit. The United Nations Food and Agriculture

Organization (FAO) was involved with the process because it cooperated with the IWC to do whale-stock assessments. By the mid-1960s, when whale stocks were clearly being depleted and the IWC was unable to pass strict quotas to protect them, FAO threatened to cease cooperation on research unless IWC adopted quotas that fit the scientific consensus for the level of management required; specifically the IWC would have to end the use of the BWU and reduce the catches of fin and sei whales below the assessed sustainable yield.[43]

The IWC commissioned additional scientific evaluations during this period of disagreement over management. The first of these was the creation of a Committee of Three in 1961 after the discussion over quotas had repeatedly broken down over disagreement about management practices and sustainable yield. This Committee was composed of experts in whale (or fish) population dynamics, and "drawn from countries not engaged in pelagic whaling in the Antarctic."[44] The Committee was later broadened to four. The committee operated from 1961 to 1964. The IWC pledged itself to heed the recommendations of this Committee. The Committee found extreme depletion of some whale stocks, and therefore recommended a complete ban on the catching of humpbacks and blue whales, as well as a low quota on fin whales. It also proposed ending the use of the BWU. The Scientific Committee concurred with most of the Committee of Three/Four's recommendations, although the Scientific Committee representatives from Japan and the Soviet Union could not agree with the recommendation to abandon the BWU, and demanded more scientific information before a change in regulatory procedure be made. Their dissent gave the commissioners from those countries what one analyst referred to as a "scientific alibi" when voting against the change.[45] The chair of the Scientific Committee threatened to resign if the new quotas were not adopted. The IWC began by protecting specific stocks through disallowing all catches of blue and humpback whales, but retained the BWU quota for fin and sei whales. It was only in 1972 that the BWU measure was finally abandoned.

Scientific discourse played an important role in the creation of the commercial moratorium. After decades of catch limits higher than the IWC's own scientists recommended it was becoming virtually certain that some stocks were so severely depleted that they could not be harvested sustainably in the short run. The initial efforts of the new management procedure, while more scientifically justified than management by BWU, did not succeed in preventing some whale stocks from becoming seriously endangered. At the same time, uncertainty about the actual size of whaling stocks remained strong in this period. When the idea of a moratorium was first proposed in 1972, the Scientific Committee argued that it was not scientifically justified. As the option was increasingly debated, opinion of some in the SC shifted with some arguing that a moratorium would allow for increased emphasis on science. Some members of the Scientific Committee as well came to believe in the precautionary principle: absent certainty that whale stocks at the time could withstand continued hunting, doing so should not be allowed so as to prevent the possibility of extinction.[46] The Scientific Committee as a whole did not propose or even support the moratorium, and other organizations such as the FAO opposed it as well. Nevertheless, the clear evidence of severely depleted whale stocks likely influenced some of the support behind the halt to commercial whaling.

The controversy over the use of science in the organization did not end with the creation of the moratorium on commercial whaling. It is argued that the organization is now failing to heed scientific advice that favors allowing whaling, when earlier it failed to heed the advice to restrict it. As part of the decision on the commercial moratorium, the Scientific Committee was directed by the IWC to do a "comprehensive assessment" of whale stocks by 1990,[47] which would guide the Commission in its decision about whether to continue or lift the moratorium. The committee reported some of its results in 1990, and by 1991 drafted a Revised Management Procedure. On minke whales, the most contested stock, it reached a variety of conclusions. It concluded that the Eastern North Pacific stock of minke whales numbered at least 21,000, had been increasing 3 per cent per year from 1967 to 1988, and might approach the region's carrying capacity. It found that the minkes in the Southern hemisphere numbered 760,000. In the North Atlantic there was a range of estimates due to survey difficulties.[48] Overall, though, its conclusions pointed to the likelihood that such whales could be harvested sustainably. Because of the politicized nature of whaling brought about in large part by non-governmental organizations (as discussed below), and the requirement of agreement of three-quarters of the IWC's membership to change the schedule, the recommendations of the Scientific Committee have not been adopted.

More recently, new scientific studies using analysis of genetic diversity suggest that the population of whales before large-scale commercial whaling began may have been larger than previously believed.[49] Since IWC estimates of sustainable harvest have been based on ensuring that stocks remain above a certain percentage of pre-exploitation size, this information could have implications for determining how many whales could be sustainably harvested. It is of particular relevance to the discussion of harvesting of minke whales, the most abundant whale species. The North Atlantic minke whale, considered by many to exist in sufficient numbers to allow harvesting, may still be considerably below its pre-exploitation numbers if this analysis is correct.

The other scientific controversy is over the use of "scientific whaling." Japan takes increasing numbers of otherwise protected whales under the exception to the ICRW for scientific research. Iceland has begun lethal scientific whaling as well. Collectively approximately 10,000 whales have been killed in scientific whaling since the moratorium began.[50]

While the former Secretary of the IWC has suggested that there is a legitimate scientific purpose served by lethal whaling studies,[51] others are skeptical of the value of or need for this lethal whale research. The IWC has passed numerous resolutions calling on Japan to curtail its lethal scientific whaling. Australian whale experts have noted that Japanese whaling research has resulted in the publication of only thirty-four peer-reviewed papers, despite eighteen years of lethal scientific whaling and the deaths of 8,300 whales.[52] This Japanese scientific whaling kills enough whales to keep the former commercial whaling industry operational and the whale meat from whales caught for these studies is sold in Japanese food markets. Moreover, testing of whale meat labeled as from minke whales has determined that one quarter of it came not from minkes but from other protected whale species, even during the period when Japan claimed to only be killing minke whales for scientific purposes.[53] It is likely, therefore, that Japanese scientific whaling serves multiple purposes.

# The Role of Non-Governmental Actors

Non-governmental actors have been central to the politics of whaling throughout its history. The whaling industry has both worked for whale conservation and, at points, attempted to undermine it. Without environmental activists it is unlikely that the moratorium on commercial whaling would have passed.

## Industry

As discussed in the history of international whaling regulation, the whaling industry was the first progenitor of efforts to protect whale stocks from depletion. Whalers are those who suffer most if the stocks are so depleted that whales become hard to catch. But whalers have also been instrumental in efforts to circumvent regulation: after all, the best regulation is one that others follow and you do not have to. Their pressure on their own governments, and as representatives on IWC committees, led to higher catch limits than turned out to be sustainable.

The whaling industry that currently exists is small. Norway, Japan, and Iceland are the only states that indicate an interest in commercial whaling at this point. As the traditional diet in these countries turns away from whale meat, it is not even clear that there is a sufficient market for the whales that are currently caught. While it is not clear whether the IWC will eventually lift the commercial moratorium, it seems likely that the whaling industry worldwide will not be a major factor in the future.

## Non-Governmental Organizations

NGOs have been some of the harshest critics of the operations of the IWC, and their influence has been unquestionable. Unlike much of the debate about whaling, it has not been conducted so much in terms of science as in terms of ethics and images. NGOs such as Greenpeace attempted to shift the terms of the debate about the regulation of whaling. They began by using the same scientific terms more broadly discussed in the organization, suggesting that depletion of whales required a commercial moratorium in order to protect the species. Ultimately, however, the organizations most central to the whaling debate believe that whales should not be seen as a resource to be exploited, but should not be killed at all.

Organizations such as Greenpeace, the Sea Shepherd Conservation Society, the Animal Welfare Institute, and many others have had a considerable effect on whaling policy worldwide through a number of types of strategies, many subverting (or even coming to redefine) the traditional role of activist organizations. They have engaged in direct action campaigns, putting themselves between whale boats and whales with the hopes of protecting the whales and, more importantly, dramatizing the whale hunt. Through this approach as well as other publicity- and awareness-raising campaigns they have worked not through their own states to change their views on whaling, but across state lines to influence the views of others in whaling states to change the policies of their own states. At the same time activist organizations worked through the international process created by the IWC, working to convince nonwhaling states to join the IWC, which is open to membership regardless of whaling activity. Because a three-quarters majority is needed to amend the schedule, convincing a sufficient number of antiwhaling states to join the organization could – and did – have an important influence on the policies adopted.

Beginning in the early 1970s, conservation organizations, primarily in the United States and England, took up the plight of the whale as an important symbol of environmentalism. Some of these groups were broader environmental organizations for whom the whale could serve as an important symbol. Other organizations, such as the American Cetacean Society, were formed solely for the purpose of protecting whales. While a number of organizations worked in standard awareness-raising fashion with a goal of influencing the political stands of their own governments, other organizations took on increasingly radical approaches that brought the issue even more publicity.

Working through national political channels should not be discounted as an effective way to change international environmental policy. Environmental activists within the United States clearly influenced the passage of the 1972 Marine Mammal Protection Act (MMPA), which effectively ended any potential remaining U.S. whaling industry and, more importantly, helped to turn the U.S. against whaling internationally. It was in the context of the MMPA that the U.S. was pressured – and able – to use the Pelly and Packwood-Magnuson Amendments to persuade whaling states to join the organization and accept its regulations. NGOs also formed branches in other IWC member states to work to convince local populations to turn against whaling. Two such states that eventually changed from pro- to anti-whaling were Argentina and Uruguay.[54] Working within the state thus was an important role for antiwhaling activists.

But working through other channels allowed these organizations to have an even greater impact. Some tactics, such as collecting evidence of violations of whaling agreements, helped raise awareness of those within the organization that current whaling regulations were not sufficiently constraining member states. Even simply documenting legal whaling practices, through videotapes of whaling vessels slaughtering the whales they caught, could help dramatize the brutality of the whaling industry to those who simply had not thought much about it previously.[55] Greenpeace activists often put themselves physically in between whaling vessels and whales, both in the hopes of preventing whalers from catching individual whales (because of the risk that an activist would be harmed in the process) and to indicate their level of commitment to the cause. In doing so, they also hoped to change the image of whaling in the minds of average people, who could see large factory whaling vessels taking on committed activists and facing defenseless whales.[56] In the case of whaling it seems likely that these actions outside of the traditional political arena were more effective at changing whaling policy than traditional political action would have been.[57]

In the short run, the greatest success of antiwhaling environmental organizations was through persuading antiwhaling states to join the IWC. In some cases this process happened through the conversion of pro-whaling states, such as

Australia, into antiwhaling states, with domestic electoral victories.[58] Some former whaling states ceased participation in the organization once they stopped whaling. The Dutch had not actually left the organization but were not active participants; environmental organizations persuaded the Netherlands to become active in the organization in the campaign to halt commercial whaling. Non-governmental organizations focused additional efforts on bringing in nonwhaling states that had never or not recently been members of the organization, so as to increase the number of votes against whaling. The Seychelles membership in the IWC in 1979 was an important victory for the antiwhaling organizations, since it was the first antiwhaling developing state to join the organization.[59] A number of states in the agreement that have traditionally not cared about whaling joined in the time period when a commercial whaling moratorium was being discussed in the organization. Antigua and Barbuda, Oman, Egypt, and Kenya, for example, are all states that joined in the early 1980s, with no previous history of concern about whaling issues, that voted consistently against commercial whaling.[60]

NGOs contributed financially to bringing states into the agreement as well. Environmental organizations have persuaded antiwhaling states to join the agreement and have assisted them with funding and representation.[61] Japan's representatives at the 47th IWC annual meeting in 1995 pointed out that "some individuals are listed as government delegates attending the preliminary meetings of working groups and sub-committees but registered as NGO observers in the plenary week."[62] While NGOs were not the only ones to play this game,[63] their efforts to recruit non- (and anti-) whaling states to the organization ultimately resulted in raising the membership of nonwhaling states in the agreement to just above three-quarters of the membership, the number required to amend the schedule to create a temporary moratorium on commercial whaling.

Through these techniques, these organizations raised awareness of the issue of whaling, and ultimately an alliance between those opposed to whaling on moral grounds and those opposed to whaling in order to replenish the stocks was sufficient to support a moratorium on commercial whaling. Although the goal of these organizations was to change the terms of the debate, they also called attention to the lack of sustainable management by the Commission over time, and thus provided the information used by those who supported the moratorium on conservation rather than preservation grounds. What resulted was an uneasy coalition of those who supported a halt to commercial whaling for a variety of different reasons, and that, through an increased voting bloc in the organization and increasing evidence of severe depletion of whale stocks, managed to create a moratorium on commercial whaling.

Their role since the moratorium, and specifically as whaling in and around IWC regulations has increased, has been to use direct action to call attention to whaling activity and, ideally, prevent some of it. Recently both Greenpeace and the Sea Shepherd Conservation Society organizations have sent ships to the Southern Ocean where they have placed themselves in between whalers and whales.[64]

# Developing Countries

Developing countries have, for the most part, not been among the primary whaling states and have therefore not had a direct concern about international regulatc ry efforts to protect whales. They have played important roles in the politics of international whaling regulation, however. Developing states have joined the IWC, which is open to membership by all states, for a variety of reasons, including an interest in protecting a species and ecosystem, concern for the international norms created by the organization, or allegiance to developed states or non-governmental organizations that promise aid.

Few developing states have strong traditions of whaling or are currently practicing it now. The ones that are involved in whaling are conducting aboriginal whaling, and some of these, such as the Philippines and Indonesia, have remained apart from the IWC, which has no involvement in their local whaling decisions. St. Vincent and the Grenadines conduct traditional whaling as overseen by the IWC.

Most developing states that participate in the IWC, therefore, are not involved for the purpose of having a say in regulation that will directly affect them. Why, then, are they involved in the agreement in such large numbers? Some, such as Mali and Mongolia, do not even have a coastline, and therefore have little direct connection with resources of the sea. Certainly it is possible to be concerned about protection of a resource you never use and hope to ensure the survival of the whales and the ecosystem of which they are a part. Some nonwhaling developing states like Argentina, a former whaling state that is now decisively antiwhaling, participate for this reason.

Others have different motivations. For many of these states their participation has to do with the creation (or avoidance) of norms within the agreement. Zimbabawe, for instance (a former member), used its participation in the IWC to argue in favor of the rights of sovereign states to harvest natural resources as long as they do so sustainably, a clear reference to its own concern about having international limits put (in other international regulatory processes) on what it could do with the elephants within its borders. Others are particularly concerned with upholding the rights of indigenous peoples.

Other developing states are likely caught up in the politics of international aid. Japan has been the primary source for aid to small developing states that then agree to join the IWC and vote against restrictions on whaling, or (as in the case of previously antiwhaling Jamaica) withdraw from participation in the organization. States whose IWC activities Japan is said to have influenced through offers of foreign aid include Brazil, Chile, Peru, Jamaica, Costa Rica, and the Philippines. Japan has also given aid to a number of Caribbean states – Grenada, St. Kitts and Nevis, Antigua and Barbuda, Dominica, and St. Vincent and the Grenadines – in the context of decisions about whaling.[65] As one IWC official reported, "We're not fools. We know the Japanese pay for these people's membership fee, for their hotel bills – even for the limousines they drive around in."[66]

Recent whaling votes have placed Pacific Island states in the middle between antiwhaling Australia, to which they have important ties, and Japan, which has targeted funding to change their allegiance. After sustained lobbying from Australia, the Solomon Islands had promised it would abstain from voting to lift the commercial whaling moratorium at the 2005 IWC meeting. But Solomon Islands officials admitted that the country received Japanese aid in return for a vote against the moratorium, which it ended up casting at the meeting.[67] Others charge that Nauru and Tuvalu were in the same position, though they deny having been influenced by Japanese funding in determining their votes.[68] Japan's recent unsuccessful effort to introduce secret voting at IWC meetings likely comes from its hope that other states could be persuaded to vote in favor of the resumption of whaling if their votes would not become public.

Antiwhaling NGOs have also persuaded developing states, such as Oman, Egypt, Kenya, and Antigua and Barbuda[69] to join the IWC as antiwhaling states. The former secretary of the IWC gave the example of a member state that signed over a check from an environmental organization to pay its dues.[70] A Greenpeace consultant admits that the organization persuaded six new states to join the organization and vote against whaling in the late 1970s and early 1980s, spending $150,000 annually to paying their dues, name commissioners to represent them, and pay other costs.[71]

Developing states are targets of these "vote-buying" efforts because their relative poverty means that aid can be provided without undue expense to influence their behavior. The fact that the IWC allows any state to join and gives equal voting power to all states means that developing states can have influence in the organization beyond what they would normally experience in world politics, even without participating in whaling themselves.

# International Cooperation
## Participation

An important difficulty faced by those who want to regulate whaling internationally is gaining the participation of all those likely to be catching whales. Several aspects of the efforts to gain full participation have been challenging in the history of whaling regulation. The first was an attempt to secure the involvement of all the whaling states in the Commission, or, failing that, to gather information on their catches that could be used to determine a sustainable harvest. The Commission passed numerous resolutions over the years aimed at encouraging nonmember whaling states to sign the agreement. The second was an effort to ensure that all IWC members actually accepted all of the regulations passed by the commission. In both cases unilateral threats of economic sanctions by the United States had the greatest effect in bringing nonmembers into the IWC, and encouraging members to accept the organization's restrictions on whaling.

The United States used domestic legislation passed initially in 1971 for the purpose of threatening states that did not accept provisions of fisheries treaties. The legislation, the Pelly Amendment to the Fisherman's Protective Act, allows the U.S. president to refuse to accept imports of fish when the Secretary of Commerce "finds that nationals of a foreign country, directly or indirectly, are conducting fishing operations or under circumstances which diminish the effectiveness" of an international fishery conservation program. The legislation was left intentionally broad, and defines "international fishery conservation program" as "any ban, restriction, regulation, or other measure in force pursuant to a multilateral agreement to which the United States is a signatory party, the purpose of which is to conserve or protect the living resources of the sea."[72] In other words, whaling was an acceptable target of the legislation, and the legislation could be – and in fact generally has been – used against states that are themselves not members of the agreement in question. A second piece of U.S. legislation was passed to decrease the amount of discretion the president has when the Secretary of Commerce has "certified" that a state is diminishing the effectiveness of the International Whaling Commission. The Packwood-Magnuson Amendment to the Magnuson Fishery Conservation and Management Act, passed in 1979, required that states certified as such under the Pelly Amendment automatically have their fishing allocation in U.S. waters cut by at least 50 per cent, and cut off entirely the following year if the issues that lead to certification have not been remedied.[73]

The main whaling states that had not initially signed the agreement were Chile, South Korea, Peru, and Taiwan. After IWC efforts failed to bring them in, the United States certified each under the Pelly Amendment, thus threatening them with the loss of the U.S. market for their fish and fish products. The U.S. certified Chile, Peru, and South Korea in 1978; all three took immediate steps to join the organization.[74] The U.S. certified Taiwan for the same reason in 1980; although it did not sign the ICRW it did agree to stop all foreign whaling and then banned whaling altogether in 1981.[75]

An additional – and in the IWC case, earlier – instance of this type of non-participation was the presence of what came to be known as "pirate whalers"; whaling ships that flew flags of states that were not members of the IWC so that their activities would remain unregulated. This nonparticipation differs slightly, however, from state-level non-compliance, because in this instance it is an individual whaling vessel that finds a way to engage in whaling without falling under international regulation.[76] The main whaling organization engaged in this type of whaling was the Olympic Whaling Company, run by Aristotle Onassis. The company's main whaling vessel, the *Olympic Challenger*, was registered in Panama; other whaling vessels run by the company registered in Honduras. The company itself was incorporated in Uruguay. Since none of these states were IWC members, the vessels were not bound by IWC regulations. In the early 1950s the *Olympic Challenger* and its associated whale catchers caught whales contravening nearly every IWC rule, while at the same time trying to negotiate deals with some of the major whaling vessels.[77] The IWC repeatedly discussed how to prevent such pirate whaling, with specific reference to the *Olympic Challenger*. Most efforts were aimed at convincing Panama, the state under which it was flagged, to join the Commission, or to at least enforce IWC provisions. The IWC had little success, however, and it is likely that had it joined at the time Onassis would simply have registered his operations elsewhere. In 1956 the Peruvian Navy seized the vessel for fishing in Peruvian waters and sold it to the Japanese,[78] ending the most serious case of individual nonparticipation in the convention process.

A second type of nonparticipation occurs when members of the organization opt out of specific commitments. While this practice is legal, it also undermines the ability of the organization to accomplish effective regulation. The practice has been widespread at points in IWC history. Unfortunately, at times, this procedure has meant that none of the major whaling states have been bound by some of the regulations passed by the organization. In 1964, for example, the IWC passed a complete ban on the catching of blue whales, which were quite endangered in the Antarctic at that point. But all five of the Antarctic whaling states objected to the quota, and thus were not bound by it. States used the objections practice strategically as well. For instance, in 1956 the Soviet Union indicated that, while it approved a lowering of the whaling quota that year, seven states objected to it, and it would not abide by the lower quota if the other major whaling states did not.[79] Such strategic use of the objections procedure makes sense in the ocean commons; if one major whaling state restricts its catches and others do not it loses twice: first by having to forego the whales it could have caught, and second because its conservation behavior will not even serve to protect the stock in the long run if others continue to catch whales.

Early efforts to remedy this situation also had little effect; in the 1970s and 1980s, U.S. threats to deny entry to fish products from states because of their whaling behavior had an important impact on the willingness of member states to accept specific whaling regulations. This influence culminated in threats that convinced the most reluctant whaling states to abide by the moratorium on commercial whaling, but has waned in more recent times. The first use of these threats came in 1974 with U.S. certification of Japan and the Soviet Union for lodging objections to the quota for minke whales in the Southern hemisphere. Both were certified under the Pelly Amendment and both agreed to abide by the quota. In 1980 Spain objected to the quota on fin whales and South Korea to the ban on the use of the cold harpoon; both withdrew their objections when the U.S. threatened certification under the Pelly Amendment.[80] The adoption by the IWC in 1982 of a moratorium on commercial whaling as of the 1986 whaling season drew official objections from many of the major whaling states, primary among them Japan, the USSR, and Norway. The U.S. certified the latter two; domestic battles over whether it was required to certify Japan were fought judicially all the way to the U.S. Supreme Court, leaving unclear whether Japan would ultimately be certified.[81] In the interim, Japan withdrew its objection, arguing later that it had done so in an "involuntary" manner, "coerced by a certain nation."[82] Norway and the Soviet Union responded by agreeing to halt whaling, but did not withdraw their objections. Russia, the successor state to the Soviet Union, no longer conducts commercial whaling.

The nonparticipation by some whaling states in IWC regulations applies not only to specific quotas on commercial whaling. The IWC in 1994 created a Southern

Ocean Whaling Sanctuary, by declaring the area around Antarctica off-limits for whaling. Japan lodged an objection to the creation of the sanctuary, and conducts much of its scientific whaling there.[83]

Finally, the possibility exists that whaling states, frustrated with the politics of the regulatory organization, will simply withdraw from the IWC altogether. There is no legal restriction to prevent them from doing so, and withdrawal is a threat Japan makes almost annually when decisions at the IWC meetings do not go its way. For awhile it looked as though a competing international organization to regulate whaling, the North Atlantic Marine Mammal Commission (NAMMCO) would become a forum for the possible regulation – but acceptance – of commercial whaling. But the organization, consisting entirely of whaling states, has yet to issue regulations and no longer seems likely to be a competitor to IWC. Because the United Nations Convention on the Law of the Sea (UNCLOS) requires that states "work through the appropriate international organization" for the "conservation, management and study" of marine mammals anywhere in the ocean,[84] if NAMMCO does not become a widely accepted international organization Japan and other whaling states could run into legal trouble if they attempt to conduct their whaling outside of the IWC.

## Compliance and Implementation

Compliance is always at least an underlying concern in international agreements; in the case of whaling this concern turns out to have been well-founded. The Convention itself has no procedure for detecting or responding to non-compliance; instead "each Contracting Government shall take appropriate measures to ensure the application of the provisions ... and the punishment of infractions ... in operations carried out by persons or by vessels under its jurisdiction."[85] As with most international agreements, data on compliance (in this case, whaling catch statistics) are self-reported. Under the ICRW, whalers transmit their catch data to the Bureau of International Whaling Statistics in Norway.[86] Though technically not part of the IWC, this bureau functions as part of the commission by deciding when, based on the information it receives, to end the whaling season each year that commercial whaling occurs.[87] This system creates several different types of incentives for non-compliance.

The first concerns the role of self-reported information used to determine the closing of the whaling season. Individual whalers who correctly report their catches run the risk of reducing the number of whales they can catch overall, as their reports serve to hasten the closing of the season. This process creates the possibility for systemic non-compliance without being able to ascribe individual responsibility. It is possible that during the final days of the whaling season as determined by the BIWS the collective catch will exceed the quota, but responsibility for this excess could be ascribed to no individual whaling vessel or state. Such a system can make non-compliance harder to detect, prevent, or punish.

From early on IWC members expressed concern over whether the whaling ships of the member states were following the rules on catch limits and sizes. There was some evidence examined by the Technical Committee suggesting that whalers were misreporting catch sizes. For instance, in 1965 when the minimum size limit for baleen whales was thirty-eight feet, 90 per cent of female baleen whales caught were reported to be between thirty-eight andthirty-nine feet long – a statistical absurdity.[88] Whalers were almost certainly catching undersize whales and reporting them at or near the minimum size. Since all information was self-reported and since the IWC only had the power to ask the individual states to investigate and punish infractions,[89] there is not much data on this type of non-compliance other than suspicions extrapolated in this manner.

Suspected lack of compliance with catch limits in the Antarctic made states overall less willing to accept substantial restrictions on their whaling activities.[90] Commission members suggested that the creation of some kind of inspections process would increase the willingness, particularly of the Antarctic pelagic whaling states, to accept greater cuts in the whaling quotas, since they could be more certain that their competitors were not defying the regulations. The IWC considered creation of an international observer scheme to address this potential problem, but the issue was contentious and the observer scheme was discussed from 1957 until it was finally implemented for the Antarctic whaling states in 1972. The ultimate scheme involved the whaling states nominating commissioners, who were then appointed to go along on Antarctic whaling voyages to monitor compliance. Such a scheme was only created for Antarctic whaling, however, and not seriously considered for whaling vessels overall.

More serious is non-compliance that was not reported or observed and was therefore hard to detect. In the 1990s reports from Russia indicated that whale statistics reported by the former Soviet Union were incorrect. The Russian Commissioner to the IWC in 1994 suggested that Soviet whale catches from the 1960s to the 1980s were nearly twice the number reported to the organization.[91] Moreover, the USSR had a systematic program to misreport which species of whale were caught, taking prohibited whales such as humpbacks and right and blue whales in large numbers, and report their catches as other species. Ernst Cherry, a member of Russia's team investigating illegal Soviet whaling, commented that "the data on violations of whaling rules contained in official Soviet reports bore no resemblance to the real situation."[92] It is likely as well that Japanese whalers knew about and even assisted such non-compliance, by buying whale carcasses at sea from Soviet vessels.[93] Before the implementation of an international observer scheme, there was no way to ascertain whether reported catches were in compliance with regulations. It is worth noting, however, that the great bulk of illegal Soviet whaling happened outside the Antarctic, and the international observer scheme could not prevent illegal whaling in areas in which it did not operate. It does suggest, however, both the advantage of such a scheme and the reasons that some of the major whaling states resisted it so mightily.

Also important is the impact Soviet non-compliance had on the use of scientific models for whale conservation. The models examined by the Scientific Committee to set whaling quotas were based on reported catch statistics; projections of stock recovery were likely thrown off by such non-compliance.[94]

Finally, the issue of non-compliance with the whaling regime shows the ease of non-compliance with international environmental regulations more broadly. In this instance, there was likely non-compliance (with size limits, for instance) by individual whaling vessels, made possible in an arena as vast and difficult to monitor as the ocean. We also saw non-compliance at the officially sanctioned state level, something that is perhaps somewhat less likely in the post-Soviet era of increased information and political openness, but not necessarily a phenomenon entirely relegated to history. Ironically, however, it also shows the importance that states accord to the perception of compliance: the USSR could easily have objected to specific quotas or withdrawn from the IWC altogether and accomplished its whaling legally. That it chose to hide its excessive whaling behind a cloak of respectability suggests that the norms of the whaling regimes, and the norms of compliance more broadly, do have some impact.

# The Future of Whaling and Whale Conservation?

Some continue to argue that no killing of whales is acceptable. "Even if humanity thinks that it has an ironclad 'scientific' banner under which to kill the whales, is that enough? Is the paradigm under ... which it is okay to take the maximum number of a particular species according to a complicated calculation of 'sustainability' defensible?"[95] Some of the states in the Commission are persuaded by this logic. The IWC delegate from the United Kingdom indicated in an opening statement to the 50th IWC annual meeting in 1998 that "We do not believe that any whaling is justified" and would like to see "the introduction of a permanent, comprehensive moratorium on all whaling other than aboriginal subsistence whaling."[96] At the same time, Norway, Japan, and Iceland are working actively to overturn the commercial moratorium and return to large-scale commercial whaling.

Others fall somewhere in the middle. They acknowledge that whaling has been poorly regulated in the past, and new revelations about Soviet non-compliance only serve to underscore the past inability of the organization to prevent depletion of whales. As witnessed in the case of elephant protection under the Convention on International Trade in Endangered Species of Wild Fauna and Flora (CITES) as well as other environmental regimes, a complete ban on an activity is easier to monitor and enforce than one that allows for but limits a potentially harmful environmental activity. Others argue that a whaling regime that does not include the major whaling states in its regulatory process (if they withdraw, as Iceland has done and Japan and Norway have threatened to do, or if they catch whales – for science or for commercial purposes – in ways not regulated by the organization while still members) would be better off relaxing its moratorium to allow its continued oversight of the process. Fewer whales may be caught under a commercial whaling regime overseen by the IWC than under an IWC moratorium with non-participation.[97]

Yet for those who find the killing of marine mammals to be morally repugnant, would such a compromise be acceptable? As Greenpeace activists continue to put themselves between whalers and whales, would they be willing to accept a politically expedient compromise that might result in the killing of fewer whales but enshrine in international law and practice the principle that killing whales is simply the acceptable harvesting of a sustainable resource? Should they be?

In the meantime, there are increasing numbers of additional threats to the health of whale populations that the IWC has been unable to address as a result of its stalemate over commercial whaling. Environmental harm to the oceans, through pollution, overharvested fisheries, or from climate change, may turn out to be a bigger threat to whales than the limited commercial hunting that could take place. The use of sonar to detect submarines (or in studies to improve its accuracy) in the ocean affects whales, which rely on sound for navigation, and may be responsible for recent marine mammal deaths off the coast of the United States.[98] The threats to whales are numerous, and the stalemate in the IWC over how to protect them may prevent these threats from being adequately addressed.

# Notes

1   Steinar Andresen, "Science and Politics in the International Management of Whales," *Marine Policy* 13(2) (April 1989): 105.

2   The extent to which this statement is true depends on the extent to which whales are simply regarded as a natural resource to be managed; that definition has been called into question politically by non-governmental actors in important ways in the last thirty years.

3   International Convention for the Regulation of Whaling (1946), Preamble.

4   Garrett Hardin, "The Tragedy of the Commons," *Science* 162 (1968): 1243–48.

5   Patricia Birnie, *International Regulation of Whaling: From Conservation of Whaling to Conservation of Whales and Regulation of Whale Watching*, vols. I and II (New York: Oceana, 1985); Steinar Andresen, "Science and Politics in the International Management of Whales," *Marine Policy* 13 (April 1989): 99–117.

6   Interview with Ray Gambell, IWC Secretary, August 1993; Ronald Mitchell, "Membership, Compliance, and Non-compliance in the International Convention for the Regulation of Whaling 1946–Present," paper presented at Harvard University, International Environmental Institutions Research Seminar, October 1992, cited with permission, 7.

7   Elizabeth R. DeSombre, *Flagging Standards: Globalization and International Environmental, Safety, and Labor Standards at Sea* (Cambridge, Mass.: MIT Press, 2006).

8   Richard Ellis, *Men and Whales* (New York: Lyons Press, 1999), 33.

9   Daniel Francis, *A History of World Whaling* (Ontario: Viking, 1990), 21–22.

10  Ibid., 31–35.

11  Ibid., 79.

12  Ibid., 143.

13  Ibid., 208.

14  Ibid., 209–10.

15  Karl Brandt, *Whale Oil: An Economic Analysis*. Fats and Oil Studies, 7 (Stanford: Stanford University Press, 1940), 92–94, quoted in Marc A. Levy, "Leviathan's Leviathan: Power, Interests, and Institutional Change in the International Whaling Commission," unpublished paper, Harvard University, June 1986.

16  Levy, "Leviathan's Leviathan," 6.

17  Francis, 210.

18  Andresen, p.101; Birnie, *International Regulation of Whaling*, 191–92.

19  International Convention for the Regulation of Whaling, Preamble.

20  Birnie, *International Regulation of Whaling*, 178.

21  J. N. Tønnessen and A. O. Johnsen, *The History of Modern Whaling* (Berkeley: University of California Press, 1982), 511.

22  Birnie, *International Regulation of Whaling*, 180.

23  If an objection is registered there is an additional ninety-day period during which other states may decide to object to the same measure. *International Convention for the Regulation of Whaling*, Article 5(3).

24  *International Convention for the Regulation of Whaling*, Article 5(2)(c).

25  The change to quotas on individual stocks was completed by this time; it had, however, begun gradually earlier with some stock quotas in the North Pacific.

26  Birnie, *International Regulation of Whaling*, 453, 461; Andresen, 106. This determination involved comparing the current population size to the maximum sustainable yield (MSY).

27  Colin W. Clark and R. Lamberson, "An Economic History and Analysis of Pelagic Whaling, " *Marine Policy* 6(2) (April 1992): 107–9.

28  Birnie, *International Regulation of Whaling*, 243, 247, 314.

29  Mitchell, 6–7.

30  Fiona Harvey, "Japan Fails to Reverse Ban on Commercial Whaling," *Financial Times*, 20 June 2006, 10.

31  "Iceland Rejoins IWC, but Exempt from Whaling Ban," *Reuters News Service*, 4 July 2001.

32  IWC, "Catches Under Objection since 1985," http://www.iwcoffice.org/_documents/table_objection.htm.

33  Elaine Lies, "Japan Plans New Pro-Whalers Group to End Hunting Ban," *Planet Ark, Reuters Environmental News Service*, 8 June 2006.

34  International Convention for the Regulation of Whaling, Article 5(2)(b).

35  Birnie, *International Regulation of Whaling*, 191.

36  D. S. Butterworth, "Science and Sentimentality," *Nature* 357 (18 June 1992): 532–34.

37  See, generally, Birnie, *International Regulation of Whaling*, for reports from the SC.

38  Butterworth, 533.

39  G. Elliot, "Failure of the International Whaling Commission 1946–1966," *Marine Policy* 3 (1979): 149–55; Birnie, *International Regulation of Whaling*, 198.

40  Birnie, *International Regulation of Whaling*, 364.

41  Steinar Andresen, "Science and Politics in the International Management of Whales," *Marine Policy* 13 (April 1989): 100.

42  Ellis, 421.

43  Birnie, *International Regulation of Whaling*, 335; M. J. Peterson, "Whalers, Cetologists, Environmentalists, and the International Management of Whaling," *International Organization* 46(1) (Winter 1992): 163.

44  Andresen, 104.

45  Ibid., 105.

46  Ibid., 107, 110.

47  International Whaling Commission schedule, 1992, ¶ 10e.

48  G. P. Donovan, "Forty-second Annual Meeting of the International Whaling Commission," *Polar Record* 24 (June 1989): 631–63.

49  Joe Roman and Stephen R. Palumbi, "Whales Before Whaling in the North Atlantic," *Science* 301(5632) (25 July 2003): 508–10.

50  IWC, "Special Permit Catches since 1985," http://www.iwcoffice.org/_documents/table_permit.htm.

51  Interview with Ray Gambell, June 1997.

52  Paul Dyer, "Whalers 'Faking' Science," *Sunday Telegraph*, 29 January 2006, 18.

53  Douglas H. Chadwick, "Pursuing the Minke," *National Geographic* 199(4) (April 2000): 58–71.

54  Patricia Birnie, "The Role of Developing Countries in Nudging the International Whaling Commission from Regulating Whaling to Encouraging Nonconsumptive Uses of Whales," *Ecology Law Quarterly* 12 (1985): 955.

55  Wapner, *Environmental Activism and World Civic Politics*, 52, 54.

56  Robert Hunter, *Warriors of the Rainbow: A Chronicle of the Greenpeace Movement* (New York: Holt, Reinhart, and Winston, 1979), 229.

57  Robert Mandel, "Transnational Resource Conflict: The Politics of Whaling," *International Studies Quarterly* (March 1984): 99–127.

58  Peterson, 175.

59  Birnie, "The Role of Developing Countries," 953.

60  Alan Macnow, a consultant to the Japan Whaling Association, argues that these states in particular, along with ten others, were recruited to the organization by antiwhaling groups. "A Whaling Moratorium Opposed by I.W.C.'s Own Scientists," Letter to the Editor, *New York Times*, 29 September 1984, 22.

61  Leslie Spencer with Jan Bollwerk and Richard C. Morais, "The Not So Peaceful World of Greenpeace," *Forbes*, 11 November 1991, 174ff. (Lexis/Nexis).

62  International Whaling Commission, "Chairman's Report of the 47th Annual Meeting" (1996), 41.

63  Pro-whaling states did what they could as well to provide support to countries that would vote in favor of continued commercial whaling. See Day, 103–5, 107; Paul Brown, "Playing Football with the Whales," *The Guardian*, 1 May 1993, 26 (Lexis/Nexis).

64  Maggie Tait, "We were Rammed, says Greenpeace," *The Advertiser*, 9 January 2006, 15.

65  Elizabeth R. DeSombre, "Distorting Global Governance: Membership, Voting, and the IWC," in Robert L Friedheim, ed., *Toward a Sustainable Whaling Regime* (Seattle: University of Washington Press, 2001), 183–99.

66  Mark Fineman, "Dominca's Support of Whaling is No Fluke," *Los Angeles Times*, 9 December 1997, A1.

67  "Japan 'Bought Whale Votes,'" *Daily Telegraph*, 19 July 2005, 10.

68  Peter Alford, "Vote on Whales 'Not Sold,'" *Daily Telegraph*, 24 June 2005, 9,

69  Note that Antigua and Barbuda is considered to have been influenced by both sides of the whaling debate in its IWC voting. Initially it was not a member and is said to have been persuaded to join by NGO pressure and incentives. Later it switched to supporting whaling after receiving Japanese aid.

70  Interview with Ray Gambell, June 1997.

71  Leslie Spencer with Jan Bollwerk and Richard C. Morais, "The Not So Peaceful World of Greenpeace," *Forbes*, 11 November 1991, 174ff.

72  United States Public Law 92-219, sec. 8.

73  16 United States Code 182.

74  Elizabeth R. DeSombre, *Domestic Sources of International Environmental Policy: Industry, Environmentalists, and U.S. Power* (Cambridge, Mass.: MIT Press, 2000), 210–11.

75  DeSombre, *Domestic Sources of International Environmental Policy*, 212.

76  This phenomenon is seen more broadly than in just whaling; ships of all sorts register in "flag of convenience" countries to get around international regulations. In the case of the Olympic Whaling Company, it chose specifically to register vessels in locations where it would not be bound by international rules.

77  Tønnessen and Johnsen, 534–38.

78  Mitchell, "Membership, Compliance and Non-compliance," 19.

79  Birnie, *International Regulation of Whaling*, 235.

80  Gene S. Martin Jr. and James W. Brennan, "Enforcing the International Convention for the Regulation of Whaling: The Pelly and Packwood-Magnuson Amendments," *Denver Journal of International Law and Policy* 17(2) (1989): 293–315.

81  The Supreme Court ultimately ruled that certification was at the discretion of the Secretary of Commerce and could not be required, but lower courts had ruled otherwise, and the possibility seemed real that Japan would be certified. *Japan Whaling Association v. American Cetacean Society*, 478 U.S. 221, 105 S. Ct., 2860 (1986); DeSombre, *Domestic Sources of International Environmental Policy*, 209.

82  International Whaling Commission, 1993, *Verbatim Record*, 198.

83  Michael McCarthy, "Save the Whale: 20 Years on and Whales are Under Threat Again," *The Independent* (London), 2 January 2006, 2.

84  UNCLOS (1982), Article 65.

85  International Convention for the Regulation of Whaling, Article IX (1).

86  Andresen claims that the true name of this organization is the "Committee of International Whaling Statistics," but it is known by its other name within the IWC. Andresen, 103.

87 It does so by informing whalers a week before it predicts the catch limits will be reached of what the closing date of the season will thus be.

88 Birnie, *International Regulation of Whaling*, 338.

89 The main form of punishment was to deny a whaler the fee from an illegally caught whale.

90 G. Elliot, "The Failure of the International Whaling Commission 1946–1966," *Marine Policy* 3 (1979): 149–55; Birnie, *International Regulation of Whaling*, 198.

91 *Greenwire*, "Worldview – Whaling: Soviet Kills Could Affect Sanctuary Decision," 22 February 1994.

92 Paul Brown, "Soviet Union Illegally Killed Great Whales," *Guardian*, 12 February, 1994, 14; Interview with Ray Gambell, IWC Secretary, August 1993. The whole Soviet whaling industry was run as a covert operation.

93 Brown, "Soviet Union Illegally Killed Great Whales," 12.

94 "Call me Smiley," *New York Times Magazine*, 13 March 1994, 14.

95 "A New Era for the IWC," *Greenpeace Magazine* (Oct.–Nov.–Dec. 1991), 5.

96 "International Whaling Commission: 50th Annual Meeting: Opening Statement by the United Kingdom Delegation," IWC/50/OS/UK, 1998.

97 Mitchell, "Membership, Compliance and Non-compliance."

98 "Whales in the Way of Sonar," *New York Times*, 7 March 2006, 20.

# 8 Biodiversity in the Amazon and Elsewhere

*The Amazon is ... a remarkable self-contained system that depends crucially on the integrity of the whole to sustain itself ... the soils are among the poorest on the planet – yet the vegetation and the unparalleled richness of living organisms seem to suggest a luxuriance that derives from the plenty rather than from deprivation. That paradox is the miracle of the rainforest.*[1]

Global biodiversity is threatened. Species are becoming extinct at rates unprecedented in human history, from habitat loss, overexploitation, nutrient changes, climate change, and the introduction of invasive species into new environments. The current wave of species loss has been referred to as the sixth major extinction, on the scale of such previous natural events as the extinction of the dinosaurs, but due instead primarily to human causes. The trends are not encouraging in areas of high biodiversity: 6 million hectares of primary forests are lost each year, 35 per cent of mangroves have been lost in the last twenty years, and coral reefs are rapidly declining. Species abundance of those wild species that are measured have declined by between 30 per cent and 50 per cent in the last thirty years. Ecosystems are increasingly fragmented.[2] The Millennium Ecosystem Assessment determined that fifteen of the twenty-four services provided by ecosystems are declining.[3] As the Secretariat for the Convention on Biological Diversity reports, "biodiversity is in decline at all levels and geographical scales."[4]

Biodiversity, the health and variability of species, ecosystems, and genetic material existing worldwide, is an unusual global environmental issue. For the most part any particular species or part of an ecosystem is located in the territory of a state and thus can be seen as a private good. For a number of reasons, however, the destruction of biodiversity and the efforts to protect it are inherently global issues. First, the concern about biodiversity is international: people all over the world care about potential future benefits, existence value, or associated environmental problems that come from biodiversity or the failure to protect it. Second, the idea of biodiversity, as separate from species protection, suggests that what is important is not only individual species or even eco-systems, but the world wide diversity of these things. No one state alone can guarantee worldwide biodiversity; in order to have a diverse array of species, ecosystems, and genetic material efforts must be made in a variety of places worldwide to protect such diversity. Third, and most controversially, the deep causes of at least some biodiversity loss, even when taking place on a primarily local level, can be international. These include pressures to overuse resources to pay back debt, international markets and multinational corporations that value the use rather than the protection of natural resources, and governments sufficiently impoverished by a number of historical (and often international) causes that they have short time horizons leading them to undervalue local resources.

This issue is thus inherently global, but because ecosystems exist in specific locations, the efforts to protect them take on a different character than other forms of international environmental cooperation. State sovereignty is an important factor, both in constraining and in inspiring solutions to biodiversity problems. Developing states, host to most of the world's biodiversity, have strongly supported wording in international declarations and treaties that supports states' "sovereign rights over their own biodiversity,"[5] and that acknowledges that "states have, in accordance with the Charter of the United Nations and the principles of international law, the sovereign right to exploit their own resources pursuant to their own environmental and developmental policies."[6] The important effect of these principles is that countries have been wary to take on any international obligations to significantly constrain what they can do with their biodiversity resources, and that developed states that place a high value on biodiversity have needed to make deals with biodiverse states in order to gain access to the resources or increase the likelihood that they will be protected. Non-governmental actors have also been particularly involved in these approaches, out of either environmental concern or interest in access to resources, and many of the most notable approaches to biodiversity protection have been private, rather than intergovernmental.

Issues pertaining to biodiversity are examined here with particular reference to the context of the Amazonian rainforest. Doing so allows a specific focus to be put on a global phenomenon and thus allows for a closer examination of both global and local activities to protect biodiversity in a particular region. Tropical forests are particularly important for biodiversity protection; the only 6 per cent of the earth's surface that is covered by tropical rainforests is considered to contain more than half of the terrestrial species on the globe.[7] The Amazon in particular is relevant both for its importance to global biodiversity and for the creativity – along with occasional failure – of the efforts to protect species and ecosystems. The Amazon rainforest, which is present in eight different South American countries,[8] has been declared by biologist Norman Myers to be one of the world's biodiversity "hotspots."[9] Tropical forests generally are considered to contain between 50 per cent and 90 per cent of all the world's species.[10] The Amazon basin constitutes only 7 per cent of the earth's land surface, but accounts for 35 per cent of its tropical forests. Sixty per cent of the rainforest is in Brazil.[11]

Although the Amazon rainforest is spread across eight countries, it functions in many ways as a unitary ecosystem. It plays an important role in the global climate system, acting as a giant "heat pump" sending energy from the tropics to moderate the climate of the colder, higher, latitudes.[12] The ecosystem functions additionally in the global climate system by acting as a carbon sink, taking up carbon dioxide that would otherwise enter the atmosphere and contribute to global climate change. In fact, with increasing deforestation worldwide, a carbon sink can be transformed into a carbon source, as cut or burned trees release the carbon they had stored. While the amount of carbon emissions from tropical deforestation vary widely, the Food and Agriculture Organization of the United Nations recently estimated that deforestation releases 2 billion tonnes of carbon annually, accounting for 25 per cent of human-generated greenhouse gas emissions.[13]

The Amazonian rainforest has importance far beyond its role in the global climate system. Tropical forests account for a large percentage of the world's species, which may become extinct with increased levels of deforestation. These species may be valued for their potential uses (as genetic material or for potential future medicinal products that can be made from them) or simply because of the belief that it is wrong to cause the extinction of species. Moreover, the ecosystem as a whole interacts; when one part of it is removed the rest has difficulty functioning. Deforestation can lead to local problems like soil erosion and decreased land productivity.

It must also be pointed out how little we know, both in the Amazon and elsewhere, about the level of biodiversity generally. It is suggested that the approximately 1.75 million species identified represent as little as 15 per cent of the total existing species.[14] For that reason, estimates of biodiversity loss vary greatly. While many estimates suggest that approximately 5 per cent of the world's species become extinct each decade, estimates even within the relatively conservative community of specialists range between 1 per cent and 11 per cent per decade.[15] Even within the region of the Amazonian rainforest, estimates differ widely as to how much land is being converted from rainforest. Two estimates from the late 1980s put the total rainforest area lost up to that point between 7 per cent and 12 per cent,[16] and more recent estimates suggest the total area of forest loss in the region is 17.3 per cent.[17]

## Threats to Amazonian Biodiversity

Biodiversity loss in the Amazonian region is caused primarily by agricultural and development activities, in addition to direct harvesting of natural resources. There are deeper causes, however, to these activities, including subsidies, social pressures, transnational capital and trade, the debt crisis, and land distribution. Additional related threats to biodiversity are the overharvesting of wild species, the introduction of non-native species (including agriculture), habitat destruction, pollution by toxins, changing nutrient balances, or physical contaminants and local or global climatic changes.

Agricultural activity of a variety of types is a major source of biodiversity loss in the Amazonian region. Estimates for the period 2000–2005 suggest that cattle ranching is responsible for at least 60 per cent of Amazonian deforestation. At least 30 per cent of deforestation in the region can be attributed to farmers who cut or burn down trees in order to plant crops,[18] including farmers from other regions who migrate into the rainforest in an effort to support themselves.[19] Palm, rubber, and oil plantations add to the rainforest destruction.[20] More importantly, the increased wealth of local populations contributes to more, rather than less, pressure on the land, as wealthier rainforest settlers are likely to see cattle ranching, among the most land intensive of rainforest activities, as a route to a better life.[21]

Development broadly construed also contributes to the loss of Amazonian rainforest biodiversity. Brazilian government policies to "open up" the rainforest to settlement and economic activity began as early as 1946.[22] These policies generally involved the construction of major highways. The first major effort of this sort came in 1956 with the construction of a highway through the rainforest between several major cities, which made possible the colonization of rainforest land, increased the flow of foreign capital into Brazil, and increased the dependence of the Brazilian economy on oil.[23] Further road projects made access to the Amazon even easier. The most controversial of these road building exercises was the Polonoreste project, financed by the World Bank to pave a major highway cutting through the Brazilian state of Rondônia. This project began as military rule in Brazil was ending in the early 1980s and people moved at great speed into areas of the Amazon the military had previously controlled as national security zones. But the military presence had at least kept order in this region, and without it, land conflicts in the region increased. While the World Bank included provisions in the project designed to protect the environment and indigenous people, activists believed that increased ease of transportation would simply increase settlement and deforestation in the area, at the expense of indigenous populations. As a result of multinational protests the World Bank suspended payments to Brazil in 1985.[24] Despite this controversy, efforts for Brazil to make the Amazon more accessible to populations and those wanting to engage in economic activity has had a clear impact on deforestation.

Finally, natural resource extraction is a major threat to biodiversity in the Amazon region as well as outside the region. The most obvious activity of this sort is logging. In the Brazilian region of Amazônia logging and the associated wood products industries have been among the fastest growing contributions to the national economy. Commercial logging intersects with agricultural use, because once an area has been stripped of its trees settlers and subsistence farmers often move in. The roads created by the logging industry make access by settlers possible into areas of the rainforest that would have been previously impenetrable.[25] Additionally, mining of copper and other minerals can have a huge impact on the biodiversity of the region. The Brazilian Amazon contains what some suggest is the world's largest deposit of iron ore, manganese, and other minerals. While mining can theoretically be done in a way that has minimal impact on the surrounding ecosystem, the development of this region includes an open ore mine and a variety of smelters, with serious environmental impacts.[26] Similarly, mining for gold, found in some rivers of the Amazon region, leads to an influx of people and pollution of the rivers by mercury, which is used (often illegally) to amalgamate gold.[27] Oil, present in various places in the Amazon but particularly in Ecuador, is extracted by companies that travel far into the forest by helicopter, clear the forest for oil drilling, and often then leave waste products or spill oil in the process of transporting it out.

Underlying these specific rainforest destruction activities are broader social forces and policies that create the incentives for the patterns of land use and development seen in the Amazon region. Social pressures created by poverty and population growth are important background factors that force settlers into the rainforest in search of subsistence and land. The rainforest has often functioned as a "safety valve" for social and agrarian crises,[28] allowing people room to expand or escape local difficulties. Population growth and unequal distribution of non-forested land gives incentives to people to claim and deforest land.[29]

These factors combine with governmental policies that give incentives to those who settle in the rainforest. At minimum, the land tenure system in Brazil, in which 5 per cent of farmers occupy 70 per cent of the land, and 70 per cent occupy 5 per cent,[30] suggests that there is little nonforested room for expansion. Government policies designed to deal with these problems grant land to people in the rainforest. In the Brazilian region of Amazônia "the right to possession of land is granted to the party who clears it,"[31] which gives an obvious incentive to those who destroy rainforested area rather than conserve it. Between 1982 and 1986 approximately half a million people moved to Rondônia, lured by grants of between 100 and 250 hectares per family to farm. During this time period, the forest area of the region decreased dramatically. The World Bank estimates that 24 per cent of the Brazilian state of Rondônia was burned, in efforts to make it suitable for agricultural use.[32] Brazil has spent more than $2.5 billion subsidizing cattle ranching in previously forested areas,[33] which allows ranchers to make a profit even if cattle ranching is an otherwise inefficient source of income. And it frequently is; previously rainforested land tends to not be especially productive either agriculturally or for grazing of cattle.[34]

Also important is the incentive that the international market gives to cattle ranchers or lumber companies. The spread of cattle ranching to the Amazonian region can be at least partially attributed to the demand in North America for inexpensive beef.[35] Oil exports, primarily from exploitation in the Amazon, account for up to half of Ecuador's export income.[36] In Brazil, it is argued, the "international market to a large extent determines the course of development,"[37] with increases in the international price of tropical timber increasing the incentive to cut down trees as earlier international demand for rubber increased the use of the rainforest for rubber plantations. But a decrease in prices does not have the beneficial effect that relationship might suggest. Rather, as world prices for commodities fall, countries that depend on their exports for generating income must export more, rather than less.[38]

Debt is a major underlying factor in development strategies to provide income from the Amazon. The pressures work in several ways. First, the need to pay increasingly large debt service gives an incentive to states to increase their exports, to bring in foreign currency with which to pay the debt. Doing so by increasing the export of primary products found in the rainforest (timber, oil, minerals) is a traditional method for debt-strapped states to earn money to help pay off their debt. Beginning in the 1960s in Brazil small coffee farms were replaced with large-scale agriculture pushing into the Amazon region to produce soybeans for export; in the 1960s alone these new agricultural activities caused the eradication of 400 million trees from coffee plantations in the rainforest.[39] In order to pay their debt service, countries may be forced to cut social programs, which also result, in the case of Amazonian countries, in more people moving into the forest to try to make a living off of the land.[40] In addition, the more a country is indebted, the higher an interest rate it must pay. This translates into what is called a higher discount rate, or a shorter time horizon. In other words, the state values gains in the present much more than gains in the future, as it struggles to pay off its debt. That also leads to an increased desire to use resources to gain economic advantages in the present, rather than taking a longer run view of the advantages of biodiversity. In a particularly interesting example of this phenomenon, Nicaragua allowed a Taiwanese timber company to log one-eighth of its remaining forests in return for a $30 million loan to help Nicaragua pay its foreign debt.[41] The debt crisis in Latin America in the 1980s certainly correlates with increased deforestation, with 9.2 million hectares per year of rainforest lost in the 1970s and 16.8 million hectares per year lost in the 1990s.[42] These numbers have decreased somewhat with the easing of the debt crisis; estimates from 2000–2005 suggest a loss of 4.3 million hectares annually.[43]

# Approaches to Biodiversity Protection

## International Agreements

There are few international agreements that provide serious protection for biodiversity as a whole, though the development of international cooperation over the last century has included a number of approaches to protect or conserve specific species. These types of agreements were among the first international cooperative efforts on environmental and resource issues, beginning at the end of the nineteenth century and focusing first on migratory species or those in danger from overhunting. Among the most important international species protection agreements is the Convention on International Trade in Endangered Species of Wild Fauna and Flora (CITES), signed in 1973, which restricts trade in species listed on several appendices to the treaty. Also important is the Convention on Migratory Species, signed in 1979, which focuses on species that cross international space of their own accord, and encourages range states for a given species to negotiate agreements to protect them. Both these processes have likely been responsible for the increased protection of some individual species, but are unlikely to have a large impact on biodiversity as a whole. They also demonstrate the difficulties of undertaking intrusive restrictions to protect natural resources. By regulating only trade in endangered species CITES protects state sovereignty by allowing states to do whatever they want with species inside their own borders. While that arrangement makes the agreement more politically palatable, it prevents it from addressing the underlying causes for species decline.

Given the important role of forests in biodiversity generally and Amazonian biodiversity in particular, it is also worth mentioning the International Tropical Timber Agreement. The agreement was created initially in 1983, renegotiated in 1994 and renegotiated once more in 2006. This commodity agreement attempts indirectly to conserve tropical forest resources by addressing uncertainty and fluctuation in the international market for tropical timber, with the idea that a more stable international market will allow states to choose when to harvest and sell their forest resources, rather than being driven to do so by market pressures or opportunities. The 1994 renegotiation focused more directly on sustainable use of tropical timber, setting an (unreached) goal for producers of tropical timbers to be able to export only sustainably harvested timber by the year 2000,[44] and by setting up the Bali partnership fund to "assist producing members to make the investments necessary" to meet the sustainability objective.[45] The 2006 renegotiation addresses illegal logging and forest certification, and claims <u>sustainable forest management</u> as one of its two central objectives. It is not clear that the treaty has fulfilled its main effort to facilitate (and regularize) trade in tropical timber, and even less clear that it has contributed significantly to an increase in sustainable management of these forests. The treaty organization itself suggested that at the end of the 1990s less than 1 per cent of tropical forests were under sustainable management.[46]

The international agreement most directly concerned with the protection of the world's biodiversity, the <u>Convention on Biological Diversity (CBD)</u>, was negotiated in conjunction with the <u>United Nations Conference on Environment and Development (UNCED)</u> in Rio di Janeiro, Brazil, in 1992. This agreement is a framework convention, to which the <u>Cartagena Biosafety Protocol</u> was added in 2000.

In large part due to the level of uncertainty about current levels of biodiversity and the extent of existing threats, the major substantive obligation of the CBD is the identification, monitoring, and assessment of existing biodiversity. Countries are required to determine the extent of their biological diversity and monitor it on an ongoing basis, particularly those aspects "requiring urgent conservation measures."[47] The agreement requires all parties to develop "national strategies, plans or programmes for the conservation and sustainable use" of biodiversity.[48] The treaty also puts forth an obligation to protect existing biodiversity resources, though it leaves the form of implementation entirely to the discretion of the states involved. As such it is hardly a substantive obligation to which states could be called to account. An additional important aspect is the funding mechanism, described in Article 20 of the treaty and implemented by the Global Environment Facility. Developed countries accept the obligations to pay the "full incremental costs" that developing countries incur in meeting the obligations of the treaty.

Recently the CBD has taken up the goal of achieving "by 2010 a significant reduction of the current rate of loss of biological diversity," and has persuaded the major international species protection agreements and the participants at the World Summit on Sustainable Development in Johannesburg in 2002 to adopt this objective.[49] Though this effort raises awareness, gives organizations and states a shared goal, and focuses attention on ways to evaluate progress toward it, it does not involve specific policy approaches that necessarily change how states and international organizations were operating.

The CBD continues the move in international law away from the principle of "free access" by anyone to biodiversity resources. Again "recognizing the sovereign rights of States over their natural resources," the treaty agrees to facilate access to genetic resources, but requires that such access be on the basis of prior informed consent and "on mutually agreed terms."[50] It thus increases the ability of states to keep others from their biodiversity resources to a much greater extent than it requires them to protect such resources. The idea in part may be that states, when guaranteed control over their own resources, will be able to profit from them in a way that will increase the likelihood of preserving them. Nevertheless, short-term considerations will often trump the long-run advantages to an individual state of protecting a piece of the world's biodiversity heritage. The sovereignty rights affirmed by states in the CBD were made possible primarily because states cannot be forced to join international environmental agreements. Since most biodiversity is located within the territory of states, those states with high biodiversity resources were loathe to accept specific restrictions but eager to increase their control over their resources. These states had the ability to keep substantive conservation obligations from the agreement. What resulted was a treaty that provides a general approach to protection of biodiversity and an agreement that doing so is important, while requiring little substantive action to accomplish that goal. The funding mechanism and the information generated from national biodiversity inventories are likely to be among the most important features of the agreement, largely because they will reduce some of the uncertainty and scientific disagreement associated with discussions of biodiversity.

The one existing protocol to the CBD is the Cartagena Biosafety Protocol (2000), again showing a concern by developing countries to protect their territorial integrity from outside interference, rather than an obligation to preserve ecosystems in any way. The Protocol concerns trade in what it calls Living Modified Organisms (LMOs) (a subset of genetically modified organisms that are "capable of transferring or replicating genetic material").[51] Trade in these organisms is regulated through a prior-informed-consent-like procedure termed Advanced Informed Agreement (AIA). Under this process, countries that wish to export LMOs must inform and receive consent from the importing country before such an activity can take place.[52] Additional obligations require all states to notify each other in the case of unintentional transboundary release of LMOs and take responsibility for the removal of any LMOs illegally transferred. The agreement spells out the ability of states to restrict imports of LMOs based on risk assessment, "carried out in a scientifically sound manner."[53]

While the biosafety protocol may serve to protect ecosystems from being taken over by genetically modified organisms unwittingly imported and thus help conserve biodiversity, the converse argument is made as well: that increased use of biotechnology will allow more people to be fed using less land and with less damage to ecosystems, and thus ultimately benefit biodiversity.[54] More importantly, the fact that the first protocol to the CBD is again about protecting the rights of the countries in which the most biodiversity is found, rather than requiring obligations of them, suggests the importance of the issue structure in determining what types of biodiversity protection may be most useful.

# Private Solutions

The nature of the biodiversity conservation problem suggests that states are likely to be most moved by measures to protect biodiversity that enable them to profit from the protection of their resources. While to some extent sustainable use of any resource, and in particular the protection of rainforest ecosystems that otherwise are subject to soil degradation and erosion, is in the interests of the countries in which the resource is located, that interest is collective and long-term. The forces that lead to rainforest destruction tend to be individual (as farmers or ranchers move into the Amazon, in search of profits) and driven by short-term considerations. A number of innovative private solutions have helped to mitigate some of the underlying causes of rainforest destruction. They provide benefits to individuals as well as to the state for protecting nature, and increase the likelihood that the long-term benefits of protecting biodiversity resources will be accomplished. These efforts rely predominantly on actions of non-governmental actors, who also play a broader role in general pressure to address issues of biodiversity protection.

## Debt-for-Nature Swaps

One of the most inventive initial strategies for protection of biodiversity was the idea of debt forgiveness in exchange for conservation activities undertaken by the indebted country. This concept was important in the late 1980s and early 1990s, but is not currently being practiced as designed, for structural reasons. As first proposed by Thomas Lovejoy of the World Wildlife Fund in 1984,[55] this process begins when a seriously indebted country is unlikely to be able to pay back its debt. The bank to which it owes the debt sells the debt at a discounted rate on the secondary market, for fear that it will not receive the full payment from the country in question. A non-governmental organization (NGO), interested in conservation, buys a piece of the country's debt at a discounted rate. The NGO then negotiates with the environment and finance ministries of the indebted country for some amount of money – usually higher than the NGO paid for the debt but lower than the actual value of the debt – to be put in national currency into local conservation. The first Debt-for-Nature (DFN) swap, in Bolivia in 1987, required the setting aside of specific land areas for conservation. Concerns about sovereignty and disrespect of local priorities led to a general shift of approach allowing DFN funding to be put to any agreed-upon conservation goal, including environmental education, increases in the budgets of the national parks, funding for a local conservation organization, or employment of rangers to patrol protected areas. Swaps still almost always focus on increasing conservation in a specific area of the indebted state.

DFN swaps build on the idea that highly indebted countries are likely to use natural resources unsustainably in order to meet their immediate economic needs. Because of the Latin American debt crisis the mechanism was also able to build on the advantages of a secondary market in debt to increase the value of money NGOs put towards conservation. Rather than simply donating money to a country to convince it to protect its biodiversity, the NGO invests that money in buying debt and thus multiplies the amount of conservation its donation can buy. For example, Conservation International spent $750,000 on a DFN swap in Brazil. If it had simply donated that amount of money to Brazilian conservation, it would have purchased $750,000 in conservation measures in Brazil. Instead, it purchased $2.2 million in debt and (in a slight departure from the average process), Brazil agreed to put all of the funding toward conservation locally.[56] The NGO thus spent $750,000 to purchase $2.2 million in conservation measures in Brazil. That is the marvel of the DFN swap mechanism.

Between 1987 and 1994 (the height of the first generation DFN swaps) there were thirty-two swaps completed in fifteen states, which reduced foreign debt by $177 million and generated approximately $130 million in local conservation funding.[57] Most swaps were in Latin America. Early DFN swaps in the Amazon region included two in Bolivia, two in Ecuador, and one in Brazil.[58] Later DFN swaps followed a different pattern, with governments forgiving debt in exchange for conservation measures. The first of these was done with Germany forgiving $500 million in Kenyan debt in exchange for environmental protection.[59] The United States Tropical Forest Conservation Act of 1998 promised to provide $325 million for DFN swaps.[60] As of 2005, eight states – Bangladesh, Belize, Colombia, El Salvador, Jamaica, Panama, Peru, and the Philippines—had negotiated agreements with the United States under this agreement, which resulted in pledges of conservation efforts valued at nearly $100 million.[61] Other states plan or have executed these types of programs as well, although the original momentum for undertaking them seems to have decreased.

It is clear that DFN swaps are a mechanism more suited to addressing conservation needs than solving the debt crisis given the relatively small amount of debt that is forgiven overall,[62] although that may change with second generation, bilateral, swaps. But the mechanism has had a noticeable impact on conservation. For example, the first Ecuadorian DFN swap relieved only $1 million in debt of an overall debt of $8.3 billion. But the amount put to conservation more than doubled the budgets of the national parks.[63]

There are criticisms of this mechanism even within the framework of conservation, however. These focus either on the failure of external NGOs to effectively influence domestic conservation or on the ethics of doing so. The first concern is that funding does not necessarily accomplish much; Rhona Mahoney complains that DFN swaps produce only "paper parks" that give the illusion of environmental protection without actual on-the-ground conservation. She points out that "protected areas are invaded by loggers, miners, or the landless."[64] While this observation is certainly true in some instances, NGOs have learned from DFN failures and have designated increased funding to help protect park borders and provide alternative economic activities for people impacted by the protection of land they might otherwise occupy. A study of ninety-three national parks in tropical areas concluded that 83 per cent of the parks were unaffected by agricultural encroachment, and also suffered less than nearby areas from other human-induced change such as hunting, grazing, and logging.[65]

Others point to the inflationary pressure that can be created domestically by the influx of currency used to pay for environmental measures.[66] This particularly happens if the government responds to the need to put local funding into conservation by simply printing additional currency. States do not have to follow that approach, however, and in most cases the amount of internal money generated in a debt-for-nature swap is small enough relative to the overall national budget to have at most a minimal inflationary impact. In addition, it is suggested that the mechanism rests on an incorrect assumption of a relationship between debt and deforestation.[67] While it is clear that debt is not the only or even necessarily the primary factor leading to Amazonian deforestation, the fact that DFN swaps have provided increased funding for conservation, while reducing small amounts of debt, renders this criticism irrelevant. Whether deforestation in the Amazon is caused by debt, the fact that it can be ameliorated by a mechanism that involves debt relief seems clear.

A bigger concern may be ethical. The mechanism has been called "eco-imperialistic."[68] Developing countries may see such agreements as threats to sovereignty, which may have prevented some from participating. Some are concerned that the mechanism takes place without developed countries acknowledging their role in environmental degradation, and operates by

*[handwritten margin notes: "ethics of intervention" and "inflation pressure"]*

impacting the lives of local subsistence farmers in the Amazon rather than changing the lifestyles of people in the wealthy industrialized countries.[69] It is also suggested that no real transfer of funding takes place, since the funding from NGOs goes to the banks, and the country protects biodiversity with its own money. While these criticisms are to some extent fair, if conservation of biodiversity is a relevant goal, the actions of debt-for-nature swaps have been one way to accomplish it. The fact that states may choose not to participate removes at least some of the sovereignty concerns. To the extent that biodiversity conservation is advantageous in the long run for the country it takes place in, DFN swaps may be one way to help states realize their own long-term self-interest.

It is also interesting to note that initial DFN swap successes helped sow the seeds of their own decline. During the height of the Latin American debt crisis debt could be bought for a highly discounted rate on the secondary market, because banks believed the chances of being paid back were slim. Few others wanted to buy debt that was so unlikely to be paid back and so the price was low. During the 1990s the price of Latin American debt on the secondary market increased, largely because banks became more cautious about lending money to those who had previously failed to pay it back and there was thus less debt to be sold. Even in cases where the price of debt decreased, governments have responded to increased NGO demands for swaps by agreeing to put a lower percentage of the swapped debt value into conservation. So while the price of Costa Rica's debt on the secondary market fell from 30 cents per dollar of debt to only 10 cents in the first few years of the mechanism's operation, the country responded by moving from paying 75 per cent of the debt's face value for conservation goals to paying only 30 per cent.[70] While bilateral governmental debt forgiveness in exchange for conservation measures may be of increasing importance in the future, first generation debt-for-nature swaps appear to have been a time-limited mechanism.

## Bioprospecting

Since one of the arguments for protecting the rainforest is the potential future use of its products for medical advances, ensuring that states in which it exists benefit from those medical advances could help increase the odds that those states will undertake measures to protect their biodiversity. Since 1990 global sale of products derived from traditional medical practices in tropical countries earned $32 billion annually.[71] A study of new small-molecule drugs introduced to the market between 1981 and 2002 indicated that 61 per cent were inspired by, or could trace their development to, natural products,[72] with that number reported as high as 80 per cent since then. It is estimated that that two-thirds of anticancer drugs are derived from natural products.[73]

Bioprospecting involves the extraction and examination of biological samples from an area to determine whether they are useful for pharmacological purposes. While this activity is not new – Eli Lilly and Co. developed cancer treatments from the rosy periwinkle native to Madagascar in the 1950s,[74] and specific removal and use of local plants likely dates back to colonial times – its specific contribution to conservation is. The countries in which bioprospecting takes place, buoyed by increasing international safeguards on their rights to their own resources, demand compensation for allowing pharmaceutical countries to examine their resources. This compensation comes in several forms: companies may pay states to protect an area in which they want to bioprospect and simply to allow them access, local people may be paid to collect and evaluate samples and are provided with technology and training to do so, and if a product is developed from this process the state that has a bioprospecting deal with the company has likely negotiated for some share of the royalties. More generally, the idea is that a state will itself gain the incentive to protect an area that might be the source of economic benefits in the near future, particularly if threats to the area originally came for economic reasons.[75]

The first large bioprospecting deal took place not in the Amazon but in Costa Rica in 1991, when the pharmaceutical company Merck paid that country approximately $1.1 million plus access to royalties (half of which are to be put into conservation) in return for samples and protection of a specific region. Merck and Costa Rica renewed the contract in 1994 for an additional $1 million,[76] and INBio, the National Biodiversity Institute of Costa Rica with which the Merck deal was made, has negotiated several bioprospecting agreements with other companies since then,[77] though no drugs have yet been brought to market from this agreement.

There have been some bioprospecting agreements specifically in the Amazon region. An early effort was undertaken by a firm called Shaman Pharmaceuticals, Inc., which hoped to draw on the knowledge of practicers of traditional medicine in the Amazon to identify which plants might have medicinal potential. Working in the Amazon, among other locations, this firm included biodiversity conservation as part of its mission and shared the benefits of its developments with the communities in which it worked, through a nonprofit organization it created called "Healing Forest Conservancy." It employed local people. In its operations in Peru, the company made an agreement with a federation representing 30,000 indigenous people to harvest plant samples for its operations.[78] While Shaman had remarkable success at finding products to bring to drug trials, however, the cost of conducting these trials, and the failure of some of its products to perform, led the company to declare bankruptcy in 2001. Initially following bankruptcy the firm continued to operate, focusing its efforts on dietary supplements, which require less government oversight. But it has now ceased even these efforts, though it was granted twenty patents from its efforts to identify useful drugs.[79]

The Massachusetts Institute of Technology (MIT) began a $5 million bioprospecting project in the Amazon region of Brazil. Under this arrangement, MIT agreed to establish a biotechnology center in the Amazon region, and make use of faculty resources to help develop a variety of appropriate economic activities for the region. In addition, the plan called for screening natural resources in the area for suitability for pharmaceutical use. Brazil had previously been wary of entering into bioprospecting agreements, but this one differed from the standard model in that development of any products with commercial potential was to take place inside Brazil, rather than in pharmaceutical industries outside the country.[80] Unfortunately, this agreement was never fully implemented, and MIT pulled the plug with the project in arrears when Brazil did not contribute the funding it agreed to provide.[81]

Other problems have befallen bioprospecting efforts, especially as concern for the interests of indigenous populations grows. In 2000 the Government of Mexico blocked the implementation of existing bioprospecting agreements out of concern that indigenous populations were being exploited by organizations that attempted to develop drugs based on indigenous knowledge.[82] The Convention on Biological Diversity acknowledges the power that states have to authorize permits for scientific collections of biodiversity, and more states appear to be using this power to prevent private deals from taking place that they determine may be detrimental to their populations.

In theory, bioprospecting agreements appear to be a way for states to earn funding from their biodiversity resources and thus increase the reasons to protect it. Certainly some of these agreements fulfill that function, though the examples given here suggest that initial optimism was likely overstated. There are dangers, additionally, in the widespread use of this approach. One is that the mechanism may be likely to be less profitable as it becomes more popular, in ways similar to debt-for-nature swaps. The more states there are with high levels of biodiversity that are willing to agree to enter into bioprospecting agreements, the less each state's negotiating advantage becomes. This is observed particularly with respect to the negotiation for royalties from the rainforest products that lead to successful drug development. Where once the expected range for royalties was between 1 per cent and 15 per cent,[83] royalties in some cases now range as low as 0.2 per cent.[84]

The usefulness of bioprospecting for biodiversity conservation may be geographically limited. Efforts to find uses for biological resources have taken place in the locations of highest biological diversity, such as tropical rainforests and coral reefs, which are controlled by sovereign states. But other promising locations for research, such as the deep seabed and Antarctica (where searches for organisms referred to as "extremophiles" for their ability to tolerate or thrive in environments that are unusually hot, cold, or subject to high pressure are conducted),[85] are explicitly outside the legal or practical control of states. The same incentive structure that can increase the likelihood that states with biodiversity resources will protect them because of the prospect of earning money from doing so may have the opposite effect when resources are not under sovereign control. International regulation of common spaces requires the consent of the governed, and those who want access may therefore refuse to participate in protection.

Another criticism of the mechanism is that even when royalties are substantial, little may go to the actual communities in which the bioprospecting takes place.[86] Eli Lilly receives profits of up to $100 million annually from the drugs developed from the rosy periwinkle and Madagascar receives none of these profits.[87] Even when local communities are expected to receive the profits, the timeframe is longer than may be ideal to help prevent more immediately profitable and less sustainable uses of forest resources. The first marketed product from Shaman's Amazon bioprospecting, a dietary supplement to treat AIDS diarrhea derived from the Amazonian *Croton lechleri* (or Dragon's Blood) tree, reached the market in 2000, nearly fifteen years after the company first began bioprospecting in the Amazon. This product appeared sooner than it otherwise would have because the company, dismayed by delays by the United States Food and Drug Administration, decided to offer it for sale as a dietary supplement,[88] a category with less strict regulation (but also probably lower profits). Even so, this timeline is not unusual; it is estimated that the average time for a pharmaceutical company to develop and bring a new drug to market is between twelve and fifteen years.[89] Some pharmaceutical companies, initially interested in bioprospecting deals, have recently been unable to accomplish their goals and have given up. Pharmaceutical giant Pfizer apparently tried to buy access to a three-hectare plot of land in Ecuador for $1 million, working on the details of the deal for nearly four years before Ecuador cancelled the deal without explaining why.[90]

A similar but more fundamental critique of the idea of bioprospecting is that it can become – either potentially or inherently – what people refer to as "biopiracy." Some object to the mere idea of patenting a life form or something derived from it, and thus suggest that any pharmaceutical companies that do so (such as Merck) are fundamentally engaged in illegitimate activity. Ironically, the criticism is more often applied to smaller firms like Shaman that rely specifically on indigenous knowledge to help identify local uses of natural products and thus increase the likelihood of finding effective medical treatments. These firms are seen as taking and patenting local knowledge, with the (generally unsubstantiated) critique that local people will no longer be able to use traditional remedies. It is true that these groups do not then profit from the sale of resulting products to the same extent that the companies that develop them do. While local people may earn income from gathering plant samples for bioprospecting agreements, the agreements themselves are ultimately between the government of the country and the pharmaceutical company, and thus indigenous people may not see the prospective future income from royalties.[91] The jury is out about whether the advantages of environmental protection outweigh the seeming unfairness of such a situation. More serious yet are the true biopirates – those who come to take samples without permission and then use them to develop and profit from drugs. The rights of ownership to genetic material agreed to in the CBD, which is one of the reasons for the reluctance of the United States to fully participate in the agreement, is an effort to prevent or mitigate such outcomes.

## Alternative Rainforest Products

From Ben and Jerry's "Rainforest Crunch" ice cream to Body Shop toiletries made from "sustainably" harvested rainforest product, the world has been made aware that products from the Amazon can be harvested in a way that can provide local economic benefits without destroying the ecosystem. The most influential academic argument in this effort came in a 1989 article in *Nature* in which the authors argued that rainforest land in the Amazon could be more economically valuable when sustainably harvested than when logged and converted to agricultural uses, even in the short run. They came to this conclusion after studying an area of Amazon rainforest in Peru, and concluded that production rates and world prices of rainforest products in the area would yield two to three times the value of the harvested timber of the region, and would be available over the long run if harvested sustainably.[92]

One of the best known efforts to put this observation into practice comes from the non-governmental organization Conservation International (CI). CI's "Sound Environmental Enterprise Development" program began in 1990 with the Tagua Initiative. This project focuses on encouraging sustainable harvesting of the tagua nut, which has properties much like ivory, and linking local suppliers with manufacturers nationally and internationally who can make use of products derived from this nut. In particular, CI worked on this project with the Fundacion de Capacitacion e Investigation para el Desarollo Socioambiental (CIDESA), an Ecuadorian community development organization, and with residents of a buffer zone of an Amazonian ecological reserve, from which the nuts could be harvested.[93] By 1995 the initiative had sold 1,600 tonnes of tagua nuts within Ecuador, and the price had increased 200 per cent. It had also involved more than 1,500 people and resulted in the sales, at that point, of more than 35 million buttons.[94] The government of the region in which the initiative operates agreed to create a reserve to protect forests and also refused to allow the clearing of forested land in the area for a banana plantation.[95] Other Conservation International programs work to bring alternative forestry products to market from eleven countries with tropical forest resources.[96]

One of the major recent developments in alternative rainforest products is the entry of local firms into the business. In Brazil, a company called Natura has become the largest cosmetics company in the country and is expanding internationally. It develops cosmetics with sustainably harvested products from the Amazon rainforest, gaining certification for its forest management programs from an NGO.[97]

There are dangers from the successes in creation of a demand for sustainably harvested forest products that less scrupulous organizations will use the marketing advantage of selling to environmentally concerned customers without taking the care that NGOs like Conservation International do to ensure the protection of the ecosystem from which such products are harvested. R. David Simpson suggests that "virtually anything that can be harvested from a diverse natural forest can be even more profitably cultivated in that same area by eradicating competing species."[98] While there is little evidence so far of widespread occurrence of this phenomenon with the tagua initiative, his example of such a danger, some have noted that a typical forest where tagua products are being harvested "bears little resemblance to an undisturbed primary forest."[99] Later studies have suggested that the economic advantage to the use of alternative rainforest products is less than half what the *Nature* article suggested.[100]

## Ecotourism

Opening the Amazon, or other areas of high biodiversity, to environmentally friendly tourism offers another option for earning income from the resource and thus increasing the advantages to making sure it is protected. Additionally, bringing people to threatened ecosystems can increase support by tourists for biodiversity conservation. Cited as the fasted growing form of tourism but without a generally accepted definition, ecotourism generally involves enticing people to visit (presumably in an ecologically responsible manner) the very places one hopes to protect from destruction. Some argue that "of all the economic alternatives contemplated for threatened habitats in the developing world, none appears to hold as much commercial promise as the business of accommodating people who wish to experience those habitats firsthand."[101]

Ecotourism in biodiversity hotspots is growing. The United Nations Environment Programme and Conservation International estimate that ecotourism in the most important and threatened ecosystems more than doubled between 1990 and 2003.[102] Some of the most widely practiced ecotourism takes place in Kenya, Costa Rica, and the Galapagos Islands of Ecuador,[103] but ecotourism in the Amazon region is increasing. Brazil in 1997 launched a $200 million program to help an ecotourism industry develop in the Amazon region. At that point, Latin American states overall had invested approximately $21 billion to develop ecotourism.[104] Tourism in Brazil increased by more than 300 per cent during the 1990s.[105]

There are numerous examples of specific ecotourism programs in the Amazon region, many of which appear genuinely to return money to the local community in which they take place, and may have the effect of increasing concern for biodiversity protection among those who take part in them. One Brazilian example is the Silves Association for Environmental and Cultural Preservation, which began an ecotourism program when the area's fishing industry had overharvested the fish stocks. The funding from ecotourism goes to fund ranger patrols, habitat restoration, and education for the local fishers.[106] In the Ecuadorian Amazon, the Kapawi lodge aims to help an indigenous tribe protect its lands and earn an income, while protecting its local culture. This venture is jointly run by a for-profit tourism agency and the local tribe's federation. The lodge was built by the local people using materials from the forest, and people who visit learn about both the local ecosystem and culture.[107] For every ecotourism project that carefully protects the area in which it operates and returns funding to the local community, however, there are plenty that prey on the desire of tourists to visit nature, without actually protecting it along the way.[108]

Ecotourism is another mechanism that can sow the seeds of its own demise. In essence it succeeds when it is profitable, but profit as a driving motive can overtake environmental protection. Any visitors to endangered habitats can have an impact on the ecosystems, and large numbers of visitors create problems of erosion and solid waste. At its extreme, tourism in fragile ecosystems may sufficiently impact the environment, or even simply the ability to enjoy being "alone" with nature, that it can lead to either a total destruction of the area or a decline in true opportunities for ecotourism.[109] Moreover, the infrastructure needed to make ecotourism desirable and thus profitable, such as roads into remote areas, can then create opportunities for depletion of the resources of the area by commercial actors, such as loggers more able to reach virgin forest.[110]

Other concerns expressed are for the well-being of local people in remote areas. While they may gain income from ecotourism, and thus be able to avoid engaging in (or being subject to) activities that destroy the ecosystems on which they have traditionally depended, their own cultural diversity may suffer. Particularly in previously unvisited areas of the Amazon, local peoples become part of a cash economy that they may not have previously participated in, and are exposed to Western lifestyles they may not have previously encountered.[111] While it is as paternalistic to deny indigenous people the opportunity to change their lifestyles if they want to as it is to impose a new way of life upon them, this potential impact of ecotourism poses ethical concerns about its benefits for the very people it may be intended to help.

# International Aid

Aid from external governments, non-governmental organizations, or international organizations can provide funding for study or conservation of biodiversity, as seen in a number of such efforts underway in the Amazon region. Often this aid is in conjunction with some of the abovementioned private initiatives or international agreements, but is worth mentioning separately nonetheless.

The Global Environment Facility (GEF), established in 1990 with provision of funding for biodiversity conservation as one of its four original focus areas, was later also designated the funding mechanism for the Convention on Biological Diversity. The GEF receives its funding from developed states. The largest portion of its funding has gone to address issues of biodiversity. As of 2005, $1.89 billion had been given in GEF grants for biodiversity-related projects which had been matched by an additional $3.8 billion in cofinancing from governments, non-governmental organizations, and other development agencies.[112]

This funding included not only projects and "enabling activities" for states (including those in the Amazon region) to do national biodiversity surveys and create national biodiversity plans under the CBD, but also a number of projects focused specifically on protecting Amazonian biodiversity. These include a project on the Conservation and Sustainable Use of Biodiversity by the Indigenous Ashanika Population in Peru at a cost of $1.55 million, and an Amazon-wide "Regional Strategy for the Conservation and Sustainable Use of Natural Resources in the Amazon," funded at $5.35 million.[113] The most ambitious is the Amazon Regional Protected Areas project, a joint undertaking by the Global Environment Facility, the World Bank, the NGO World Wide Fund for Nature (WWF) and the Brazilian government. This ten-year project was launched at the 2002 World Summit on Sustainable Development, and aims to protect 50 million hectares of Brazilian land in all twenty-three Amazonian eco-regions.[114] The parties have committed to spend $89.35 million on this ambitious project.[115]

Other governmental funding for Amazonian biodiversity comes from governments outside the GEF framework. In 1991 the G-7, European Union, and the Netherlands pledged $250 million for a "Pilot Program for the Protection of the Tropical Forests" to be managed by the World Bank. This project was intended to increase education about the contribution of the Amazon to global emissions of greenhouse gases, to demonstrate the potential compatibility between economic and environmental objectives in tropical forests, and protect genetic resources.[116]

Given that uncertainty both of the number and types of species and about the role of biodiversity in other environmental issues has been a stumbling block in efforts to protect ecosystems, many international programs attempt to provide financial or technical aid to help answer these questions. One important such initiative in the Amazon is the Large Scale Biosphere-Atmosphere Experiment in Amazonia (LBA). This project is an international effort to understand the "climatological, ecological, biogeochemical and hydrological systems" of the Amazon region. The project operated between 1996 and 2005, and used satellite data to measure environmental changes and impacts from various activities. This project was headed by Brazil's Ministry of Science and Technology, but received assistance from a wide variety of states and relied on satellite images provided by many sources.[117]

# Science, Risk, and Uncertainty

A major underlying factor in the protection of biodiversity is uncertainty. We simply do not know how many species there are worldwide, or how resilient they are to threats. Despite that lack of knowledge, however, uncertainty has not been a major political difficulty in addressing biodiversity. No one disagrees with the need to better understand biodiversity resources, and much of the initial cooperation has involved the requirement that states evaluate their own biodiversity and create and report on their own plans for protecting it. Much international funding has gone into supporting this process of research.

Further, the scientific research underpinning biodiversity has been relatively less politicized than in other issues examined in this book. In addition, even though the specifics of species vulnerability may not be completely understood, the basic causal links between cutting down rainforests (for example) and the decreasing abundance of endemic species in an area are not especially controversial. The debates that transpire may concern the prioritization of agriculture or roads over biodiversity, but do not generally question the causal relationships.

There is, however, some concern that the Convention on Biological Diversity has made international research on biodiversity more difficult because of the protections it grants individual states to determine access to their resources. Efforts to prevent biopiracy spill over into a distrust of basic research, and scientists report that gaining visas for basic biodiversity research has become harder, and more costly, under rules states have implemented under the CBD regime.[118]

# Non-Governmental Actors

Non-state actors have played central roles both in threatening and in protecting biodiversity in the Amazon region and more generally. While the threats to biodiversity by non-state actors might be the most apparent, the role of conserving biodiversity is especially notable. As Cord Jakobeit put it in his discussion of debt-for-nature swaps, non-governmental actors are "leading the way"[119] in addressing biodiversity protection. While states hold the trump card – their sovereignty – in allowing or denying access to their biodiversity, it is often both environmental organizations and various industries that are more able to offer states incentives to protect their biodiversity than can other states. This experience suggests the importance of non-state actors, not only in influencing the behavior of states in which they operate, but in making reasonably direct changes in the environmental policies of other states.

## Industry

Much of the specific activity detrimental to biodiversity conservation is undertaken by industry actors, although they operate within governmental structures that create the framework for land use. Some industry actors have also been influential in efforts to protect biodiversity.

While to some extent the characterization of industry as responsible for environmental degradation applies to most environmental issue areas, it is particularly relevant for some of the threats to biodiversity in tropical rainforests. The cattle ranching that is the primary cause of deforestation in the Brazilian Amazon is industrial scale export ranching. And, although subsistence farming is the second biggest cause of deforestation, commercial agriculture is increasing, and commercial logging is also a significant contributor. These activities, moreover, result in the creation of roads and settlements that increase access by others into previously forested areas, and thereby help perpetuate destruction of the ecosystem.

Oil exploitation in the Amazon has been increasingly controversial, most recently in Ecuador, where indigenous groups have protested against the actions of multinational oil firms. Accessing this oil may represent Ecuador's best opportunity for funding with which to pay off its foreign debt, but at serious risk to the biodiversity of the region and the lives of local inhabitants. The International Monetary Fund conditioned a loan to Ecuador in 2000 on Ecuador's passage of a law that would permit foreign companies to build and operate pipelines.[120] Major protests in Ecuador, along with court cases in foreign courts, point to the controversy caused by this kind of activity.

Industry has also participated in some of the innovative efforts to create incentives for biodiversity conservation, most notably the idea of bioprospecting. Large pharmaceutical corporations in search of new products are the entities likely to have the financial and practical resources to pay for access to biodiversity resources to screen them for their usefulness. On a smaller scale it has been businesses eager to create a reputation as socially responsible that have worked to market alternative rainforest products. Though these arrangements by industry actors on behalf of biodiversity have not been without controversy, they represent a novel effort by industries that gain from biodiversity to contribute to protecting it.

## NGOs

Non-governmental organizations have played several important roles in biodiversity conservation: raising awareness of the problem (which includes basic research), and promoting or implementing specific solutions. Many of the major international environmental non-governmental organizations have their origins in efforts to protect species or land. Conservation organizations have frequently focused on endangered species, particularly those that some refer to as "charismatic megafauna," as high-profile ways to tap public interest in environmental protection. It has been more difficult to garner public concern for biodiversity conservation, a more nebulous concept, but many of the organizations that focus in public on species undertake action on behalf of ecosystems or biodiversity more generally.

One important role of some of these organizations has been monitoring of biodiversity and of measures to protect it, both generally and in the Amazon in particular. The World Conservation Monitoring Center (now a part of the United Nations Environment Programme, but originally an independent organization) created the Biodiversity Management program, designed to help states produce sufficient information to create national strategies to assess and protect biodiversity. On other biodiversity-related issues, NGOs such as the organization TRAFFIC have been invaluable players in the effort to monitor trade in endangered species. Concern about biodiversity, in the Amazon and beyond, reaches across borders and past governments, as a wide variety of actors contribute to efforts to better understand and protect it.

Many of the private solutions to the problem of biodiversity conservation, discussed above, are primarily undertaken by NGOs. Conservation organizations have been central to the creation of first-generation debt-for-nature swaps, the creation of alternative rainforest products (in cooperation with for-profit businesses), and ecotourism projects.

# The Role of Developing States

Developing states have had a fair amount of influence in determining the shape of some biodiversity policies. Much of the world's biodiversity is located in developing states, for two reasons. One is simply that warmer areas tend to have greater biodiversity, and more developing states are located in warmer areas. But the "development" that separates states conceptually has historically been responsible for the loss of biodiversity. Biodiversity already lost in the developed world is unrecoverable, so the focus now is primarily on biodiversity loss in the developing world. The influence of developing states in international negotiations on this issue has been tempered somewhat by the structure of the issue area. Developed states are less concerned about biodiversity collectively than about some of the other issues examined in this book, although it is also the case that most of the pressure internationally for biodiversity conservation has come from developed states. But states are not prevented from protecting their own biodiversity resources by the lack of action by others, in the same way they would be prevented from successfully protecting the ozone layer over their territories if some states remained outside the regulatory process. Any given developing state is less central to the cooperation process, and therefore likely to have less influence. The primary source of influence of developing states is their control over their own physical territory and access to it. These characteristics come largely from the structure of the biodiversity issue, as discussed below.

In negotiations on the CBD, developing countries won the guarantee of "new and additional financial resources" that will be used to "enable developing country Parties to meet the agreed full incremental costs to them of implementing measures which fulfill the obligations of this Convention."[121] They had less success, however, in determining how that funding would be distributed. The developing countries did not want the GEF to be the financial mechanism for the Convention on Biological Diversity, but the CBD adopted the GEF nonetheless. Developing country parties to the CBD were able to gain a stronger pledge for technology transfer than parties to other international agreements had accomplished. Article 16 addresses a wide variety of types of access to technology that are promised to developing countries, and indicates that transfer of technology is "essential … for the attainment of the objectives of this Convention." As one developing country negotiator said, "we have the biodiversity, they have the technology."[122] In addition, that the first protocol negotiated concerned biosafety, at the behest of developing states and the reluctance of many developed states, suggests the negotiating power of these states on this issue.

# International Environmental Cooperation

## Issue Structure

Biodiversity is to a large extent a private good with externalities. It is both subtractable and excludable. Subtractability comes because when the resources are consumed or destroyed they are not available for use by others. Excludability has to do with the characteristics of the resource. With the exception of a few migratory species (or ecosystems that exist at the edges of bordering states or in the ocean), species exist within one geographic area, over which states have sovereign control. On the whole states can exclude others from the benefits of their biodiversity. Note, though, that because of excludability, the character of subtractability shifts as well – it would be difficult for someone outside of the state where the resource exists to consume it unsustainably. Although the health of an ecosystem may be impacted by atmospheric pollution originating elsewhere and it is conceivable that this type of destruction could be used as a threat, it is a much less direct form of consumption than subtractability usually implies.

The issue exhibits many of the predicted outcomes for an issue that is both subtractable and excludable. We see a number of private agreements entered into by those countries with the greatest degree of biodiversity. Such agreements have done more to protect biodiversity so far than the large-scale multilateral effort, the Convention on Biological Diversity, has. These private deals have resulted in greater benefits for the developing countries entering into them than alternate forms of biodiversity protection would have. Countries without important biodiversity (and in the case of debt-for-nature swaps, without available discounted debt) have been unable to benefit from these types of arrangements, however. The subtractable nature of the resource does give some overall power to developing countries as well, and that has resulted in some strong language on technology transfer in the CBD, and negotiation priorities that first favor issues of less direct consequence to protection of biodiversity but that are of particular concern to developing countries.

## Implementation and Effectiveness

It is difficult to evaluate the implementation of efforts to protect biodiversity. The CBD does not require much in the way of specific protection of biodiversity; the implementation of vague commitments to conserve biodiversity cannot reasonably be measured. The underlying scientific uncertainty is central to the inability to evaluate efforts to protect biodiversity: if we do not know how many species there are and what their conditions were prior to CBD-led efforts to protect them, it is impossible to judge the impact of the agreement. It will be interesting to oberve the CBD's efforts to evaluate progress toward its 2010 goal, to determine whether the organization can truly ascertain the overall level of protection of biodiversity.

We can begin to judge some of the private efforts in their relevant contexts: do commitments to protect land in exchange for forgiveness of debt lead to actual conservation? Initial evidence is mixed but suggests that with the exception of some of the early DFN swaps that did not carefully define the conservation to be achieved states have lived up to their conservation commitments. Other efforts, such as the marketing of sustainably-harvested rainforest products, ecotourism, or even bioprospecting, are harder to judge. In all of these cases, moreover, the benefits to a specific local area may be apparent, but the question of the overall condition of biodiversity in light of them is harder to judge. For instance, if a state agrees to protect land in one area but diverts the industrial activity that might have taken place there to another location, is it a net gain for biodiversity? If ecosystems in one state are protected well, but elsewhere they are destroyed, has the diversity and range of species worldwide been improved? The goals and methods of biodiversity conservation are sufficiently unclear that it is currently unrealistic to judge their effectiveness in any systematic way.

## Conclusion

The differences between biodiversity conservation, which may conceptually be part of the common heritage of humankind, and climate change, ozone depletion, and whaling, which are truly global commons issues, is that biodiversity protection can simultaneously be accomplished and avoided by different states. No one state can undermine biodiversity protection worldwide, nor can any one state accomplish it fully.

Biodiversity protection has implications for a wide range of both local and global environmental issues. Locally, protecting ecosystems helps prevent soil degradation, erosion, and desertification. Globally, forests (as well as other plants) are carbon sinks that may mitigate human impact on the climate. In fact, a U.S. "Greening of the Globe" initiative proposed in 2000 by then President Clinton specifically to reduce greenhouse gas emissions included a proposed $37 million in debt-for-nature swaps, suggesting that biodiversity protection can help address other global environmental problems. Likewise, increases in such transboundary pollution problems as acid rain in Latin American can harm biodiversity in the Amazon. And biodiversity loss is more broadly associated with the very underpinnings of modern environmental problems: increased industrialization, population pressure, and international economic incentives. It thus serves as a virtual canary in the coal mine, indicating the health of the global environment.

## Notes

1 Peter Bunyard, "Eradicating the Amazon Rainforests Will Wreak Havoc on Climate," *The Ecologist* 29(2) (March–April 1999): 81–84.

2 Secretariat of the Convention on Biological Diversity, *Global Biodiversity Outlook 2* (Montreal: CBD Secretariat, 2006).

3 Millennium Ecosystem Assessment, *Ecosystems and Human Wellbeing: Biodiversity Synthesis* (Washington D.C.: World Resources Institute, 2005), 5.

4  Secretariat of the Convention on Biological Diversity, 42.

5  Convention on Biological Diversity (1992), preamble.

6  Rio Declaration (1992), Principle 2. Similar wording is found in the Stockholm Declaration from 1972 and elsewhere in customary international law.

7  David R. Simpson, "The Price of Biodiversity," *Issues in Science and Technology* 15(3) (Spring 1999): 65–70.

8  Bolivia, Brazil, Colombia, Ecuador, Guyana, Peru, Suriname, and Venezuela are generally thought to be the states that contain part of the Amazon rainforest. The forest itself is defined to some extent as the watershed of the Amazon river, leading to some disagreement about where its actual boundaries lie.

9  Norman Myers, Russel A. Mittermeier, Cristina G. Da Foseca, A. B. Gustavo, and Jennifer Kent, "Biodiversity Hotspots for Conservation Priorities," *Nature* 403 (24 February 2000): 853–58.

10  World Resources Institute, *World Resources 1992–1993* (New York: Oxford University Press, 1992), 128.

11  Mohammed Dore and Jorge Nogueira, "The Amazon Rain Forest, Sustainable Development, and the Biodiversity Convention: A Political Economy Perspective," *Ambio* 23(8) (December 1994): 492.

12  Bunyard, 81–84.

13  FAO, "Incentive to Curb Deforestation Needed to Counter Climate Change," Press Release, 9 December 2005, http://www.fao.org/newsroom/en/news/2005/1000176/index.html.

14  Peter H. Raven and Jeffrey A. McNeely, "Biological Extinction: Its Scope and Meaning for Us," in Lakshman D. Guruswamy and Jeffrey A. McNeely, eds., "Protection of Global Biodiversity: Converging Strategies" (Durham, N.C.: Duke University Press, 1998), 15.

15  Ibid., 20.

16  Rachel McCleary, "Development Strategies in Conflict: Brazil and the Future of the Amazon," *Pew Case Studies in International Affairs 501* (Washington D.C.: Institute for the Study of Diplomacy, 1990), 6.

17  Alex Bugge, "Farms Destroying Lungs of the World," *Courier Mail*, 20 May 2005, 19.

18  Rhett A. Butler, "Amazon Destruction," http://www.mongabay.com/about.htm.

19  McCleary, 6.

20  Norman Myers, "The Anatomy of Environmental Action: The Case of Tropical Deforestation," in Andrew Hurrell and Benedict Kingsbury, eds., *The International Politics of the Environment: Actors, Interests, and Institutions* (Oxford: Clarendon Press, 1992), 432.

21  Laura Murphy, Richard Bilsborrow, and Francisco Pinchon, "Poverty and Prosperity Among Migrant Settlers in the Amazon Rainforest Frontier of Ecuador," *Journal of Development Studies* 34(2) (December 1997): 35–66.

22 McCleary, 10.

23 Ibid., 11.

24 Margaret E. Keck and Kathryn Sikkink, *Activists Beyond Borders: Advocacy Networks in International Politics* (Ithaca: Cornell University Press, 1998), 137–40.

25 McCleary, 10.

26 Ibid., 8.

27 Ibid., 9.

28 Andrew Hurrell, "The Politics of Amazonian Deforestation," *Journal of Latin American Studies* 23 (1991): 203.

29 Myers, 444.

30 Ibid., 445.

31 McCleary, 7.

32 Alex Shoumatoff, *The World Is Burning* (Boston: Little, Brown, and Company, 1990), 85.

33 Myers, 443.

34 Dore and Nogueira, 496; McCleary, 6.

35 Myers, 434.

36 Graciela Chichilnisky, "Sustainable Development and North–South Trade," in Lakshman D. Guruswamy and Jeffrey A. McNeely, eds., *Protection of Global Biodiversity: Converging Strategies* (Durham, N.C.: Duke University Press, 1998), 105.

37 Dore and Nogueira, 494.

38 Charles Arden-Clarke, "South–North Terms of Trade, Environmental Protection and Sustainable Development," *International Environmental Affairs* 4(2) (Spring 1992), 123.

39 Shoumatoff, 84.

40 Dore and Nogueira, 493.

41 A. Sarkar, "Debt-Relief for Environment: Experience and Issues," *Journal of Environment and Development* 3(1) (1994): 124.

42 Moritz Kraemer and Jorg Hartmann, "Policy Responses to Tropical Deforestation: Are Debt-for-Nature Swaps Appropriate?" *Journal of Environment and Development* 2(2): 41–65.

43 FAO, Global Forest Resources Assessment 2005 (Rome: FAO, 2005).

44 International Tropical Timber Agreement (1994), Article 1(d).

45 International Tropical Timber Agreement (1994), Article 21(1).

46 Cited in Edith Brown Weiss, "The Five International Treaties: A Living History," in Edith Brown Weiss and Harold Jacobson, *Engaging Countries* (Cambridge, Mass.: MIT Press, 1998), 124.

47 CBD 1992, Article 7(a through d).

48 CBD 1992, Article 6(a).

49  Johannesburg Plan of Implementation, Section IV (44).

50  CBD 1992, Article 15.

51  Cartagena Protocol on Biosafety to the Convention on Biological Diversity (2002), Article 3(g) and (h).

52  Cartagena Protocol, Articles 7 through 9.

53  Cartagena Protocol, Article 15(1).

54  Robert B. Horsch and Robert Fraley, "Biotechnology Can Help Reduce the Loss of Biodiversity," in Guruswamy and McNeely, 49–65.

55  Thomas Lovejoy, "Aid Debtor Nation's Ecology," *New York Times*, 4 October 1984, 31.

56  Cord Jakobeit, "Nonstate Actors Leading the Way: Debt-for-Nature Swaps," in Robert O. Keohane and Marc A. Levy, eds., *Institutions for Environmental Aid* (Cambridge, Mass.: MIT Press, 1997), 137.

57  Jakobeit, 128.

58  Ibid., 136–37.

59  Ibid., 140.

60  United States Congress, House of Representatives, 105th Congress, "Tropical Forest Conservation Act of 1998," *Report 105-443*.

61  USAID, "Tropical Forest Conservation Act (TCFA) Program Descriptions," http://www.usaid.gov/our_work/environment/forestry/tfca_descs.html

62  Janeen Klinger, "Debt-for-Nature Swaps and the Limits to International Cooperation on Behalf of the Environment," *Environmental Politics* 3(2): 241.

63  B. Thapa, "Debt-for-Nature Swaps: An Overview," *International Journal of Sustainable Development and World Ecology*," 5(4): 260.

64  Rhona Mahoney, "Debt-for-Nature Swaps: Who Really Benefits?" *The Ecologist* 22(3): 97–102.

65  A. G. Bruner, R. E. Gullison, R. E. Rice, and G. A. B. da Fonseca, "Effectiveness of Parks in Protecting Tropical Diversity," *Science* 291 (5 January 2001): 125–27.

66  Sarkar, 123–36.

67  Kraemer and Hartmann, 41–65.

68  Thapa, 260.

69  Roque Sevilla, "Banks, Debt, and Development – II," *International Environmental Affairs* 2(2) (1990): 150–52.

70  Diana Page, "Debt-for-Nature Swaps: Experience Gained, Lessons Learned," *International Environmental Affairs* 1(4) (1989): 286.

71  "Indigenous People's Knowledge: Pharmaceuticals and their Business," *Nuestra Amazonia* (July 1996): 7.

72  D. J. Newman, G. M. Cragg, and K. M. Snader, "Natural Products as Sources of New Drugs over the Period 1981–2002," *Journal of Natural Products* 66(7) (2003): 1022–37.

73 Julia Jabour Green, "Report of the Workshop on Bioprospecting in the High Seas," University of Otago, Dunedin, New Zealnad, 28–29 November, 2003, available at http://www.fish.govt.nz/current/deepsea/workshop-report-bioprospecting-in-the-high-seas.doc, 2.

74 Christopher J. Hunter, "Sustainable Bioprospecting: Using Private Contracts and International Legal Principles and Policies to Conserve Medicinal Materials," *Boston College Environmental Affairs Law Review* 25 (1997): 130.

75 C. Joyce, *Earthly Goods: Medicine Hunting in the Rainforest* (Boston: Little, Brown, and Co, 1994).

76 Michele Zebich-Knos, "Preserving Biodiversity in Costa Rica: The Case of the Merck–INBio Agreement," *Journal of Environment and Development* 6(2) (June 1997): 180–86.

77 John Eberlee, "Assessing the Benefits of Bioprospecting in Latin America," *IDRC Reports*, 21 January 2000, http://www.idrc.ca/en/ev-5571-201-1-DO_TOPIC.html.

78 International Development Research Centre, "Shaman Pharmaceuticals: Socially Responsible Drug Development," 25 October 1996, http://idrc.ca/books/reports/1996/30-02e.html.

79 Roger Alex Clapp and Carolyn Crook, "Drowning in the Magic Well: Shaman Pharmaceuticals and the Elusive Value of Traditional Knowledge," *Journal of Environment and Development* 11(1) (March 2002): 79–102.

80 Ricard Bonalume Neto, "MIT's Amazon Outpost," *Nature* 365 (9 September 1993): 101.

81 Anthony Sisky, Project Coordinator, MIT, email message received 6 June 2001.

82 "Political Uncertainty Halts Bioprospecting in Mexico," *Nature* 408 (2000): 278.

83 S. Watson, "Are Licensing Agreements Key to Technology Transfer?" *Legal Intelligencer*, 14 June, 1994, 13ff. (Lexis/Nexis).

84 Joseph Henry Vogel, *The Successful Use of Economic Instruments to Foster Sustainable Use of Biodiversity* (Quito: Facultad Latinoamericana de Ciencias Sociales, 1996), 3.

85 Salvatore Arico and Charlotte Sapin, Bioprospecting of Genetic Resources in the Deep Seabed: Scientific, Legal, and Policy Aspects, UNU-IAS Report (Tokyo: UNU-IAS, 2005).

86 Douglas Southgate, *Alternatives for Habitat Protection* (Washington D.C.: Interamerican Development Bank, 1997), 36.

87 Robert L. Ostergood, J. Matthew Tubin, and Jordan Altman, "Stealing from the Past: Globalisation, Strategic Formation and the Use of Indiggenous Intellectual Property in the Biotechnology Industry," *Third World Quarterly* 22(4) (2001): 651. It should be noted, however, that Eli Lilly did not specifically have a bioprospecting agreement with Madagascar.

88 Shaman Botanicals, "Shaman: About Us," http://www.shamanbotanicals.com/aumaster.htm (2001).

89 Katy Moran, "Compensating Forest-Dwelling Communities for Drug Discovery: The World of the Healing Forest Conservancy," *Unasylva* 47 (1996): 42.

90 Christopher Locke, "Forest Pharmers Go Bioprospecting," *Red Herring*, (12 April 2001), http://www.redherring.com.

91 Jennifer Pepall, "Putting a Price on Indigenous Knowledge," 7 July 1998 (International Development Research Centre), http://www.idrc.ca/books/reports/1996/30-01e.html.

92 Alwyn Gentry, Charles Peters, and Robert Mendelsohn, "Valuation of the Amazonian Rainforest," *Nature* 339 (29 June 1989): 655–56.

93 United Nations Environment Programme, "Partnerships for Sustainable Development: The Role of Business and Industry" (London: Flashprint Enterprises, for UNEP and the Prince of Wales Business Leaders Forum, 1994), 13–16.

94 Conservation International, "Rainforest Buttons Get Wider Distribution," press release, 14 March 1995, http://conservation.org/WEB/NEWS/pressrel/95-0314.htm.

95 United Nations Environment Programme, "Partnerships for Sustainable Development," 14.

96 Conservation International, "Agroforestry and Forest Products" (n.d.), http://www.conservation.org/xp/CIWEB/programs/enterprises/.

97 Cristen Bolan, "Natura Sustains its Growth," *Global Cosmetic Industry* (November 2005), 22–23.

98 R. David Simpson, "The Price of Biodiversity," *Issues in Science and Technology* 15(3) (1999): 68.

99 Southgate, 25.

100 Simpson, 65–70; Christopher B. Barrett and Travis J. Lybbert, "Is Bioprospecting a Viable Strategy for Conserving Tropical Ecosystems?" *Ecological Economics* 34 (2000): 293–300.

101 Southgate, 7.

102 Christian Amodeo, "Tourists Flock to Nature's Hotspots," *Geographical* 17(12) (December 2003): 97.

103 Megan Epler Wood, "Global Solutions: An Ecotourism Society," in Tensie Whelan, ed., *Nature Tourism: Managing for the Environment* (Washington D.C.: Island Press, 1991), 201.

104 Martha Honey, *Ecotourism and Sustainable Development* (Washington D.C. and Covelo, Calif.: Island Press, 1999), 18.

105 Amodeo, 97.

106 Abigail Rome, "Amazon Adventure," *E* 10(2) (March 1999): 48.

107 Jennifer Bogo and Tracey C. Rembert, "Close to Nature," *E* 10(6) (November 1999): 46.

108 Honey, 32–59.

109 Tensie Whelan, "Ecotourism and Its Role in Sustainable Development," in Tensie Whelan, ed., *Nature Tourism: Managing for the Environment* (Washington D.C.: Island Press, 1991), 11.

110 Southgate, 1.

111 Ray Ashton, "The Natural Alternative: Planning for Success in Latin American Ecotourism Projects," *Latin Finance* 67 (May 1995): 16.

112 GEF Secretariat, "Focal Areas," http://thegef.org/Projects/Focal_Areas/focal_areas.html.

113 GEF Secretariat, "Project Database" (n.d.), http://gefonline.org/projectList.cfm.

114 World Bank, "Brazil to Triple Amount of Protected Amazon Rainforest over 10 Years," 5 September 2002.

115 GEF Secretariat, "Project Database."

116 Thelma Krug, "Space Technology and Environmental Monitoring in Amazonia," *Journal of International Affairs* 51(2) (Spring 1998): 655–75.

117 Oak Ridge National Laboratory, "LBA," http://www-eosdis.ornl.gov/LBA/misc_amazon.html.

118 Andrew C. Revkin, "Biologists Sought a Treaty; Now They Fault It," *New York Times*, 7 May 2002, 1.

119 Jakobeit, 127.

120 Matt Finer and Leda Huta, "Yasuni Blues: the IMF, Ecuador and Coerced Oil Exploitation," *Multinational Monitor* 26(5–6) (May–June 2005): 29–33.

121 Convention on Biological Diversity (1992), Article 20(2).

122 Kal Raustiala and David G. Victor, "Biodiversity Since Rio – The Future of the Convention on Biological Diversity," *Environment* 38(4) (1996): 18–20, 37–45.

# 9 Acid Rain and Regional Transboundary Air Pollution Agreements

## Chapter Outline

The Environmental Problem
Regulatory History
Science, Risk, and Uncertainty
Non-Governmental Actors
The Role of Developing Countries
Issues of International Cooperation
Conclusion

*If acid rain controls were cheap, there wouldn't be any disagreement on the science.*
William Ruckleshaus, EPA Administrator[1]

Acid rain is the same phenomenon, with minor variations, in most places it occurs. Industrial activity, such as transportation or power generation, emits air pollutants like sulphur dioxide ($SO_2$) nitrogen oxides ($NO_x$), ammonia ($NH_3$) and volatile organic compounds (VOCs). These and related substances are changed chemically to sulphuric and nitric acids, and carried by air currents until they are deposited in areas away from where the pollutants were initially generated.[2] Wind patterns may affect the way pollution is distributed, characteristics of the natural environment may vary in their ability to absorb acidification without suffering serious damage, and the types of industrial activities practiced in a given region may influence the components of the air pollutant precursors to acidification. But in general the problem is a common and commonly experienced effect of industrial activity.

It is a fundamentally different type of atmospheric pollution problem, for several reasons, than ozone depletion or global climate change. These differences have important implications for the ways it has been addressed internationally. In terms of the nature of the problem, the primary difference is that it has a directional character. How affected a country is by acid rain has everything to do with prevailing wind patterns and its own geographical characteristics, and, most importantly, where the emissions come from. Unlike ozone depletion where a ton of ozone-depleting substances emitted anywhere in the world has the same impact on the ozone layer as the same amount emitted anywhere else, location matters for acid rain. States can be net importers or net exporters of acidifying substances, depending on whether they receive more acid rain than they send out on wind currents, or vice versa. This directionality has enormous impacts for political efforts to address the problem.

Another important difference is the role of science and uncertainty. While the causes and effects of the environmental problem are now well understood and there is little uncertainty about most aspects of it, understanding the phenomenon that has come to be called acid rain took a different, and in many ways more traditional, path, than that of more global atmospheric pollutants. While the impact of coal burning on acid levels in the air was known as of the 1850s and the term "acid rain" coined as early as 1872,[3] the modern discussion of transboundary acid rain began in Sweden in the 1950s and 1960s. Swedish scientists monitoring lakes over decades began to notice an increase in lake acidity. While in 1968 a scientist argued the likely cause was air pollutants travelling long distances from other areas of Europe,[4] this assertion was widely disputed, and the true cause of acidification of the Scandinavian ecosystem not fully understood for more than a decade. The initial scientific discussion broke down into at least two separate questions that had to be addressed separately: whether sulphur dioxide could travel long distances, and whether its deposition from the air could harm local ecosystems.[5] This environmental issue thus was addressed beginning with the observation of an environmental problem and leading to the search for its cause, followed by a regulatory process, a model quite different from some other current international environmental issues.

Also interesting, however, is that despite the similarity of the acid rain problems experienced in different geographic areas and shared scientific understanding, the regulatory process to address acid rain has followed a somewhat different timetable and pattern in the various locations where it has been addressed. The most serious problems of acidification, and the most developed efforts to address acid rain, are in North America and Europe. The process in North America has taken a longer period of time and resulted in generally weaker obligations.

The specifics of the obligations differ as well. In the European experience a wider range of pollutants, including those that are not directly related to acid rain, has been regulated. The European experience has also, though imperfectly, addressed the issue of targeting emission reductions to the sources that cause the most environmental damage, based on a consideration of a combination of emissions, wind patterns and natural vulnerability of areas to acidification. Recently the European rules have made an effort to regulate multiple pollutants in conjunction with each other. Both processes allow a lot of latitude in how specific reduction obligations will be implemented domestically. Perhaps not surprisingly the ways that Canada and the United States have chosen to reduce their transboundary air pollution allow for a greater use of market mechanisms than do those undertaken in Europe. These differences exist despite the fact that the United States and Canada participated in the European regulatory process and are signatories to the European framework convention to protect against acid rain and some of its protocols, and despite the fact that they were taking place at roughly the same time and with access to the same scientific information.

The European cooperation that has resulted from this acid rain regulation has been impressive. States have changed their positions on emissions cuts and abatement policies more generally, in part due to public pressure and in part due to a scientific process that made the effects of the problem more clearly visible to those who did not realize they were suffering from it. The directional nature of the problem, however, makes the political dynamics of cooperation more difficult, as those who cause but do not suffer as much from the problem are less willing to change their behavior than those who experience the greatest impacts. This dynamic is even more apparent in the North American context. The power of those who want to resist regulation based on self-interest is thus clear in this instance, and an important lesson to remember in global environmental politics.

Because acid rain is a problem of industrialization, it is spreading to new geographic areas as they industrialize more intensively. Though there are no other strong regional agreements in other regions to address acid rain, the problem is being felt in Asia, and new cooperative programs are emerging that will have different types of challenges because of the characteristics of the region. In addition, new evidence suggests that acidifying substances can travel transcontinentally, much further than previously known. It will be interesting to see whether this new information influences the shape of international regulation. Examining the different regional efforts to address a common problem allows for analysis of the different characteristics that might affect the shape of international regulation.

## The Environmental Problem

The precursor pollutants to acid rain can stay in the atmosphere for up to twenty days and can travel several hundred kilometers or more. The acidity, or pH, of rainfall varies naturally to some extent, but industrial activities have greatly changed the composition of precipitation in many areas.[6] Acidification can also be deposited in dry form. Moreover, there is something like a tipping point for acidification in many contexts; until a threshold point additional acid deposition may cause little damage, but afterward small additional deposition can be responsible for extensive environmental damage.

There are a number of environmental problems that result from acid deposition. The pH of lakes and other bodies of water can be lowered to the point where they cannot sustain aquatic life. Forests can suffer damage from acid deposition. Soils can be made more acidic which, if they do not have substances with which to buffer the acid, can influence plant growth. Acid rain is also corrosive and has caused damage to buildings, statues, and cultural artifacts.

## Regulatory History

International discussion of European acid rain began at the United Nations Conference on the Human Environment in Stockholm in 1972 at the behest of Scandinavian states, although no actual negotiations about the problem took place at the conference. Following Stockholm, the Organization for Economic Cooperation and Development (OECD) decided to study the issue, in part through monitoring. A report from this process published in 1977 suggested that long-range transport of air pollutants took place and had significant impacts on many of the European countries involved in the study.[7]

Meanwhile, diplomatic efforts following the 1975 Helsinki Conference on Security and Cooperation in Europe were searching for a low-politics issue on which East and West Europe could negotiate a cooperative agreement. The United Nations Economic Commission for Europe (ECE) suggested that an environmental issue would provide a suitable avenue for negotiation, and ultimately selected acid rain.[8] These negotiations were thus pushed by Eastern bloc countries for political reasons and Scandinavian countries for environmental reasons, with mild resistance from much of the rest of Western Europe. Negotiations toward a convention took place in 1978 and 1979, and the Convention on Long-Range Transboundary Air Pollution (LRTAP) was signed in 1979. Canada and the United States participated in the LRTAP process, as signatories to the framework convention and participants in negotiations, probably in part because of the security goals of negotiating East–West cooperation.

Due in large part to the lack of environmental concern about the problem in most Western European countries, LRTAP was negotiated as a framework convention with little in the way of substantive abatement requirements. Signatory states agree in principle to limit and reduce their production of air pollutants. Parties commit to the idea that transboundary flows of air pollutants should be reduced as much as possible, as long as doing so is economically feasible.[9] The treaty also includes a process for collaboration in research and exchange of information on emissions and transboundary flows of air pollutants, abatement technology, and the effects of the major air pollutants.[10]

Efforts were then made to negotiate protocols to create specific obligations. The first effort was for regulations to control sulphur dioxide. The Scandinavian countries had been pushing for a commitment to a 30 per cent reduction of $SO_2$ emissions since before LRTAP negotiations were even completed, but this proposal met with resistance particularly from the rest of Western Europe. Some in the East were willing to agree, although the Soviet Union was concerned that it only be required to reduce its transboundary flows of pollutants rather than emissions more generally. Research presented during the period of negotiations indicated that forests could be harmed by acid rain and that Germany's famous Black Forest was experiencing problems. Germany then joined the call for large cuts in $SO_2$ emissions. In 1983 a number of states committed to 30 per cent reductions despite the lack of formally agreed obligations to do so. By the end of 1984 twenty states had joined the "30 per cent club," and an agreement became possible.[11]

The second protocol to be discussed, on control of nitrogen oxides, was proposed by the Scandinavian countries in 1985, immediately after the completion of the sulphur protocol. An important disagreement was over how to regulate emissions from mobile sources, as automobile emissions are one of the major sources of $NO_x$. The extent of the emissions controls were also controversial, with several states pushing for 30 per cent reductions, with others calling only for a freeze in emissions or even allowing for an increase. When in 1988 the middle option prevailed, a new 30 per cent club formed, with half the signatory states also signing (nonbinding) pledges to decrease their emissions by 30 per cent from 1987 levels by 1995. The Protocol also suggests that states will work to decrease emissions further, and will begin to apply the idea of critical loads.[12] A critical load is the amount of pollutant a particular area can receive before suffering negative environmental consequences. The idea is that emissions should ultimately be regulated to below that point, which requires different states to have different abatement obligations.

A third protocol, on the control of volatile organic compounds, was negotiated beginning in 1989. Controversy here was more pronounced, with no agreement on the type of emissions controls. Many states were willing to reduce their emissions by 30 per cent, but some that did not suffer domestic damage from their own VOC emissions wanted only to reduce the transboundary flow of their pollutants. Eastern European states, newly transitioning to democracy and capitalism, were unsure of their ability to comply with rigorous cuts and therefore suggested only a freeze on emissions. The protocol, agreed to in 1991, lists three types of regulatory options from which states must choose (along with the base year from which reductions will be calculated) upon signing the agreement. A state can choose to reduce VOC emissions by 30 per cent, it can specify certain management areas that are the sources of transboundary flows of VOC pollutants and reduce emissions from those areas by 30 per cent (along with a national freeze by 1999 at 1988 levels) or it can implement a freeze by 1999 at 1988 levels alone if 1988 VOC emissions were sufficiently low.[13] Bulgaria, Greece, and Hungary had emissions low enough and chose the third option, Norway and Canada chose the second option, and most states have taken on the first option for reductions.[14]

By the time negotiations later over a second sulphur protocol took place in the 1990s the approach had changed from one that focused on flat-rate reductions undertake by all signatories to scientifically based differentiated reduction commitments to take account of the differing effects of emissions by and on states in different geographic and ecological situations.[15] Although accepted as scientific principle, the process of determining politically acceptable implementation of this concept in its purest form proved difficult. The second sulphur protocol calls for states to ensure "as far as possible, without entailing excessive costs," that their deposition of acid rain from sulphur compounds do not exceed critical loads. The specific obligations are set out in an annex and involve a complex array of different emissions reductions required for each state over a set of years, determined in part by environmental circumstances and in part by what states were willing to accept.[16] It entered into force in August 1998.

Additional protocols expand the focus of LRTAP. Two other protocols, negotiated in 1998, on the control of heavy metals and persistent organic pollutants,[17] address transboundary pollutants that are not directly related to the issue of acid rain. An additional protocol deals with the financing of the Cooperative Programme for the Monitoring and Evaluation of the Long-Range Transmission of Air Pollutants in Europe.

The most important recent development in the process of regulation is the 1999 Protocol "to Abate Acidification, Eutrophication, and Ground-Level Ozone." It takes most previously agreed reductions even further based on critical loads and the cost effectiveness of reductions. These control measures signal an important shift in LRTAP policy-making, acknowledging that following a critical loads approach requires regulating many pollutants simultaneously. In addition, the protocol sets limits for emissions from specific sources (such as power plants and automobiles) and requires the use of "best available techniques" of emission control. The agreement aims, once fully implemented, to achieve a reduction of 63 per cent of sulphur emissions, 41 per cent of $NO_x$ emissions, 40 per cent of VOC emissions, and 17 per cent of ammonia emissions from 1990 levels.[18] It entered into force in 2005.

Discussion of regulation of transboundary acid rain in North America began in the late 1970s. Both the United States and Canada had domestic air pollution laws regulating the substances that are involved in acid rain production already. Some even mentioned the need to prevent transboundary damage, but did not have any specific regulatory mechanism to do so. The Canadian Minister of the Environment called in 1977 for negotiations toward an agreement, which led to the formation of the Bilateral Research Consultation Group on the Long-Range Transport of Air Pollutants, but no actual negotiations. The United States Senate passed a "sense of the Senate" resolution in 1978 that asked the President to negotiate an agreement with Canada, driven in part by U.S. concerns about new construction of Canadian coal-burning power plants near the border.[19] When Canadian officials responded by pointing out the effects of U.S. emissions on Canada, discussions went nowhere fast. After continued Canadian pressure the U.S. agreed in 1980 to a Memorandum of Intent (MOI). It committed the two states to upholding existing domestic air pollution agreements, and created five working groups to study the issues. Negotiations began as intended by the Memorandum, but were suspended shortly thereafter.

Canada attempted at several points to persuade the United States to undertake domestic regulations. In 1982 it proposed that the U.S. adopt a 50 per cent reduction in $SO_2$ emissions, but then-President Reagan refused to consider such an option. Meanwhile, the various scientific processes set up by the MOI and other independent groups made available more information about the transport of and damages from acid rain. Canada also signed the sulphur protocol to LRTAP, committing it to reductions in $SO_2$ emissions of 30 per cent. By 1985 the two heads of state appointed special envoys to study the issue. Their report eventually called for increased funding on research for new ways to produce less $SO_2$ in the process of coal-burning.[20] A report by the U.S. National Research Council involving both Canadian and American scientists released in 1986 indicated that acid deposition was occurring as a result of emissions of $SO_2$, but the U.S. would agree only to further research, arguing that the problem was not serious enough to justify expensive abatement measures.[21] The National Acid Rain Precipitation Assessment Program (NAPAP), a U.S.-based evaluation of acid rain initiated in 1980, released its interim report in 1987 with its summary report concluding that the effects of acid rain were not serious or widespread. It was inconsistent with most other assessments of the problem and was accused of being highly politicized.[22] Its release only made negotiations on the issue between the U.S. and Canada more difficult. In the interim, Canada took steps to reform its own domestic regulations, taking leadership in controlling the emission of pollutants that contribute to acid rain.

Canada continued to push the United States rhetorically on acid rain. In 1989, after George H. W. Bush became U.S. President, discussions began again in earnest. The United States was at the same time revising its national Clean Air Act to include provisions to respond to acid rain. The U.S. executive branch proposed regulations in which $SO_2$ reductions would take place through creating a tradable permits system, which would make U.S. reductions less costly and more efficient. With these measures passed as the Clean Air Act Amendments of 1990, the United States was once again willing to negotiate with Canada.[23] Negotiations began in 1990 and were concluded in the space of less than a year. The final result, eleven years after the MOI, and twelve years after both countries had already committed themselves to mitigating acid rain under LRTAP, was the United States–Canada Air Quality Agreement.

This agreement creates the bilateral obligations to mitigate acid rain. Its provisions are fairly general. It commits both states to set specific reductions to "reduce transboundary flows of ... acidic deposition precursors."[24] It also commits the parties more generally to environmental impact assessment, prior notification, and mitigation measures, and to conduct coordinated or cooperative scientific, technical, and economic research.[25]

An Annex to the agreement set specific reduction targets for $SO_2$ and $NO_x$ for each state. Canada committed to reducing $SO_2$ emissions in its seven eastern provinces to 2.3 million tonnes per year by 1994, not to exceed that level annually through 1999, and to set a permanent annual cap of 3.2 million tonnes any time after 2000. The United States committed to reduce $SO_2$ emissions to 10 million tonnes below 1980 levels by 2000 (with several exceptions relating to existing domestic legislation), a permanent cap on national emissions at 8.95 million tonnes for electric utilities by 2010, and the creation of new limits on $SO_2$ from industrial sources if they are expected to exceed 5.6 million tonnes annually.[26]

For $NO_x$, Canada agreed to reduce emission from stationary sources by 2000 to "100,000 tonnes below the year 2000 forecast level of 970,000 tonnes," and develop further reduction requirements by 2005 at the latest. For mobile sources the agreement sets out a minimum control program for motor vehicles that depends on the size and age of the vehicles. The United States agreed to a goal of reducing overall annual emissions of $NO_x$ by 2 million tonnes from 1980 levels by 2000. For stationary sources it would do so by an agreed-upon emission rate for boilers and the requirement that the Environmental Protection Agency set emission standards for other types of boilers and some other stationary sources of $NO_x$ by 1997. For mobile sources the U.S. agreed to a minimum control program that is more elaborate but comparable to the standards accepted by Canada.[27] How these reductions are made is left up to the states.

The two states in 2000 created an "ozone annex" to the agreement. It restricts the emissions of $NO_x$ and VOCs, the precursors to tropospheric ozone pollution,[28] in specified areas that include the Midwestern and Northeastern United States and in the provinces of Ontario and Quebec in Canada. The two states agree largely to implement pre-existing domestic laws to reduce the pollutants in question, but both states also pledge to "develop and implement standards to further reduce emissions of $NO_x$ and VOC." In the United States these should lead to an annual $NO_x$ reduction in the control areas by 27 per cent of 1990 levels by 2007 and 36 per cent by 2010 (with summer reductions of 35 per cent by 2007 and 43 per cent by 2010), as well as a reduction of annual VOC levels by 35 per cent from 1990 levels by 2007 and 38 per cent in 2010 (with summer reductions of 39 per cent in 2007 and 36 per cent in 2010). Canada's actions should lead to annual $NO_x$ emission reductions in regulated areas of 39 per cent from 1990 levels by 2007 and 44 per cent by 2010, and VOC emission reductions of 18 per cent from 1990 levels by 2007 and 20 per cent by 2010.[29]

Through participation in the LRTAP process the United States and Canada have undertaken some obligations in that forum as well, despite the fact that their emissions do not contribute to European acid rain. Canada signed the first sulphur protocol although the United States has not. Both states signed and ratified the $NO_x$ protocol (without the additional pledge of 30 per cent reductions). Canada signed and ratified the VOC protocol, choosing a 30 per cent reduction in specified areas. Canada has signed, and was one of the early states to ratify, the second sulphur protocol under LRTAP; the U.S. has neither signed nor ratified. Canada was one of the first states to have ratified the 1998 LRTAP protocols on heavy metals and persistent organic pollutants, and though it has signed the multieffect protocol it had not, as of early 2006, ratified it. The United States has signed and ratified the heavy metals protocol and the multieffect protocol.[30]

Currently Asia is experiencing increasing acute problems from acid rain and is beginning to work out ways to address the issue. Japan was the first country to experience the problems of acid rain, and although it has imposed strong domestic controls on emissions from automobiles and power generation, it cannot on its own address emissions coming from elsewhere. The major external source of Japan's acid rain is probably China,[31] though other studies have found that South Korea is a major source as well.[32] China's emissions affect many other states in the region as well, most prominently North Korea and Vietnam. As China industrializes with coal as its primary energy source, the problem will increase. Though China initially denied its responsibility for transboundary acid rain, it acknowledged in 1992 that its emissions could have effects outside of China,[33] and has accepted Japanese aid for mitigation technology and research.

Thus far the major cooperative effort has focused on monitoring causes and effects. The East Asian Acid Deposition Monitoring Network (EANET) began operations in 2001. Japan initially proposed its creation, and it has expanded to include states throughout East Asia, including China. The organization involves a secretariat, a Scientific Advisory Group, and National Focal points operating within member states.[34] EANET's first major task has been to standardize acid rain monitoring in the region which has been difficult since each member state has its own techniques for monitoring and analysis. The organization aims to work for the reduction of regional sulphur dioxide emissions, though it has not yet done so. Such an effort will almost certainly face major political difficulties, since the willingness by China to subordinate its development goals to regional environmental concerns is unlikely. Given China's large size and decreasing environmental quality, however, its willingness to impose controls that will improve its domestic environmental situation may be more likely, and may result in lower transboundary emissions as well. Moreover, historical tensions between Japan and other states complicate economic and political discussions.[35]

# Science, Risk, and Uncertainty

The resolution of unknown factors about acid rain in the European process, particularly about its negative effects, contributed to the increasing willingness by states in the region to undertake environmental controls. Uncertainty – or its resolution – can legitimately be seen to have played a role in European acid rain negotiations. When discussions began in the early 1970s there was little available evidence indicating that pollutants could travel such long distances or cause serious acidification of ecosystems. The research begun by the negotiating process and institutionalized within LRTAP contributed new understanding of the existence and extent of long-range transboundary air pollution. Although not traceable solely to the resolution of uncertainty, the increased willingness to negotiate further cuts in emissions and include new substances is certainly related to new scientific evidence about the extent of acidification and, in particular, the damages that have resulted. Moreover, the willingness to base cuts in emissions, at least in theory, on the idea of critical loads, reflects an acceptance of the scientific understanding of transport of air pollutants and ecological vulnerability that would not have been seen a decade earlier.

Scientific uncertainty does not explain the differences in timing or content between European and North American regulations, however. Uncertainty about the acid rain problem was given as the main reason for delay in the North American regulatory process. For example, during the negotiations following the MOI, the United States took the position that more research was required to confirm that there even was a cause-and-effect relationship between pollution and transboundary acid rain.[36] While it is true that there are region-specific differences in weather patterns and ecosystems that need to be understood, the overall scientific understanding available because of the European regulatory process gives convincing evidence of the existence and mechanisms of acid rain. If uncertainty were the cause of inaction, the regulations in North America, beginning slightly later than those in Europe, should in fact have proceeded more quickly and with greater depth, since they could build on the scientific understanding gleaned in the European case. As signatories to LRTAP the U.S. and Canada participated in and had access to the scientific research used in that regulatory process. The fact that most U.S. claims of uncertainty were not about geographically-specific elements of acid rain but were calling into question the scientific understanding of the process more generally indicates that uncertainty functioned at least partly as a smokescreen to hide other reasons for lack of cooperation.

## Politics of Science

The politics of science has been found to differ in the two regions generally. Sheila Jasanoff and others have examined the way that European and North American decision-making relating to harmful pollutants operates, arguing that similar concerns lead to varied outcomes in part because of the way science is used in the process. In the case of chemical regulation, for instance, the United States was found to insist on common regulations and address the broadest range of substances, taking risk assessment strongly into consideration, whereas Britain regulated in an entirely opposite way, and German regulations fell on the continuum between the two.[37] Jasanoff points to features of political culture that influence the way science is interpreted and acted upon, not necessarily in consciously self-interested ways.

In the case of acid rain it is argued that the way in which research was conducted influenced its acceptability to the process. Roderick Shaw suggests that the scientific evidence in the European context was widely accepted because it was conducted as part of the overall regulatory process, by the regulatory organization (the United Nations Economic Commission for Europe).[38] Also important was that it was conducted internationally. The lack of acceptance by U.S. actors of the scientific evidence for harm from acid rain could possibly be attributed to the fact that much of the basic research was done in a European context, although given that it was a context in which the U.S. participated, that explanation seems weak. Interestingly, studies on U.S. regulatory styles suggest generally that the United States is more willing to respond to situations of risk than other states and that it is less cost-conscious in the process of doing so.[39] The case of North American acid rain regulation would suggest the opposite.

More important than the issue of scientific uncertainty per se or even institutional constraints on the interpretation of science may be the way that science is used within the decision-making process by those with predetermined interests. The U.S. distrust of the mounting scientific evidence of damage from acid rain was certainly self-serving, and helped to delay agreement in North America. Some have argued that in the North American context more generally the institutions that sponsor reports "seem to shade the assessment results more than might be expected just from national differences."[40] Scientists may be unwitting but important players in this process. Oran Young explains that the scientific community addressing the question of acid rain presented "the relevant scientific evidence in ways that both sides in the debate have been able to exploit for partisan purposes."[41] It is clear that the United States used the spectre of scientific uncertainty as a way to avoid taking international regulatory action it would prefer not to take. In Europe as well states that would prefer not to bear the costs of international regulation, such as Britain, pointed to scientific uncertainty to justify their reluctance. But while it is important to acknowledge the political uses to which uncertainty can be put, it is not clear that self-interested use of uncertainty alone provides a sufficient explanation for the differences between the North American and European processes.

# Non-Governmental Actors

Interestingly, the role of non-governmental actors has not been as strong in the politics of acid rain as in other issue areas. Perhaps because power generation is the largest contributing activity and is, in many locations, a governmentally controlled activity, non-state industry actors have been less directly concerned. In the United States, where power generation is undertaken by private companies, industry opposition to increasingly strict air pollution regulations has been important in preventing or weakening acid rain regulations. But the large size of the United States means that there are domestic environmental impacts from acid rain generation by U.S. industry, and there has been pressure from within for action to mitigate the problem.

In Europe some non-governmental organizations have been active in lobbying for strong controls on transboundary air pollution. Central among these is the Swedish NGO Secretariat on Acid Rain, which provides excellent data on emissions and effects in Europe. Despite this pressure, however, non-state actors have in general been less central on this issue than on others examined in this book.

# The Role of Developing Countries

Acid rain is a problem of industrial development and, as such, has the potential to engage issues of the role of developing countries in international environmental politics. Because the existing international approaches to addressing the issue are regional, the differences in levels of development among cooperating countries have been smaller than might be the case with global regulatory regimes, a circumstance that is especially true in the North American context. The differences in economic and industrial development levels in Europe have played a role in the efforts to address the problem, however, and the nascent regime in Asia is likely to be affected by the profoundly different levels of development in the region.

In Europe, where the general level of economic development is high, the variations of wealth across LRTAP member states has had at least some impact on how the obligations of the agreement have been crafted and implemented. The poorer states in southern Europe have been less willing to undertake emissions reductions without some promise of assistance, and have been granted less strict obligations than other states.[42] But the willingness of other LRTAP states to agree to lower obligations for these states may be attributable more to the fact that their location in the atmospheric currents means that their emissions are less likely to have harmful effects than to the power that comes from poverty. The recent efforts to apply a critical loads approach do suggest that the costs of action are taken into consideration despite the effort to implement an environmentally based outcome.

Issues of development are far more likely to play a role in acid rain politics in Asia, where the levels of development vary dramatically across states in the region. It seems unlikely that states such as North Korea and Vietnam will be willing to reduce emissions that affect wealthy Japan without Japanese assistance. Even China's small efforts thus far to deal with transboundary air pollution have come with the assistance of funding and technology from Japan. The scope of the problem, with China's increasing industrialization and reliance on coal, however, is likely to be far more than can be funded by Japan. The priority China gives to economic development is likely, for the time being, to swamp any interest in acid rain controls.

# Issues of International Cooperation

International regulation to address acid rain has several implications for the consideration of international cooperation more broadly. The directional nature of the environmental problem affects the incentives of states involved in negotiations. The interests of actors in this case made regulation difficult, but those who were not especially interested in acid rain controls have ultimately been persuaded to take some action. The comparison between regional experiences with the same problem also suggests that the power of recalcitrant states may be different in multilateral versus bilateral contexts. It also appears that states are more willing to undertake international action when they have already regulated domestically. And, ultimately, cooperative efforts to mitigate acid rain in North America, and especially in Europe, have been implemented by states and are beginning to show some signs of effectiveness.

## Issue Structure

The environmental problem of transboundary acid rain looks structurally different than other atmospheric pollution problems, because it is a directional problem. Although it has the issue structure of a common pool resource problem, in that it is both nonexcludable and subtractable, states do not contribute to or suffer from the problem equally. For some states, that changes how they experience the issue structure, making the issue closer to one of public goods from their perspective.[43] How does that impact the efforts to address the issue internationally?

If there were any circumstance in which it makes sense to impose different levels of obligations on states based on where the pollutants have the greatest effect, a directional pollution problem would be that scenario. While the agreements in both Europe and North America create differential obligations for participants, what is striking is that they differentiate as little as they do. In the initial efforts at crafting obligations in the European context in the first three abatement protocols, obligations were to be undertaken on an equal basis (such as a 30 per cent reduction in sulphur dioxide emissions) regardless of environmental impact. The radical shift embodied by the critical loads approach represents one of the first moves away from equality of obligations in multilateral environmental agreements, but also demonstrates the difficulty of regulating based on effects.

What is also notable in the case of European acid rain regulations is the moral suasion exerted by those states that would, because of the issue structure, seem likely to have the least power in the negotiations. The Scandinavian states bear the greatest consequences, because of their geographic position and ecosystem vulnerabilities, from acid rain on the continent. But their leadership in accepting regulations (as well as in pushing the issue more generally) helped translate into greater obligations by others, rather than a lower level. On the other hand, the southern European states that have fewer obligations under LRTAP, by virtue of their location, do not have a major impact on continental acid rain. The efforts to address directional pollution issues are influenced, but not necessarily determined, by geography.

The most important differentiation in the North American agreement is not that there are different requirements for the United States and Canada, a factor that can be traced to domestic politics rather than to environmental efficacy. But the agreement also is crafted to address emissions based on their location of impact. Because both of the direction of prevailing winds and the specific vulnerability of ecosystems, the eastern half of the continent is much more affected by acid rain than elsewhere, and the North American agreement does focus on preventing emissions that will have the greatest impact on that region. Acid rain agreements, then, have made some effort to craft mitigation efforts that take the directional characteristics of the environmental problem into consideration, albeit imperfectly.

## Interests of Actors

The interests of the individual states involved with an international problem are likely to have an impact on the extent and type of regulation, nowhere more than in a directional pollution problem in which interests are likely to differ. These interests collectively can shape both the extent to which a cooperative outcome is likely and the particular form of an agreement that does emerge. Realist international relations theory at its most basic, seeing any international cooperation that does emerge as epiphenominal, would suggest that the interests of the individual states are paramount. This phenomenon is, if anything, more likely in issues relating to the environment. Detlef Sprinz and Tapani Vaahtoranta are among those who see states as rational self-interested actors. Specifically, they expect states that are the victims of pollution to seek international environmental protection, and those that are net contributors to the problem to resist. [44]

Their hypothesis can be easily used to explain responses to acid rain in both Europe and North America, as well as the differences between the two regions. The directional character of acid rain, combined with differences in the natural ability of various ecosystems to resist harm from acidifying substances, means that the extent to which states are harmed by acid rain varies, often through no action of their own. Some states are net exporters and some are net importers of acid rain. Examining the interests of a state as a single entity of course oversimplifies the situation, since within any of the states examined there are actors who are harmed by acid rain or who would be harmed by the regulation of emissions to prevent acid rain. Nevertheless, there are certain wider generalizations that can help explain the negotiating positions taken by various states. In both the European and North American cases, the net exporters are less willing to undertake cooperative action than the net importers. In the case of North America, more than 50 per cent of the acid rain Canada receives is thought to come from the United States, while only 15 per cent of U.S. acid rain is thought to originate in Canada. In addition, Canada is more vulnerable to acidification, not necessarily for ecological reasons, but because it relies more heavily for income on the natural resources (such as forestry products and fisheries) that are harmed by acid rain than does the United States. [45] Given those overall statistics, it is not surprising that the United States was a reluctant participant in negotiations. With U.S. reluctance, agreement was likely to be problematic.

Sprinz and Vaahtoranta examine their interest-based approach in the context of acid rain in Europe, specifically looking at the first sulphur protocol. They suggest that a variable combining the ecological vulnerability of a state and the cost to that state of reducing the pollutants that cause acid rain can explain the willingness of a state to adopt the first sulphur protocol. Although their theory cannot account for the case of the United Kingdom, judged to have high ecological vulnerability and low abatement costs (and which did not sign the protocol),[46] it otherwise explains the actions of states that chose to push for, go along with, or refuse to participate in European acid rain controls.

## Negotiation Arithmetic – Power and Number of Actors

Other factors that contribute to explaining the outcomes in both regions include factors that many who examine international negotiations more broadly consider important: the role of power and the number of actors involved in a negotiation. While power is difficult to define and more difficult to conceptualize in an environmental context, the fact that acid rain cut to the heart of industrial activity and was initially negotiated in a security context suggests that the power of the actors is likely to be important. Powerful actors certainly played influential roles in acid rain negotiations in both Europe and North America. Germany's transformation into a supporter of emissions controls was an important factor in allowing regulation to move forward in Europe. The disparity in power in the North American case was certainly influential in slowing down the agreement and in keeping its provisions somewhat weaker than those that have been undertaken in Europe. In both economic and security terms Canada is far more dependent on the United States than the reverse, although the United States did rely heavily on Canada as a source for energy.[47] It is important to note, though, that the power of the United Kingdom did not prevent agreement in Europe the way that the power of the United States slowed it down in North America. Power alone is not a full explanation for the actions of states in international cooperation in the two regions, though the ability of important actors to throw their weight around in international environmental negotiations should not be overlooked more generally.

Also important to discuss in conjunction with power is the number of actors involved. Most international relations theory models international cooperation as a two-player game, and most international agreements are indeed bilateral. But in the realm of global environmental politics much is now done through multilateral agreement, and the number of actors involved may make a difference. In the case of acid rain, negotiations in Europe involved a large number of participants compared to the bilateral U.S.–Canada negotiations, and may therefore be a possible source of the different outcomes. Hypotheses about the difficulty of negotiations with greater numbers of actors do not explain the increased difficulty of negotiating the North American Air Quality Agreement, and the decreased stringency of its provisions, however. They would suggest exactly the opposite.

The case of acid rain across regions suggests that the issues of power and of number of negotiating states might need to be considered together. In a situation of small numbers, when the most powerful state is a laggard on international cooperation it has a considerable drag on the potential for meaningful cooperation. But when there are more states the ability of a powerful and recalcitrant state to prevent cooperation is diminished. And, as the exampes of both Germany and the United Kingdom in LRTAP demonstrate, some degree of participation in a multilateral process can change the interests of even those states that have been resisting serious action.

What does the negotiation arithmetic suggest will transpire in Asian efforts to address acid rain? Two states in the region – Japan and China – are powerful, in somewhat different ways, and China is the most likely laggard. Efforts to address acid rain are thus far multilateral, which decreases the odds that a laggard state can prevent meaningful cooperation. But China's location as a largely "upstream" polluter does give it the ability to prevent some meaningful action on acid rain, and the actions of other states – such as North Korea and Vietnam, which are sources of at least some of the acid rain experienced by Japan – would also be important. Asia will stand as an important test case for ideas about the number and power of states in directional pollution issues.

## Domestic Sources of International Environmental Policy

An important related element in international environmental negotiation is the actions undertaken by states prior to international negotiations on an issue, or the actions they would take absent international agreement. There is evidence that industrial actors already subject to domestic environmental regulations will work to push for international regulations so that their competitors will have to bear similar costs.[48] States that have regulated unilaterally, or are willing to, to address a collective issue will benefit greatly if they can persuade others to do so as well. International cooperation can therefore be a reasonable activity by those who have regulated domestically; the question is whether it causes them to undertake action they would not have otherwise taken.

Much of the action undertaken by states in both regions to mitigate acid rain damage reflects what they had already done domestically or would have done absent international cooperation. In Europe, Levy points out, Norway, Sweden, and Germany would have undertaken their LRTAP-related obligations absent any international agreement; these states reduced their emissions before they had international obligations to do so.[49] Similarly, France dropped its initial objection to the first sulphur protocol when it realized that its aggressive nuclear energy program would allow it to meet the proposed obligations without changing existing activity.[50] By the time of the second sulphur protocol, Barbara Connolly points out, most states had exceeded the 30 per cent reductions required in the first protocol, many because of domestic reasons, unrelated changes in energy policy, or European Union regulation.[51]

In North America, the Air Quality Agreement finally emerged once the U.S. had already taken domestic action, under the 1990 Clean Air Act Amendments, to mitigate the creation of acid rain. The bulk of the Ozone Annex commits both states to implement existing domestic law. Perhaps states are only willing to accept internationally what they have already adopted domestically, or what they are likely to adopt anyway. While that pessimism overlooks the role of the international scientific process, particularly under LRTAP, in persuading states that their interests are at stake, it does suggest that domestic regulation can be an important precursor to international environmental action.

## Implementation and Effectiveness

The implementation of LRTAP's obligations has been impressive. Emissions of most of the regulated substances have fallen in the major states. Sulphur dioxide emissions (from land-based sources) in Europe fell by 70 per cent between 1980 and 2000. Emissions of nitrogen oxides in Europe rose in the decade following 1980 (before the $NO_x$ Protocol entered into force) but had decreased by 30 per cent overall by 2000.

But not all of the decrease in emissions can be attributed to LRTAP obligations, though teasing out cause and effect can be difficult. The United Kingdom switched from coal as a major energy source during this period, for reasons largely unrelated to the existence of LRTAP. And as was the case with greenhouse gas emissions, the sulphur and nitrogen emissions from Eastern Europe and the former Soviet Union dropped dramatically with the economic and industrial changes brought about by the end of the Cold War and the disintegration of the Soviet Union. Recently EU policy, rather than LRTAP obligations, has been an influence on the emissions of EU member states, though it may be that the existence of LRTAP obligations influences EU policy.

Nevertheless, the behavior of some states in Europe has been changed by the existence of LRTAP, particularly such states as Austria, Finland, the Netherlands, and Switzerland that learned of their vulnerability from studies undertaken in the context of LRTAP.[52] And for the rest of the states that might have changed their behavior for other reasons, LRTAP provided them with a context to commit to these changes collectively.

Most importantly, there have been optimistic environmental results from changed European emissions behavior. The area of Europe that receives acid deposition beyond critical loads has decreased from 34 per cent in 1990 to 11 per cent in 2000. And while in 1980 approximately 200 million hectares of European ecosystems were determined to be harmed by acidification, that area in 2000 was reduced to only about 38 million, with the area continuing to decrease since then.[53]

The situation in North America is less clear. Both the United States and Canada have broadly followed the requirements of the agreement, though U.S. emissions of $SO_2$ have been somewhat higher than planned due in part to increases in the price of gas and a decrease in use of nuclear energy. U.S. $SO_2$ emissions overall were 32 per cent below 1990 levels by 2003 (and 38 per cent below 1980 levels). Canada's total $SO_2$ emissions have decreased by 50 per cent since 1980 (including a reduction of 28 per cent more than required in the eastern provinces where the ecosystems are the most vulnerable), which is greater than required by either domestic or international rules.[54] Recent changes in U.S. air pollution regulations have involved jockeying between branches of government with implications for U.S. continued implementation of its obligations under the regional agreement. In 2002 the U.S. Environmental Protection Agency decided to relax rules that had previously required that old and highly polluting power plants upgrade their pollution control technology when undertaking other upgrades. This policy was challenged in court by several states and environmental organizations. In 2005 the U.S. Court of Appeals upheld the bulk of the policy change,[55] but a ruling on a related case in 2006 overturned a number of its central provisions.[56] These cases may be appealed and other related cases are pending. They will determine, in part, whether the United States continues to meet its obligations under the Air Quality Agreement.

The vast majority of the rules under the North American agreement are those already required domestically by both states, so the primary benefit of the agreement seems to be in information exchange and reporting. In terms of environmental effects, the reduced emissions, whether their cause is primarily domestic or international regulation, is translating into environmental benefits. Ambient sulfate levels in the United States have decreased by 30 per cent, and the amount of sulphate deposition in the Northeastern United States has declined by 39 per cent. Some lakes and streams are recovering from previous acidification.[57] The results in Canada are also encouraging but suggest that the problem is far from being solved. Since the early 1980s the area of Eastern Canada that receives a significant amount of acid deposition has decreased by 61 per cent. But although 33 per cent of lakes in the region had reduced acidity during this time period, 11 per cent became more acidic and the others showed no improvement.[58]

# Conclusion

In both Europe and North America, states have undertaken increasingly strict actions to limit their production, from industrial and transportation sectors, of substances that contribute to acid rain. What began as a concern by Swedish scientists about lake acidification has ultimately led to an understanding that a wide variety of air pollutants can travel long distances across national borders to impact other states, and a willingness to take action based on this knowledge.

The directional element of this pollution provides an example of a situation where neither contribution to, nor suffering from, environmental damage is universally distributed across states. Despite this directional character, however, the first approach to addressing international environmental problems tends to be equality of obligations, even if it is not the most effective way to resolve directional environmental problems. In Europe, where the process of regulating air pollutants based on efforts to prevent the greatest damage has gone the farthest, regulation based on "critical loads" is imperfectly applied because of the difficulty of imposing differential obligations on states. But the trend has been toward increasing differentiation of obligations, despite the political and economic difficulties of doing so, to address the problem more efficiently.

The collective scientific undertaking generated by the LRTAP process convinced states that they had interests in controlling acid rain they might otherwise not have discovered independently until much later.[59] Germany may have become an advocate of strong mitigation measures when it discovered its own forest damage from acid rain. That looks to be an example of self-interest, but it was self-interest made possible by the resolution of scientific uncertainty. A counterpoint to the political ways states choose to use science for self-interested reasons is the fact that scientific information may inform and thereby change self-interest in a way that can make cooperation or regulation more likely.

The role the number of actors plays in a negotiation becomes more useful when taken in conjunction with other explanations. In particular, the smaller numbers in the North American context meant that if one of the actors wanted to undermine the process it could do so in a way that was less likely in Europe with far more actors. Moreover, when that actor is the more powerful of the two, it has an easier time undermining cooperation. When you combine the issues of interests and numbers in this case you see that the directionality of the environmental problem actually made it more likely that a larger group of (smaller) states would be able to agree to collective mitigation measures than a smaller group of states with less mutual geographic dependence. If the European case had involved negotiations only between Germany and the UK the scenario might have looked similar to what happened in North America.

But it is unlikely that domestic preferences account for all the activity we see in the case of acid rain. Levy points to the "tote-board diplomacy" effect of essentially shaming states into agreeing to emissions cuts because other states have publicly accepted them. So states may take action they wanted to take domestically, but take it publicly in a way that may help induce others to do so as well. Similarly, some of the domestic action may be undertaken in the service of trying to persuade others to regulate. In the North American context, Canada increased the stringency of its acid rain protection probably in part to shame the U.S. into taking similar action (or at least because its willingness to regulate was called into question early in the process). Simply looking at what action states have already taken domestically may not take into account the strategic nature of their domestic actions.

Also worth noting in the acid rain case is that, to an extent greater than in many other international environmental agreements, states have accepted different levels and types of obligations under the various different acid rain agreements. The obligations for the United States and for Canada differ under the North American agreement. Under LRTAP there are *de facto* differences to the extent that different states may agree to different LRTAP protocols or that some states agree only to reduce their transboundary fluxes rather than overall emissions; in the later protocols the obligations undertaken by the different European states vary widely, and the trend is toward greater differentiation. This level of differentiation is unusual. Those who examine global environmental agreements are unused to seeing different levels of obligations within treaties, although it is more common in bilateral treaties where the norm of equity may be less pronounced for precisely the reasons discussed in examining the effects of numbers. It is also interesting to observe that this trend is appearing even in multilateral agreements. In agreements where states take on different levels of commitments, particularly when not tied directly to environmental conditions, the effects of numbers, uncertainty, interests, and domestic politics may be even greater than they would otherwise be.

# Notes

1 Speech delivered 26 October 1983, as quoted in Robert B. Stewart, "Negotiations on Acid Rain," in Jurgen Schmandt, Judith Clarkson, and Hilliard Roderick, eds., *Acid Rain and Friendly Neighbors: The Policy Dispute between Canada and the United States*, rev. edn. (Durham, N.C.: Duke University Press, 1988), 73.

2 John McCormick, *Acid Earth: The Politics of Acid Pollution* (London: Earthscan, 1997), 8.

3 Marc A. Levy, "European Acid Rain: The Power of Tote-Board Diplomacy," in Peter M. Haas, Robert O. Keohane, and Marc A. Levy, eds., *Institutions for the Earth: Sources of Effective International Environmental Protection* (Cambridge, Mass., and London: MIT Press, 1993), 78.

4 Svante Odén, "The Acidification of Air and Precipitation and its Conserquences in the Natural Environment," *Ecology Committee Bulletin* 1 (Stockholm: Swedish National Research Council, 1968).

5 Levy, "European Acid Rain," 80.

6 Gregory S. Wetstone and Armin Rosencranz, *Acid Rain in Europe and North America: National Responses to an International Problem. A Study for the German Marshall Fund of the United States* (Washington D.C.: Environmental Law Institute, 1983), 9.

7 Organization for Economic Cooperation and Development, *The OECD Programme on Long Range Transport of Air Pollutants: Summary Report* (OECD, 1977).

8 Levy, 81–82.

9 Convention on Long-Range Transboundary Air Pollution (1979), Articles 2 and 6.

10 LRTAP, Articles 7 and 8.

11 Levy, 91–94.

12 Protocol to LRTAP Concerning the Control of Emissions of Nitrogen Oxides or their Transboundary Fluxes (1988), Article 2.

13 Protocol to LRTAP Concerning the Control of Emissions of Volatile Organic Compounds or Their Transboundary Fluxes (1991), Article 2.

14 UNECE, "The 1991 Geneva Protocol Concerning the Control of Emissions of Volatile Organic Compounds or their Transboundary Fluxes," http://www.unece.org/env/lrtap/vola_h1.htm.

15 Helen M. ApSimon and Rachel F. Warren, "Transboundary Air Pollution in Europe," *Energy Policy* 24(7) (1996): 631–40.

16 Protocol to LRTAP on Further Reductions of Sulphur Emissions (1994), Article 2, Annex I; see also Barbara Connolly, "Asymmetrical Rivalry in Common Pool Resources and European Responses to Acid Rain," in J. Samuel Barkin and George E. Shambaugh, eds., *Anarchy and the Environment: The International Relations of Common Pool Resources* (Albany: SUNY Press, 1999), 129.

17 Protocol to LRTAP on Heavy Metals (1998) and Protocol to LRTAP on Persistent Organic Pollutants (1998).

18 UNECE, "1999 Gothenburg Protocol to Abate Acidification, Eutrophication and Ground-Level Ozone," http://www.unece.org/env/lrtap/multi_h1.htm.

19 Don Munton, "Acid Rain and Transboundary Air Quality in Canadian–American Relations," *The American Review of Canadian Studies* (Autumn 1997): 328–29.

20 Robert B. Stewart, "Negotiations on Acid Rain," in Schmandt, Clarkson, and Hilliard, 64–82.

21 Lois Ember, "U.S., Canada Still Far Apart on Acid Rain Accord," *Chemical and Engineering News*, 8 February 1988, 15.

22 Kim J. DeRidder, "The Nature and Effects of Acid Rain: A Comparison of Assessments," in Schmandt, Clarkson, and Roderick, 62.

23 Vicki L. Golich and Terry Forrest Young, "United States–Canadian Negotiations for Acid Rain Controls," *Pew Case Studies in International Affairs*, Case 452 (1993), 21, 24.

24 Agreement Between the Government of Canada and the Government of the United States on Air Quality (known colloquially as the U.S.–Canada Air Quality Agreement) (1991), Article IV(2).

25 Article III(2)(b).

26 Annex I, Paragraph 1(A)(B).

27 Annex I, Paragraph 2(A)(B).

28 Note that at ground level ozone is a pollutant with health risks for humans, whereas in the stratosphere (as discussed in Chapter 6) it provides beneficial protection from ultraviolet radiation.

29 Protocol Between the Government of Canada and the Government of the United States of America Amending the "Agreement between the Government of Canada and the Government of the United States on Air Quality," 2000.

30 UNECE, "Status of Convention on Long-Range Transboundary Air Pollution and its Related Protocols (as of 13 January 2006), http://www.unece.org/env/lrtap/status/Status%20of%20the%20Convention.pdf.

31 Miranda Schreurs, "Shifting Priorities and the Internationalization of Environmental Risk Management in Japan," in The Social Learning Group, *Learning to Manage Global Environmental Risks*, vol. I (Cambridge, Mass.: MIT Press, 2001), 203.

32 Anna Brettell, "Security, Energy, and the Environment: The Atmospheric Link," in In-take Hyun and Miranda Schreurs, eds., *The Environmental Dimensions of Asian Security: Conflict and Cooperation Over Environment, Energy and Natural Resources* (Washington, D.C.: United States Institute of Peace Press, forthcoming).

33 Miranda Schreurs, "Japan: Elite Newspaper Reporting on the Acid Rain Issue from 1972 to 1992," in William C. Clark and Nancy M. Dickson, eds., *The Press and Global Environmental Change: An International Comparison on Elite Newspaper Reporting on*

the Acid Rain Issue from 1972–1992 (Cambridge, Mass.: Center for Science and International Affairs, Kennedy School of Government, 1995).

34  EANET Secretariat, "East Asian Acid Deposition Monitoring Network," http://www.eanet.cc/eanet.html.

35  Brettell.

36  Stewart, 67.

37  Sheila Jasanoff, "Cross-National Differences in Policy Implementation," Evaluation Review 15(1) (February 1991): 103–19.

38  Roderick W. Shaw, "Acid Rain Negotiations in North America and Europe: A Study in Contrast," in Gunner Sjöstet, ed., International Environmental Negotiation (Newbury Park, London, and Delhi: Sage, 1993), 88.

39  Sheila Jasanoff, "American Exceptionalism and the Political Acknowledgment of Risk," Daedalus 119(4) (Fall 1990): 63–78.

40  Jurgen Schmandt, Judith Clarkson, and Hilliard Roderick, "Introduction," in Schmandt, Clarkson, and Roderick, 5.

41  Oran Young, "Science and Social Institutions: Lessons for International Resource Regimes," in Steinar Andresen and Willy Ostreng, eds., International Resource Management: The Role of Science and Politics (London and New York: Bellhaven Press, 1989), 10.

42  Connolly, 124.

43  Ibid., 123.

44  Detlef Sprinz and Tapani Vaahtoranta, "The Interest-Based Explanation of International Environmental Policy," International Organization 41(1) (Winter 1994): 77–105.

45  Golich and Young, 11–12.

46  Interestingly, they point to Britain's distrust of scientific findings as a possible cause of its reluctance on this issue. Sprinz and Vaahtoranta, 100.

47  Golich and Young, 12.

48  Elizabeth R. DeSombre, Domestic Sources of International Environmental Policy: Industry, Environmentalists, and U.S. Power (Cambridge, Mass.: MIT Press, 2000).

49  Levy, "European Acid Rain," 76.

50  Ibid., 93.

51  Connolly, 129.

52  Levy, "European Acid Rain," 119.

53  Swedish NGO Secretariat on Acid Rain, "Acidification," http://www.acidrain.org/pages/acidEutrophications/sub3_1.asp#Areas.

54  Canada–United States Air Quality Agreement Progress Report 2004, at http://www.ec.gc.ca/pdb/can_us/2004CanUs/intro_e.html.

55 Michael Janofsky, "U.S. Court Backs Bush's Revisions in Clean Air Act," *New York Times*, 25 June 2005, 1.

56 Michael Janofsky, "Judges Overturn Bush Bid to Ease Pollution Rules," *New York Times*, 18 March 2006, 1.

57 U.S. EPA, "Acid Rain Program 2003 Progress Report," http://www.epa.gov/airmarkets/cmprpt/arp03/summary.html.

58 Environment Canada, "Acid Rain: What's Being Done?" http://www.ec.gc.ca/acidrain/done-canada.html.

59 Levy, 76, for example.

# 10 Conclusion

The experience of responding to global environmental issues suggests a number of conclusions. Addressing environmental issues is not easy, but it is possible. The right combination of information and interests, and politics and persuasion, can bring states to commit to changing behavior, and people to actually do so, in ways that influence the environment beneficially. People's ability to degrade the environment is increasing, but so is our understanding of how natural systems work and intersect, and the same technological and economic innovation that can be seen as creating environmental destruction can also be harnessed to mitigate it.

The cases examined here suggest that it is not only difficult to gain international cooperation to protect the environment, as in the case of global climate change, but also that it is difficult to ensure compliance with international agreements, as demonstrated by illegal Soviet whaling and the black market in ozone-depleting substances. Even when there is large-scale behavior change, as with developed countries' near complete phase-out of ozone-depleting substances, the environment does not necessarily respond quickly. Under such circumstances, it can be difficult to determine whether lack of environmental improvement is due to an inaccurate or incomplete understanding of the environmental problem, undetected cheating, or natural environmental fluctuations. More importantly, it can be politically difficult to take potentially costly action, when the outcome is uncertain or will be beneficial in the distant future.

The cases nevertheless also demonstrate the willingness of states to work together, and non-state actors to undertake cooperative action with states, in order to address problems that affect the global environment. There are strong (and in Europe, innovative) controls on emissions of acid rain, despite the varying impacts to states from acidifying substances. There are innovative policies that bring together industry or environmental organizations with governments in efforts to protect biodiversity in the Amazonian rainforest. A commercial whaling moratorium was declared when it became clear that human activity had sufficiently depleted whaling stocks that they would not be able to recover without drastic action. And, though efforts to mitigate climate change are only in their early stages, protection of the global atmosphere through strict regulation on ozone-depleting substances has been among the most successful international efforts to protect the environment.

Certainly self-interest has played an important role in making these policies possible. But it is interesting to note a subtle redefinition of what constitutes self-interest, from one based on strict power resources of states. When Germany dropped its opposition to acid rain controls after scientific processes initiated by the Convention on Long-Range Transboundary Air Pollution indicated that it too was harmed by acid rain, did it change its interests, or simply learn new information that allowed it to realize its broader interest in protecting its environment? When the United States passed restrictions on the use of ozone-depleting substances in nonessential aerosols after citizens demanded alternatives and scientists expressed precautionary concern about a potential environmental problem, the state was reflecting the concerns of some of its component parts to protect the environment over the long term, at the expense of other, traditionally more politically powerful, elements. This then gave regulated industry an incentive to internationalize that regulation. When industrialized states provide funding to developing countries to assist them in their implementation of global environmental agreements, it can help the donor states by making possible a collective environmental action that could not be achieved without the participation of states for whom protection of the ozone layer or the global climate system may be a lower priority than domestic economic or environmental concerns. Environmental politics also makes strange bedfellows out of political actors, when domestic industries may work together with environmentalists on international environmental policy; the latter concerned about the well-being of the earth and the former concerned about their international competitiveness.

Studying the politics of addressing global environmental problems also suggests broader lessons for those who examine international relations. The nature of international relations has likely changed across a number of issues areas in the last century. The extent of international cooperation, the role of uncertainty, the influential position of developing states, and the importance of non-governmental actors are all factors examined in international relations more broadly but that stand out particularly in efforts to manage the global environment.

While few who study international relations truly believe the characterization of the world as composed of unitary self-interested state actors, there are few areas of international relations in which non-state actors matter more, and in more varied ways, than in the realm of environmental politics. Scientists, not only as generators of knowledge, but as political actors, bring issues to the attention of environmental activists. These activists do not always follow the simple political model of lobbying the policy makers of their own states (although they also do that) to change international negotiating positions. The standard model of the role of activists is linear: people's concerns filter up to policy makers, who work them out internationally, agree to policies states will follow, and then states implement those policies domestically, restricting activities by their citizens. And that is, indeed, sometimes the way global environmental politics works. Initial efforts to regulate whaling followed this model to some extent: whalers wanted to be able to continue their livelihood and ensure that only as many whales be caught as could be sustained, and expressed these concerns to their governments, which negotiated an international agreement that thus regulated the activities of the whalers. But on this and other issues we also see citizens' groups working across borders to influence the actions of other states, disseminating information to other activists. We see environmental organizations buying tracts of land to preserve them, or buying and then forgiving commercial debt of foreign countries that do so. We see international organizations of scientists, willing to contradict the political wishes of their states in announcing their findings on climate change. And we see people changing their behavior not because they are required to by international or domestic regulations, but because they have been made aware of an environmental problem and want to help fix it. Since it is the actions of those who are not states whose behavior will have to change in order to protect the environment, it is notable that non-state actors have been so influential in efforts to create a situation in which others will do so.

And yet states do still matter as actors in international environmental politics. They are the ones that sign international agreements, and that – in some cases, anyway – have the ability to make rules that change the behavior of environmentally destructive actors within their boundaries. Some of the traditional elements of international relations are thus present in global environmental politics. The disconnect between political and ecosystemic boundaries may make cooperation to protect the global environment more difficult at the same time that it makes it more necessary. States cannot address environmental problems by themselves but must cooperate to manage any problems of the global commons. Even issues like deforestation that would seem to be purely local have both international causes and international consequences. Environmental politics, while sometimes stymied by the concerns of states for their own well-being, can also be helped by that same concern, as states recognize that they cannot address global environmental problems on their own.

The nature of environmental politics gives influence to some states, as well, that would not traditionally be seen as powerful. States that have biodiversity resources the rest of the world cares about located within their borders have the ability to dictate the terms on which the rest of the world can gain access to them, or the conditions under which these resources will be protected. Developing countries whose future (or, in the case of climate change, current) behavior may influence the ability of states to manage a global environmental problem can gain great influence by refusing to undertake action to protect the resource unless it is on their terms. Their threat to refuse to participate is generally credible. Even if they may be harmed by the environmental problem, their time horizons are generally shortened by the need to meet the basic needs of their current populations. And they have an ethical card to play as well: is it fair to ask developing countries to foreswear development in the ways that benefited the currently industrialized states? Developing countries have thereby seized great negotiating power in efforts to protect the global environment.

Global environmental issues not addressed in depth in this volume follow and may expand many of the patterns explored here. Some examples: The Basel Convention on the Control of Transboundary Movement of Hazardous Wastes and Their Disposal (1989) reflected the recognition by developing countries that they could not always control their borders and required that exporters obtain prior informed consent before any shipments of hazardous wastes are sent for disposal. The International Convention for the Prevention of Pollution from Ships (1973/1978) attempted to restrict intentional oil pollution in the oceans in several different ways, gaining the most success when it focused regulations on smaller numbers of easily monitored larger actors (shipbuilders) than large numbers of small actors (ship operators) with incentives to cheat. The United Nations Convention to Combat Desertification in Those Countries Experiencing Serious Drought and/or Desertification (1994), in which developing states initially failed to leverage significant new sources of funding for their environmental goals, suggests that the influence of developing countries in international environmental agreements may be relevant but is limited in issues that are not subtractable. The problems are becoming more complicated as well; the presence of organochlorides in the food chain far from where they are produced or consumed suggests an interconnectedness of natural systems even greater than we previously believed. And what these and still other environmental issues all have in common is the international implications of domestic activities, and the uncertainty about the severity of the environmental problems and the costs and benefits of fixing or preventing them.

There are many additional factors one should take into consideration when examining global environmental politics, that have arisen implicitly in the cases examined in this volume. Population pressures are at the root of almost all environmental problems; at minimum, more people put more stress on environmental resources. Issues of development are important as well, since many environmental problems can be traced to industrialization. The issue of whether the less developed global South will follow the same industrialization path as its predecessors in Europe and North America is essential in determining what will happen to the global environment. To the extent it would be better for the environment if development happened differently, how to accomplish that goal, in a manner that is both fair and politically feasible, will be one of the most important questions to address.

The globalizing influence of trade and culture are mirrored in environmental issues: to a large extent, all environmental politics is global. People are more capable of environmental destruction as the industrial revolution reaches further around the globe and people find more efficient ways of harvesting resources at the same time that their activities result in greater levels of pollution. And the more we understand about the science of ecosystems, the more we realize that very local activities have ultimately global effects, and that the effects of environmental problems that appear to be only global (such as climate change or ozone depletion) are felt in specifically local ways. If ever there were an issue to remove the distinction between domestic politics and international relations, the study of the politics of the global environment is the one. In removing this distinction, efforts to protect the global environment can often succeed.

# Bibliography

Adler, Emanuel, and Peter M. Haas. 1992. "Conclusion: Epistemic Communities, World Order, and the Creation of a Reflective Research Program." *International Organization* 46(1) (Winter): 367–90.

*Agreement Between the Government of Canada and the Government of the United States on Air Quality.* 1991.

Alford, Peter. 2005. "Vote on Whales 'Not Sold.'" *Daily Telegraph*, 24 June: 9.

Allenby, Braden R. 1999. *Industrial Ecology: Policy Framework and Implementation.* Upper Saddle River, N.J.: Prentice Hall.

Alliance for Responsible CFC Policy. 1986. *A Search for Alternatives to the Current Commercial Fluorocarbons* (February).

Amodeo, Christian. 2003. "Tourists Flock to Nature's Hotspots." *Geographical* 17(12) (December): 97.

Andresen, Steinar. 1989. "Science and Politics in the International Management of Whales." *Marine Policy* 13 (April): 99–117.

ApSimon, Helen M., and Rachel F. Warren. 1996. "Transboundary Air Pollution in Europe." *Energy Policy* 24(7) (July): 631–40.

Arden-Clarke, Charles. 1992. "South–North Terms of Trade, Environmental Protection and Sustainable Development." *International Environmental Affairs* 4(2) (Spring):122–38.

Arico, Salvatore, and Charlotte Sapin. 2005. *Bioprospecting of Genetic Resources in the Deep Seabed: Scientific, Legal, and Policy Aspects, UNU-IAS Report.* Tokyo: UNU-IAS.

Arnt, Ricardo. 1993. "The Inside Out, The Outside In: Pros and Cons of Foreign Influence on Brazilian Environmentalism." In *Green Globe Yearbook 1992*, edited by Helge O. Bergesen, Magnar Norderhaug, and Georg Parmann, 15–23. Oxford: Oxford University Press.

Ashton, Ray. 1995. "The Natural Alternative: Planning for Success in Latin American Ecotourism Projects." *Latin Finance* 67 (May): 16.

Axelrod, Robert. 1984. *The Evolution of Cooperation.* New York: Basic Books.

Bäckstrand, Karin. 2003. "Civic Science for Sustainability: Reframing the Role of Experts, Policy-Makers and Citizens in Environmental Governance." *Global Environmental Politics* 3(4) (November): 24–41.

Baldocchi, Dennis. 2005. "The Carbon Cycle Under Stress." *Nature* 437(22): 483–84.

Ball, Jeffrey. 2005. "Ford to Study How Steps to Curb Global Warming Might Affect It." *Wall Street Journal*, 31 March: 7D.

Baram, Michael S. 1994. "Multinational Corporations, Private Codes, and Technology Transfer for Sustainable

Development." *Environmental Law* 24(1) (Winter): 33–66.

Barbera, Anthony J., and Virgina D. McConnell. 1990. "The Impact of Environmental Regulations on Industry Productivity: Direct and Indirect Effects." *Journal of Environmental Economics and Management* 18: 56–65.

Barkin, J. Samuel, and George E. Shambaugh. 1999. "Hypotheses on the International Politics of Common Pool Resources." In *Anarchy and the Environment: The International Relations of Common Pool Resources*, edited by J. Samuel Barkin and George E. Shambaugh, 1–25. Albany: SUNY Press.

Barrett, Christopher B., and Travis J. Lybbert. 2000. "Is Bioprospecting a Viable Strategy for Conserving Tropical Ecosystems?" *Ecological Economics* 34: 293–300.

Benedick, Richard Elliot. 1998. *Ozone Diplomacy: New Directions in Safeguarding the Planet*, enlarged edition. Cambridge, Mass.: Harvard University Press.

Berejekian, Jeffrey. 1997. "The Gains Debate: Framing State Choice." *American Political Science Review* 91(4) (December): 789–805.

Biermann, Frank. 2002. "Institutions for Scientific Advice: Global Environmental Assessments and Their Influence in Developing Countries." *Global Governance* 8: 195–219.

Bin Mohd, Rusli, and Jan G. Laarman. 1994. "The Struggle for Influence: US Nongovernmental Organizations and Tropical Forests." *Journal of Forestry* 92(6) (June): 32–36.

Birnie, Patricia. 1985. *International Regulation of Whaling: From Conservation of Whaling to Conservation of Whales and Regulation of Whale Watching*, vols. I and II. New York: Oceana.

Birnie, Patricia. 1985. "The Role of Developing Countries in Nudging the International Whaling Commission from Regulating Whaling to Encouraging Nonconsumptive Uses of Whales." *Ecology Law Quarterly* 12: 937–75.

Birnie, Patricia, and Alan E. Boyle. 1992. *International Law and the Environment*. Oxford: Clarendon Press.

Bodansky, Daniel. 1991. "Scientific Uncertainty and the Precautionary Principle." *Environment* 33(7) (September): 4–5, 43.

Boettcher III, William A. 1995. "Context, Methods, Numbers, and Words: Prospect Theory in International Relations." *Journal of Conflict Resolution* 39(3) (September): 561–83.

Bogo, Jennifer, and Tracey C. Rembert. 1999. "Close to Nature." *E* 10(6) (November): 46.

Bolan, Cristen. 2005. "Natura Sustains its Growth." *Global Cosmetic Industry* (November): 22–3.

Bramble, Barbara J., and Gareth Porter. 1992. "Non-Governmental Organizations and the Making of U.S. International Policy." In *The International Politics of the Environment*, edited by Andrew Hurrell and Benedict Kingsbury, 313–53. Oxford: Clarendon Press.

Breitmeier, Helmut, and Volker Rittberger. 1998. "Environmental NGOs in an Emerging Global Civil Society." Nr. 32. Tübingen, Germany: Center for International Relations/Peace and Conflict Studies, Institute for Political Science, University of Tübingen.

Brettell, Anna. Forthcoming. "Security, Energy, and the Environment: The Atmospheric Link." In *The Environmental Dimensions of Asian Security: Conflict and Cooperation Over Environment, Energy and Natural Resources*, edited by In-take Hyun and Miranda Schreurs. Washington D.C.: United States Institute of Peace Press.

Breyer, Stephen J. 1993. *Breaking the Vicious Circle: Toward Effective Risk Regulation*. Cambridge, Mass.: Harvard University Press.

Brickman, Ronald, Sheila Jasanoff, and Thomas Ilgen. 1985. *Controlling Chemicals: The Politics of Regulation in Europe and the United States*. Ithaca and London: Cornell University Press.

British Antarctic Survey. 2005. *British Antarctic Survey Bulletin* (19 December) http://www.theozonehole.com/ozonehole2005.htm.

Brown, Paul. 1993. "Playing Football with the Whales." *The Guardian*, 1 May: 26.

Brown, Paul. 1994. "Soviet Union Illegally Killed Great Whales." *The Guardian*, 12 February: 12.

Brown Weiss, Edith. 1998. "The Five International Treaties: A Living History." In *Engaging Countries: Strengthening Compliance with International Environmental Accords*, edited by Edith Brown Weiss and Harold K. Jacobson, 89–172. Cambridge, Mass.: MIT Press.

Brühl, Tanja. 1998. "NGOs and Formation of International Environmental Regimes: Explaining Their Inclusion." Paper presented at the Third Pan-European International Relations Conference, September, Vienna, Austria.

Brunnée, Jutta, and Stephen J. Toope. 1997. "Environmental Security and Freshwater Resources: Ecosystem Regime Building."

*American Journal of International Law* 91(1) (January): 26–59.

Bruner, A. G., R. E. Gullison, R. E. Rice, and G. A. B. da Fonseca. 2001. "Effectiveness of Parks in Protecting Tropical Diversity." *Science* 291 (5 January): 125–27.

Bruno, Kenny. 1992. "The Corporate Capture of the Earth Summit." *Multinational Monitor* 13 (July–August): 15–20.

Bruyninckx, Hans. 2006. "Sustainable Development: The Institutionalization of a Contested Policy Concept." In *Palgrave Advances in International Environmental Politics*, edited by Michele M. Betsill, Kathryn Hochstetler, and Dimitris Stevis, 265–98. Basingstoke and New York: Palgrave Macmillan.

Bunyard, Peter. 1999. "Eradicating the Amazon Rainforests Will Wreak Havoc on Climate." *The Ecologist* 29(2) (March–April): 81–85.

Burns, William C. G. 2000. "From the Harpoon to the Heat: Climate Change and the International Whaling Commission in the 21st Century." An Occasional Paper of the Pacific Institute for Studies in Development, Environment, and Security.

Burns, William C. G. 2005. "Introduction to Special Issue on the Precautionary Principle and Its Operationalisation in International Environmental Regimes and Domestic Policymaking." *International Journal of Global Environmental Issues* 5(1/2): 1–9.

Butler, Nick. 2000. "Companies in International Relations." *Survival* 42(1) (Spring): 149–64.

Butler, Rhett A. n.d. "Amazon Destruction." http://www.mongabay.com/about.htm.

Butterworth, D.S. 1992. "Science and Sentimentality." *Nature* 357 (18 June): 532–34.

Cairncross, Frances. 1990. "Cleaning up." *Economist*, 8 September: S1ff.

Cairncross, Frances. 1991. *Costing the Earth*. Boston: Harvard Business School Press.

"Call Me Smiley." 1994. *New York Times Magazine*, 13 March: 14.

*Canada-United States Air Quality Agreement Progress Report 2004*. http://www.ec.gc.ca/pdb/can_us/2004Ca nUs/intro_e.html.

Cashore, Benjamin, Graeme Auld, and Deanna Newsom, 2004. *Governing Through Markets: Forest Certification and the Emergence of Non-State Authority*. New Haven: Yale University Press.

*Cartagena Protocol on Biosafety to the Convention on Biological Diversity*. 2000.

Catan, Thomas, and Fiona Harvey. 2005. "BP Earmarks 8bn for Green Investment." *The Financial Times*, 29 November: 22.

CCX. n.d. "About CCX." http://www.chicagoclimatex.com/about/.

Chadwick, Alex. 2001. "The Treasured Islands of Palmyra." *National Geographic* 199(3) (March): 46–56.

Chadwick, Douglas H. 2001. "Pursuing the Minke," *National Geographic* 199(4) (April): 58–71

Charnovitz, Steve. 1997. "Two Centuries of Participation: NGOs and International Governance." *Michigan Journal of International Law* 18 (Winter): 183–286.

Chasek, Pamela S. 1997. "The Convention to Combat Desertification: Lessons Learned for Sustainable Development." *Journal of Environment and Development* 6(2): 147–69.

Chasek, Pamela S., David L. Downie, and Janet Welsh Brown. 2006. *Global Environmental Politics*, 4th edn. Boulder, Colo.: Westview Press.

Chayes, Abram, and Antonia Chayes. 1995. *The New Sovereignty: Compliance with International Regulatory Agreements*. Cambridge, Mass.: Harvard University Press.

"Chemical Production: Holed Up." 1995. *Economist*, 9 December: 63.

Chichilnisky, Graciela. 1998. "Sustainable Development and North–South Trade." In *Protection of Global Biodiversity: Converging Strategies*, edited by Lakshman D. Guruswamy and Jeffrey A. McNeely, 101–17. Durham, N.C., and London: Duke University Press.

Choucri, Nazli. 1991. "The Global Environment and Multinational Corporations." *Technology Review* 94(3) (April): 52–59.

Cities for Climate Protection. n.d. "Members." http://www.iclei.org/index.php?id=642.

"Citizens' Groups: The Non-Governmental Order – Will NGOs Democratise, or Merely Disrupt, Global Governance?" 1999. *Economist*, 11 December: 20.

Clapp, Jennifer. 1996. "Multinational Corporations and Environmental Hazards in the Asia-Pacific Region." Paper prepared for the International Studies Association Annual Meeting, San Diego, April.

Clapp, Jennifer. 2005. "The Privatization of Global Environmental Governance: ISO 14000 and the Developing World." In *The Business of Global Environmental Governance*, edited by David L. Levy and Peter J. Newell, 223–48. Cambridge, Mass.: MIT Press.

Clapp, Jennifer, and Peter Dauvergne. 2005. *Paths to a Green World: The Political Economy of the Global Environment*. Cambridge, Mass.: MIT Press.

Clapp, Roger Alex, and Carolyn Crook. 2002. "Drowning in the Magic Well: Shaman Pharmaceuticals and the Elusive Value of Traditional Knowledge." *Journal of Environment and Development* 11(1) (March): 79–102.

Clark, Colin W., and R. Lamberson. 1992. "An Economic History and Analysis of Pelagic Whaling." *Marine Policy* 6(2) (April): 107–9.

Clark, D. A., S. C. Piper, C. D. Keeling, and D. B. Clark. 2003. "Tropical Rain Forest Tree Growth and Atmospheric Carbon Dynamics Linked to Interannual Temperature Variation During 1984–2000." *PNAS* 100(10) (13 May): 5852–56.

Clark, John. 1990. *Democratizing Development: The Role of Voluntary Organizations*. West Hartford, Conn.: Kumarian Press.

"Climate Change: The Big Emitters." 2005. *BBC Online* (4 July). http://news.bbc.co.uk/1/hi/sci/tech/3143798.stm.

Conca, Ken. 2006. *Governing Water: Contentious Transnational Politics and Global Institution Building*. Cambridge, Mass.: MIT Press.

Connole, Patrick. 1999. "Ford Exits Anti-Kyoto Climate Change Group." *Reuters News Service* (7 December).

Connolly, Barbara. 1999. "Asymmetrical Rivalry in Common Pool Resources and European Responses to Acid Rain." In *Anarchy and the Environment: The International Relations of Common Pool Resources,* edited by J. Samuel Barkin and George E. Shambaugh, 122–54. Albany: SUNY Press.

Conservation International. 1995. "Rainforest Buttons Get Wider Distribution." Press release, 14 March. http://conservation.org/WEB/NEWS/pressrel/95-0314.htm.

Conservation International. n.d. "Agroforestry and Forest Products." http://www.conservation.org/xp/CIWEB/programs/enterprises/.

*Convention on Biological Diversity*. 1992.

*Convention on Long-Range Transboundary Air Pollution*. 1979.

*Convention to Combat Desertification*. 1994.

*Copenhagen Amendments to the Montreal Protocol*. 1992.

Cox, Susan Jane Buck. 1985. "No Tragedy on the Commons." *Environmental Ethics* 7 (Spring): 49–61.

Cunningham, William P., and Barbara Woodworth Saigo. 1997. *Environmental Science: A Global Concern*. Dubuque, Ia.: William C. Brown.

Cutler, A. Claire, Virginia Haufler, and Tony Porter, eds. 1999. *Private Authority and International Affairs*. Albany: SUNY Press.

Daley, Beth. 2004. "Region Struggles on Greenhouse Emissions Goals." *Boston Globe*, 15 March: A1.

Daley, Beth. 2006. "Big Gaps in State's Plans for Emissions." *Boston Globe*, 17 January: A1.

Daniels, Lee. 2000. "Texaco Buys 20% Stake In Energy Conversion Company." *Reuters News Service*, 7 June.

Darst, Robert G. 2001. *Smokestack Diplomacy: Cooperation and Conflict in East–West Environmental Politics*. Cambridge, Mass.: MIT Press.

Dasgupta, Chandrashekhar. 1994. "The Climate Change Negotiations." In *Negotiating Climate Change*, edited by Irving Mintzer and J. A. Leonard, 138–39. Cambridge: Cambridge University Press.

Day, David. 1987. *The Whale War*. San Francisco: Sierra Club Books.

De Aragão, Murillo, and Stephen Bunker. 1998."Brazil: Regional Inequalities and Ecological Diversity in a Federal System." In *Engaging Countries: Strengthening Compliance with International Environmental Accords*, edited by Edith Brown Weiss and Harold K. Jacobson, 475–509. Cambridge, Mass.: MIT Press.

De Oliveira, Miguel Darcy, and Rajesh Tandon. 1994. "An Emerging Global Civil Society." In *Citizens: Strengthening Global Civil Society*, edited by Miguel Darcy de Oliveira and Rajesh Tandon, 1–17. Washington, D.C.: Civicus: World Alliance for Citizen Participation.

DeRidder, Kim J. 1988. "The Nature and Effects of Acid Rain: A Comparison of Assessments." In *Acid Rain and Friendly Neighbors: The Policy Dispute Between Canada and The United States*, edited by Jurgen Schmandt, Judith Clarkson, and Hilliard Roderick, 31–63. Durham, N.C.: Duke University Press.

Dernbach, John C. 1998. "Sustainable Development as a Framework for National Governance." *Case Western Reserve Law Review* 49(1) (Fall): 93.

Desai, Uday. 1998. "Environment, Economic Growth, and Government in Developing Countries." In *Ecological Policy and Politics in Developing Countries: Economic Growth, Democracy, and the Environment*, edited by Uday Desaim, 1–45. Albany: SUNY Press.

Desai, Uday. 1998. "Poverty, Government, and the Global Environment." In *Ecological Policy and Politics in Developing Countries*, edited by Uday Desai, 295–301. Albany: SUNY Press.

DeSimone, Livio D., and Frank Popoff. 1997. *Eco-Efficiency: The Business Link to Sustainable Development*. Cambridge, Mass.: MIT Press.

DeSombre, Elizabeth R. 1996. "Compliance Implications of the Multilateral Fund." *International Conference On Ozone Protection Technologies*. Conference Proceedings. Washington D.C. (21–23 October): 910–19.

DeSombre, Elizabeth R. 1998. "International Environmental Policy." In *Environmental Management in Practice: Analysis, Implementation, and Policy*, edited by B. Nath, L. Hens, P. Compton, and D. Devust, 361–77. New York: Routledge.

DeSombre, Elizabeth R. 2000. "Developing Country Influence in Global Environmental Negotiations." *Environmental Politics* 9(3) (Autumn): 23–42.

DeSombre, Elizabeth R. 2000. *Domestic Sources of International Environmental Policy: Industry, Environmentalists, and U.S. Power*. Cambridge, Mass.: MIT Press.

DeSombre, Elizabeth R. 2001. "Distorting Global Governance: Membership, Voting, and the IWC." In *Toward a Sustainable Whaling Regime*, edited by Robert L. Friedheim, 183–99. Seattle: University of Washington Press.

DeSombre, Elizabeth R. 2001. "United Nations Conference on the Human Environment." In *Oxford Encyclopedia of Global Change*, edited by Andrew Goudie. New York and Oxford: Oxford University Press.

DeSombre, Elizabeth R. 2001. "United Nations Conference on Environment and Development." In *Oxford Encyclopedia of Global Change*, edited by Andrew Goudie. New York and Oxford: Oxford University Press.

DeSombre, Elizabeth R. 2005. "Fishing Under Flags of Convenience: Using Market Power to Increase Participation In International Regulation." *Global Environmental Politics* 5(4) (November): 73–94.

DeSombre, Elizabeth R. 2005. "Understanding United States Unilateralism: Domestic Sources of U.S. International Environmental Policy." In *The Global Environment*, edited by Regina S. Axelrod, David Leonard Downie, and Norman J. Vig, 181–99. Washington D.C.: CQ Press.

DeSombre, Elizabeth R. 2006. *Flagging Standards: Globalization and Environmental, Safety, and Labor Regulations at Sea*. Cambridge, Mass.: MIT Press.

DeSombre, Elizabeth R. 2006. *Global Environmental Institutions*. London and New York: Routledge.

DeSombre, Elizabeth, and Joanne Kauffman. 1996. "The Montreal Protocol Multilateral Fund: Partial Success Story." In *Institutions for Environmental Aid*, edited by Robert O. Keohane and Marc A. Levy, 89–126. Cambridge, Mass.: MIT Press.

Dimitrov, Radoslav S. 2006. *Science and International Environmental Policy: Regimes and Non-Regimes in Global Governance*. Boulder, Colo.: Roman & Littlefield.

Donovan, G. P. 1989. "Forty-Second Annual Meeting of the International Whaling Commission." *Polar Record* 24 (June): 631–63.

Dore, Mohammed H. I., and Jorge M. Nogueira. 1994. "The Amazon Rain Forest, Sustainable Development, and the Biodiversity Convention: A Political Economy Perspective." *Ambio* 23(8) (December): 491–96.

Douglas, Mary, and Aaron Wildavsky. 1982. *Risk and Culture: An Essay on the Selection of Technical and Environmental Dangers*. Berkeley, Los Angeles, and London: University of California Press.

Downie, David. "Ozone Depletion and Common Pool Resources." In *Anarchy and the Environment: The International Relations of Common Pool Resources*, edited by J. Samuel Barkin and George E. Shambaugh, 97–121. Albany: SUNY Press.

Doyle, Timothy. 2004. *Environmental Movements in Minority and Majority Worlds*. New Brunswick, N.J.: Rutgers University Press.

Dyer, Paul. 2006. "Whalers 'Faking' Science." *Sunday Telegraph*, 29 January: 18.

EANET Secretariat. n.d. "East Asian Acid Deposition Monitoring Network." http://www.eanet.cc/eanet.html.

Easterbrook, Gregg. 1994. "Forget PCB's. Radon. Alar." *New York Times Magazine*, 11 September: 60–63.

Eberlee, John. 2000. "Assessing the Benefits of Bioprospecting in Latin America." *IDRC Reports* (21 January). http://www.idrc.ca/en/ev-5571-201-1-DO_TOPIC.html.

Eccleston, Bernard. 1996. "Does North–South Collaboration Enhance NGO Influence on Deforestation Policies in Malaysia and Indonesia?" In *NGOs and Environmental Policies: Asia and Africa*, edited by David Potter, 66–89. London: Frank Cass.

Elliot, G. 1979. "Failure of the International Whaling Commission 1946–1966." *Marine Policy* 3: 149–55.

Ellis, Richard. 1999. *Men and Whales*. New York: Lyons Press.

Ember, Lois. 1988. "U.S., Canada Still Far Apart on Acid Rain Accord." *Chemical and Engineering News*, 8 February: 15.

Energy Information Administration. 2006. "Emissions of Greenhouse Gases in the United States 2004 – Executive Summary." Report DOE/EIA-0573(2004/es) (March).

Environment Canada. n.d. "Acid Rain: What's Being Done?" http://www.ec.gc.ca/acidrain/done-canada.html.

"EU Industry Must Cut CO2 to Meet Kyoto Targets." 2006. *Planet Ark* (Reuters Environmental News Service), 11 January.

Fairman, David. 1996. "The Global Environmental Facility: Haunted by the Shadow of the Future." In *Institutions for Environmental Aid: Pitfalls and Promise,* edited by Robert O. Keohane and Marc A. Levy, 55–87. Cambridge, Mass., and London: MIT Press.

Falkner, Robert. 2003. "Private Environmental Governance and International Relations: Exploring the Links." *Global Environmental Politics* 3(2) (May): 72–87.

FAO. 2005. "Incentive to Curb Deforestation Needed to Counter Climate Change." *Press Release*, 9 December. http://www.fao.org/newsroom/en/news/2005/1000176/index.html.

FAO. 2005. *Global Forest Resources Assessment 2005*. Rome: FAO.

Fernandes, Ruben Cesar. 1994. "Threads of Planetary Citizenship." In *Citizens: Strengthening Global Civil Society,* edited by Miguel Darcy de Oliveira and Rajesh Tandon, 319–46. Washington D.C.: Civicus: World Alliance for Citizen Participation.

Fineman, Mark. 1997. "Dominica's Support of Whaling Is No Fluke." *Los Angeles Times*, 9 December: A1.

Finer, Matt, and Leda Huta. 2005. "Yasuni Blues: the IMF, Ecuador and Coerced Oil Exploitation." *Multinational Monitor* 26(5–6) (May–June): 29–33.

Finger, Matthias. 1994. "NGOs and Transformation: Beyond Social Movement Theory." In *Environmental NGOs in World Politics: Linking the Local and the Global,* edited by Thomas Princen and Matthias Finger, 48–66. London and New York: Routledge.

Finger, Matthias, and James Kilcoyne. 1997. "Why Transnational Corporations Are Organizing to 'Save the Global Environment.'" *The Ecologist* 27(4) (July–August 1997): 138–42.

Flatt, Victor B. 1994. "Book Reviews: Should the Circle Be Unbroken?: A Review of the Hon. Stephen Breyer's *Breaking the Vicious Circle*" *Environmental Law* 24(4) (Fall): 1707–28.

Foster, Kenneth R., Paolo Vecchia, and Michael H. Repacholi. 2000. "Science and the Precautionary Principle." *Science* 288 (12 May): 979–81.

Fox, Jonathan A., and L. David Brown. 1998. "Introduction." In *The Struggle for Accountability: The World Bank, NGOs, and Grassroots Movements*, edited by Jonathan Fox and L. David Brown, 1–47. Cambridge, Mass.: MIT Press.

*Framework Convention on Climate Change*. 1992.

Framework Convention on Climate Change, Conference of the Parties. 1997. "Methodological Issues Related to a

Protocol Or Another Legal Instrument: Draft Decision submitted by the Committee of the Whole." FCCC/CP/1997/L.5 (8 December).

Framework Convention on Climate Change, Conference of the Parties. 1998. "Actions Taken by the Conference of the Parties." 4th Session, Annex 60, FCCC/CP/1997/7/Add.1, 1997.

Francis, Daniel. 1990. *A History of World Whaling*. Ontario: Viking.

Friends of the Earth. 1990. *Funding Change: Developing Countries and the Montreal Protocol*.

Fritz, Jan-Stefan. 1998. "Earthwatch Twenty-Five Years On: Between Science and International Environmental Governance." *International Environmental Affairs* 10(3) (Summer): 173–96.

Gagosian, Robert B. 2003. *Abrupt Climate Change: Should We be Worried?* Woods Hole, Mass: Woods Hole Oceanographic Institution.

Gambell, Ray. 1993. Personal Interview. IWC Secretary. August.

Gambell, Ray. 1997. Personal Interview. IWC Secretary. 3 June.

Garcia-Johnson, Ronie. 2000. *Exporting Environmentalism: U.S. Multinational Chemical Corporations in Brazil and Mexico*. Cambridge, Mass.: MIT Press.

Gardner, Timothy. 2000. "Global Warming Business Group Cools Its Message." *Reuters News Service*, 9 November.

Gardner, Timothy. 2006. "World CO2 Emissions to Rise 75 Pct by 2030 – EIA." *Planet Ark, Reuters Environmental News Service*, 21 June.

GEF Secretariat. n.d. "Project Database." http://gefonline.org/projectList.cfm.

Gelbspan, Ross. 1997. *The Heat Is On: The High Stakes Battle over Earth's Threatened Climate*. Reading, Mass.: Addison-Wesley.

Gentry, Alwyn H., Charles M. Peters, and Robert O. Mendelsohn. 1989. "Valuation of an Amazonian Rainforest." *Nature*, 29 June: 655–56.

Global Commons Institute. 1996. "Draft Proposals for a Climate Change Protocol Based on Contraction and Convergence." Section 2.14 (September). http://www.gci.org.uk/contconv/protweb.html, date visited: 26 June 2001.

Global Environment Facility Secretariat. n.d. "Biodiversity and Amazon." http://gefweb.org.

Global Environment Facility Secretariat. 2000. "Biodiversity Projects." http://gefweb.org.

Goleman, Daniel. 1994. "Hidden Rules Often Distort Ideas of Risk." *New York Times*, 1 February: C1.

Golich, Vicki L., and Terry Forrest Young. 1993. "United States–Canadian Negotiations for Acid Rain Control." Case 452. *Pew Case Studies in International Affairs*. Institute for the Study of Diplomacy, Pew Case Studies Center, Georgetown University.

Gorrie, Peter. 2005. "U.S. Rejects Bids for Post-Kyoto Talks." *Toronto Star*, 7 December: A4.

Green, Julia Jabour. 2003. "Report of the Workshop on Bioprospecting in the High Seas." University of Otago, Dunedin, New Zealand (28–29 November), available at http://www.fish.govt.nz/current/deepsea/workshop-report-bioprospecting-in-the-high-seas.doc.

Greene, Owen. "The System for Implementation Review in the Ozone Regime." In *The Implementation and Effectiveness of International Environmental Commitments*, edited by David G. Victor, Kal Raustiala, and Eugene B. Skolnikoff, 97–98. Cambridge, Mass.: MIT Press.

Greer, Jed, and Kenny Bruno. 1996. *Greenwash: The Reality Behind Corporate Environmentalism*. Penang, Malaysia: Third World Network; New York: Apex Press.

Griffin, Dale, and Amos Tversky. 1992. "The Weighing of Evidence and the Determinants of Confidence." *Cognitive Psychology* 24: 411–35.

Grubb, Michael, Matthias Koch, Abby Munson, Francis Sullivan, and Koy Thomson. 1993. *The Earth Summit Agreements: A Guide and Assessment*. London: Earthscan.

Gutman, Pablo. 2003. "What Did WSSD Accomplish? An NGO Perspective." *Environment* 45(2) (March): 21–26.

Haas, Peter M. 1990. *Saving the Mediterranean: The Politics of International Environmental Cooperation*. New York: Columbia University Press.

Haas, Peter M. 1992. "Banning Chlorofluorocarbons: Epistemic Community Efforts to Protect Stratospheric Ozone." *International Organization* 46(1) (Winter): 187–224.

Haas, Peter M. 1992. "Introduction: Epistemic Communities and International Policy Coordination." *International Organization* 46(1) (Winter): 1–35.

Haas, Peter M., Robert O. Keohane, and Marc A. Levy. 1995. "The Effectiveness of International Environmental Institutions." In *Institutions for the Earth: Sources of Effective International Environmental Protection*, edited by Peter M. Haas, Robert O. Keohane, and Marc A. Levy, 3–24. Cambridge, Mass.: MIT Press.

Hardin, Garrett. 1968. "The Tragedy of the Commons." *Science* 162: 1243–48.

Harrison, Neil E., and Gary C. Bryner. 2004. "Toward Theory." In *Science and Politics in the International Environment*, edited by Neil E. Harrison and Gary C. Bryner, 327–50. Lanham, Md.: Rowman & Littlefield.

Hart, Stuart L., and Gautam Ahuja. 1996. "Does It Pay to Be Green? An Empirical Examination of the Relationship Between Emission Reduction and Firm Performance." *Business Strategy and Environment* 5: 30–37.

Harvey, Fiona. 2006. "Japan Fails to Reverse Ban on Commercial Whaling." *Financial Times*, 20 June: 10.

Healey, James R. 2005. "Alternative Energy not in the Cards at ExxonMobil." *USA Today*, 28 October: 5B.

Heath, Chip, Richard P. Larrick, and George Wu. 1999. "Goals as Reference Points." *Cognitive Psychology* 38: 79–109.

Heiman, Michael K. 1997. "Science by the People: Grassroots Environmental Monitoring and the Debate Over Scientific Expertise." *Journal of Planning Education and Research* 6: 291–303.

Heinzerling, Lisa. 1995. "Political Science." *University of Chicago Law Review* 62 (Winter): 449ff.

Henkin, Louis. 1979. *How Nations Behave: Law and Foreign Policy*, 2nd edn. New York: Columbia University Press for the Council on Foreign Relations.

Hepeng, Jia. 2004. "China is Second Biggest Greenhouse Gas Emitter." SciDev.net

(24 November)
http://www.scidev.net/news/index.cfm?f
useaction=readnews&itemid=1761&lang
uage=1.

Hileman, Better. 1997. "Ozone Treaty:
Successful but Pitfalls Remain."
*Chemical and Engineering News*, 15
September: 24.

Honey, Martha. 1991. *Ecotourism and
Sustainable Development*. Washington,
D.C., and Covelo, Calif.: Island Press.

Horsch, Robert B., and Robert T. Fraley.
1998. "Biotechnology Can Help Reduce
the Loss of Biodiversity." In *Protection of
Global Biodiversity: Converging
Strategies*, edited by Lakshman D.
Guruswamy and Jeffrey A. McNeely,
49–65. Durham, N.C., and London:
Duke University Press.

Hovi, Jon, Detlef F. Sprinz, and Arild
Underdal. 2004. "The Oslo–Potsdam
Solution to Measuring Regime
Effectiveness: Critique, Response, and
the Road Ahead." *Global Environmental
Politics* 3(3) (August): 74–96.

Hundewadt, Erik. 1995. "The Role of
Voluntary Associations (NGOs) in a
Democratic Society." In *The Role of
Non-Governmental Organizations in the
New European Order*, edited by Jürgen
Schramm, 7–12. Baden-Baden: Nomos
Verlagsgesellschaft.

Hunter, Christopher J. 1997. "Sustainable
Bioprospecting: Using Private Contracts
and International Legal Principles and
Policies to Conserve Raw Medicinal
Materials." *Boston College
Environmental Affairs Law Review* 25(1)
(Fall): 129–74.

Hunter, Robert. 1979. Warriors of the
Rainbow: A Chronicle of the
Greenpeace Movement. New York: Holt,
Reinhart, & Winston.

Hurrell, Andrew. 1991. "The Politics of
Amazonian Deforestation." *Journal of
Latin American Studies* 23: 197–215.

"Iceland Rejoins IWC, but Exempt from
Whaling Ban." 2001. *Reuters News
Service* 4 July.

IISD (International Institute for Sustainable
Development). 2003. "Summary of the
Ninth Conference of the Parties to the
United Nations Framework Convention
on Climate Change 1–12 December
2003." *Earth Negotiations Bulletin*
12(231) (15 December).

"Indigenous People's Knowledge:
Pharmaceuticals and Their Business."
1996. *Nuestra Amazonia* (July): 7.

Intergovernmental Panel on Climate Change.
n.d. "About IPCC."
http://www.ipcc.ch/about/about.htm,
date visited: 24 June 2001.

Intergovernmental Panel on Climate Change.
2001. "Summary for Policymakers: A
Report of Working Group I of the
Intergovernmental Panel on Climate
Change." Available at
http://www.ipcc.ch, date visited: 24
June 2001.

*International Convention for the Regulation
of Whaling*. 1946.

International Development Research Centre.
1992. *For Earth's Sake: A Report from
the Commission on Developing
Countries and Global Change*. Ottawa:
International Development Research
Centre.

International Development Research Centre.
1996. "Shaman Pharmaceuticals:
Socially Responsible Drug
Development." (25 October).
http://idrc.ca/books/reports/1996/30-
02e.html.

International Institute for Sustainable
Development. 1993. "A Brief Analysis of

the Second Session of the INCD, 13–24 September 1993." *Earth Negotiations Bulletin* 4(22) http://www.iisd.ca/linkages/vol04/04220 34e.html (24 September).

International Institute for Sustainable Development. 1994. "Summary of the Fourth Session of the INC for the Elaboration of An International Convention to Combat Desertification, 21–31 March 1994." *Earth Negotiations Bulletin* 4(44) http://www.iisd.ca/vol04/0444001e.html (31 March).

International Organization for Standardization. 2005. *The ISO Survey of Certifications*. Geneva: ISO.

*International Tropical Timber Agreement*. 1994.

International Whaling Commission. 1993. *Verbatim Record*.

International Whaling Commission. 1996. "Chairman's Report of the 47th Annual Meeting."

"International Whaling Commission: 50th Annual Meeting: Opening Statement by the United Kingdom Delegation." 1998. IWC/50/OS/UK.

IPCC. 2001. *Climate Change 2001: The Scientific Basis*. Cambridge: Cambridge University Press.

IPCC. 2004. "16 Years of Scientific Assessment in Support of the Climate Convention." (December).

IWC. 2006. "Catches Under Objection since 1985." http://www.iwcoffice.org/_documents/ta ble_objection.htm.

IWC. 2006. "Special Permit Catches since 1985." http://www.iwcoffice.org/_documents/ta ble_permit.htm.

Jacobsen, Susan Feitelberg. 1996. "North–South Relations and Global Environmental Issues – A Review of the Literature." *CDR Working Paper* 96.3. Copenhagen: Center for Development Research. (May).

Jacobson, Harold K., and Edith Brown Weiss. 1998. "A Framework for Analysis." In *Engaging Countries: Strengthening Compliance with International Environmental Accords*, edited by Edith Brown Weiss and Harold K. Jacobson, 1. Cambridge, Mass.: MIT Press.

Jakobeit, Cord. 1997. "Nonstate Actors Leading the Way: Debt-for-Nature Swaps." In *Institutions for Environmental Aid: Pitfalls and Promise*, edited by Robert O. Keohane and Marc A. Levy, 127–66. Cambridge, Mass.: MIT Press.

Jamieson, Dale. 1996. "Scientific Uncertainty and the Political Process." *Annals of the American Academy of Political and Social Sciences* 545 (May): 35–43.

Janofsky, Michael. 2005. "U.S. Court Backs Bush's Revisions in Clean Air Act." *New York Times*, 25 June: 1.

Janofsky, Michael. 2006. "Judges Overturn Bush Bid to Ease Pollution Rules." *New York Times*, 18 March: 1.

"Japan 'Bought Whale Votes.'" 2005. *Daily Telegraph*, 19 July: 10.

*Japan Whaling Association v. American Cetacean Society*. 1986. 478 U.S. 221, 105 S. Ct., 2860.

Jasanoff, Sheila. 1990. "American Exceptionalism and the Political Acknowledgment of Risk." *Daedalus* 119(4) (Fall): 63–78.

Jasanoff, Sheila. 1991. "Cross-National Differences in Policy Implementation." *Evaluation Review* 15(1) (February): 103–19.

Jasanoff, Sheila. 1992. "Pluralism and Convergence in International Science Policy." In *Science and Sustainability: Selected Papers on IIASA's 20th Anniversary*, 157–80. Laxenburg, Austria: The International Institute for Applied Systems Analysis.

Jasanoff, Sheila. 1997. "NGOs and the Environment: From Knowledge to Action." *Third World Quarterly* 18(3): 579–94.

Jervis, Robert. 1976. *Perception and Misperception in International Politics.* Princeton: Princeton University Press.

Jervis, Robert. 1992. "Political Implications of Loss Aversion." *Political Psychology.* 13: 187–204.

*Johannesburg Plan of Implementation.* 2002.

Joyce, Christopher. 1994. *Earthly Goods: Medicine-Hunting in the Rainforest.* Boston: Little, Brown, & Company.

Kahneman, Daniel, and Amos Tversky. 1979. "Prospect Theory: An Analysis of Decision Under Risk." *Econometrica* 47(2) (March): 263–92.

Kamieniecki, Sheldon. 2006. *Corporate America and Environmental Policy: How Often Does Business Get Its Way?* Stanford: Stanford University Press.

Karlsson, Sylvia. 2002. "The North–South Knowledge Divide: Consequences for Global Environmental Governance." In *Global Environmental Governance: Options and Opportunities*, edited by Daniel C. Esty and Maria H. Ivanova, 1–24. New Haven: Yale School of Forestry and Environmental Studies.

Kates, Robert W. 1962. "Hazard and Choice Perception in Flood Plain Management." *Research Paper 78*. Department of Geography, University of Chicago.

Keck, Margaret E., and Kathryn Sikkink. 1998. *Activists Beyond Borders: Advocacy Networks in International Politics.* Ithaca and London: Cornell University Press.

Keohane, Robert O. 1985. *After Hegemony: Cooperating and Discord in the World Political Economy.* Princeton: Princeton University Press.

Keohane, Robert O., and Joseph S. Nye, 1977. *Power and Interdependence: World Politics in Transition.* Boston and Toronto: Little, Brown, & Company.

Keohane, Robert O., and Elinor Ostrom. 1995. "Introduction." In *Local Commons and Global Interdependence*, edited by Robert O. Keohane and Elinor Ostrom, 1–26. London: Sage.

Kerr, Richard A. 1986. "Antarctic Ozone Hole is Still Deepening." *Science* 232 (June): 1602.

Kerr, Richard A. 2001. "Rising Global Temperature, Rising Uncertainty." *Science* 292 (April): 192–94.

Klinger, Janeen. "Debt-for-Nature Swaps and the Limits to International Cooperation on Behalf of the Environment." *Environmental Politics* 3(2) (Summer): 229–46.

Kobrin, Stephen J. 1987. "Testing the Bargaining Hypothesis in the Manufacturing Sector in Developing Countries." *International Organization* 41(4) (Autumn): 609–38.

Kowert, Paul A., and Margaret G. Hermann. 1997. "Who Takes Risks? Daring and Caution in Foreign Policy Making." *Journal of Conflict Resolution* 41(5) (October): 611–37.

Kraemer, Moritz, and Jörg Hartmann. 1993. "Policy Responses to Tropical Deforestation: Are Debt-for-Nature Swaps Appropriate?" *Journal of Environment and Development* 2(2) (Summer): 41–65.

Krasner, Steven D. 1982. "Structural Causes and Regime Consequences: Regimes as Intervening Variables." In *International Regimes*, edited by Stephen D. Krasner, 1–21. Ithaca and London: Cornell University Press.

Krug, Thelma. 1998. "Space Technology and Environmental Monitoring in Brazil." *Journal of International Affairs* 51(2) (Spring): 655–75.

*Kyoto Protocol to the Framework Convention on Climate Change.* 1997.

Landers Jr., Frederick Pool. 1997. "The Black Market Trade in Chlorofluorocarbons: The Montreal Protocol Makes Banned Refrigerants a Hot Commodity." *The Georgia Journal of International and Comparative Law* 26 (Spring): 478–79.

Leonard, H. Jeffrey. 1988. *Pollution and the Struggle for World Product: Multinational Corporations, Environment, and International Comparative Advantage.* Cambridge: Cambridge University Press.

Levinson, Arik. 1996. "Environmental Regulations and Industry Location: International and Domestic Evidence." In *Fair Trade and Harmonization: Prerequisites for Free Trade?*, vol. I: *Economic Analysis*, edited by Jagdish Bhagwati and Robert E. Hudec, 429–57. Cambridge, Mass., and London: MIT Press.

Levy, David L., and Peter J. Newell. 2004. "Introduction: The Business of Global Environmental Governance." In *The Business of Global Environmental Governance.* edited by David L. Levy and Peter J. Newell, 1–16. Cambridge, Mass.: MIT Press.

Levy, Jack S. 1996. "Loss Aversion, Framing, and Bargaining: The Implications of Prospect Theory for International Conflict." *International Political Science Review* 17(2): 179–95.

Levy, Marc A. 1986. "Leviathan's Leviathan: Power, Interests, and Institutional Change in the International Whaling Commission." Unpublished Paper, Harvard University, June.

Levy, Marc. A. 1993. "European Acid Rain: The Power of Tote-Board Diplomacy." In *Institutions for the Earth: Sources of Effective International Environmental Protection*, edited by Peter M. Haas, Robert O. Keohane, and Marc A. Levy, 74–132. Cambridge, Mass., and London: MIT Press.

Lichtenstein, Slovic, B. Fischhoff, M. Layman, and B. Combs. 1978. "Judged Frequency of Lethal Events." *Journal of Experimental Psychology: Human Learning and Memory* 4: 551–78.

Lies, Elaine. 2006. "Japan Plans New Pro-Whalers Group to End Hunting Ban." *Planet Ark, Reuters Environmental News Service*, 8 June.

Lindström, Per. 1995. "The Role of NGOs as seen by the United Nations and its Member States." In *The Role of Non-Governmental Organizations in the New European Order*, edited by Jürgen Schramm, 43–48. Baden-Baden: Nomos Verlagsgesellschaft.

List, Martin, and Volker Rittberger. 1992. "Regime Theory and International Environmental Management." In *The International Politics of the Environment*, edited by Andrew Hurrell and Benedict Kingsbury, 85–109. Oxford: Clarendon Press.

Litfin, Karen. 1993. "Ecoregimes: Playing Tug of War with the Nation-State." In *The State and Social Power in Global Environmental Politics*, edited by Ronnie D. Lipschutz and Ken Conca, 94–117. New York: Columbia University Press.

Litfin, Karen T. 1994. *Ozone Discourses: Science and Politics in Global Environmental Cooperation*. New York: Columbia University Press.

Locke, Christopher. 2001. "Forest Pharmers Go Bioprospecting." *Red Herring*, 12 April: http://www.redherring.com.

*London Amendments to the Montreal Protocol*. 1990.

Lopes, Lola L. 1992. "Risk Perception and the Perceived Public." In *The Social Response to Environmental Risk*, edited by Daniel W. Bromley and Kathleen Segerson, 57–74. Boston, Dordrecht, and London: Kluwer Academic.

Lovejoy, Thomas. 1984. "Aid Debtor Nation's Ecology." *New York Times*, 4 October: 31.

Macnow, Alan. 1984. "A Whaling Moratorium Opposed by I.W.C.'s Own Scientists." Letter to the Editor, *New York Times*, 29 September: 22.

Mahony, Rhona. 1992. "Debt-for-Nature Swaps: Who Really Benefits?" *The Ecologist* 22(3) (May–June): 97–102.

Makhijani, Arun, and Kevin R. Gurney. 1995. *Mending the Ozone Hole: Science, Technology, and Policy*. Cambridge, Mass., and London: MIT Press.

Mandel, Robert. 1984. "Transnational Resource Conflict: The Politics of Whaling." *International Studies Quarterly* (March): 99–127.

Martin, Gene S., Jr., and James W. Brennan. 1989. "Enforcing the International Convention for the Regulation of Whaling: The Pelly and Packwood-Magnuson Amendments." *Denver Journal of International Law and Policy* 17(2): 293–315.

Marx, Anthony. 2005. "Greenpeace Coal Export Protesters Held." *The Courier Mail*, 28 July: 29.

Matthew, Richard A. 1999. "Scarcity and Security: A Common-Pool Resource Perspective." In *Anarchy and the Environment: The International Relations of Common Pool Resources*, edited by J. Samuel Barkin and George E. Shambaugh, 155–75. Albany: SUNY Press.

McCarthy, Michael. 2006. "Save the Whale: 20 Years on and Whales are Under Threat Again." *The Independent* (London), 2 January: 2.

McCleary, Rachel. 1990. "Development Strategies in Conflict: Brazil and the Future of the Amazon." *Pew Case Studies in International Affairs*. Washington D.C.: Carnegie Council on Ethics and International Affairs.

McCormick, John. 1997. *Acid Earth: The Politics of Acid Pollution*, 3rd edn. London: Earthscan.

McCormick, John. 1999. "The Role of Environmental NGOs in International Regimes." In *The Global Environment: Institutions, Law, and Policy*, edited by Norman J. Vig and Regina S. Axelrod, 52–71. Washington D.C.: CQ Press.

McDermott, Rose. 1998. *Risk-Taking in International Politics: Prospect Theory in American Foreign Policy*. Ann Arbor: University of Michigan Press.

McKibben, W. M., and P. J. Wilcoxen. 2004. "Estimates of the Costs of Kyoto: Marrakesh versus the McKibben-Wilcoxen Blueprint." *Energy Policy* 32(4): 467–79.

Michaels, Patrick. 1993. "Environmental Rules Should be Based on Science." *Insight on the News*, 12 April: 21–22.

Miles, Edward L., Arild Underdal, Steinar Andresen, Jørgen Wettestad, Jon Birger Skjaerseth, and Elaine M. Carlin. 2001. *Explaining Regime Effectiveness:*

*Confronting Theory With Evidence.* Cambridge, Mass.: MIT Press.

Millennium Ecosystem Assessment. 2005. *Ecosystems and Human Wellbeing: Biodiversity Synthesis.* Washington D.C.: World Resources Institute.

Miller, Alan S. 1989. "Incentives for CFC Substitutes: Lessons for Other Greenhouse Gases." In *Coping with Climate Change: Proceedings of the Second North American Conference on Preparing for Climate Change*, edited by John C. Topping. Washington D.C.: Climate Institute.

Miller, Marian A. L. 1995. *The Third World in Global Environmental Politics.* Boulder, Colo. and London: Lynne Rienner.

Mintzer, Irving M., and J. Amber Leonard. 1994. *Negotiating Climate Change.* Cambridge: Cambridge University Press.

Mitchell, Ronald B. 1992. "Membership, Compliance, and Non-Compliance in the International Convention for the Regulation of Whaling 1946–Present." Paper for presentation at Harvard University, International Environmental Institutions Research Seminar, October, cited with permission.

Mitchell, Ronald B. 1994. *Intentional Oil Pollution at Sea: Environmental Policies and Treaty Compliance.* Cambridge, Mass.: MIT Press.

Mitchell, Ronald B. 2003. "International Environmental Agreements: A Survey of Their Features, Formation, and Effects." *Annual Review of Environmental Resources* 28: 429–61.

Molina, M. J., and F. S. Rowland. 1974. "Stratospheric Sink for Chlorofluoromethanes: Chlorine Atom-Catalyzed Destruction of Ozone." *Nature* 249: 810–12.

Montreal Protocol (as amended). 1997.

Montzka, S. A., J. H. Butler, J. W. Elkins, T. M. Thompson, A. D. Clarke, and L. T. Locke. 1999. "Present and Future Trends in the Atmospheric Burden of Ozone-Depleting Halogens." *Nature* 398 (22 April): 690–93.

Moran, Katy. 1996. "Compensating Forest-Dwelling Communities for Drug Discovery: The World of the Healing Forest Conservancy." *Unasylva* 47: 42.

Morgenthau, Hans J. 1967. *Politics Among Nations: The Struggle for Power and Peace*, 4th edn. New York: Alfred A. Knopf.

Multilateral Fund for the Implementation of the Montreal Protocol. 2005. *Creating a Real Change for the Environment.* Montreal: Multilateral Fund Secretariat.

Multilateral Fund for the Implementation of the Montreal Protocol. 2006. http://www.multilateralfund.org/.

Munton, Don. 1997. "Acid Rain and Transboundary Air Quality in Canadian-American Relations." *The American Review of Canadian Studies* (Autumn): 327–55.

Murphy, Laura, Richard Bilsborrow, and Francisco Pichon. 1997. "Poverty and Prosperity Among Migrant Settlers in the Amazon Rainforest Frontier of Ecuador." *Journal of Development Studies* 34(2) (December): 35–66.

Myers, Norman. 1992. "The Anatomy of Environmental Action: The Case of Tropical Deforestation." In *The International Politics of the Environment: Actors, Interests, and Institutions*, edited by Andrew Hurrell and Benedict Kingsbury, 430–54. Oxford: Clarendon Press.

Myers, Norman, Russell A. Mittermeier, Cristina G. Mittermeier, Gustavo A. B. da Fonseca, and Jennifer Kent. 2000.

"Biodiversity Hotspots for Conservation Priorities." *Nature* 403 (24 February): 853–58.

Na, Seong-lin, and Hyun Song Shin. 1998. "International Environmental Agreements Under Uncertainty." *Oxford Economic Papers* 50(2) (April): 173–85.

Najam, Adil. 2003. "The Collective South in Multinational Environmental Politics." In *Policymaking and Prosperity: A Multinational Anthology*, edited by Stuart Nagel, 197–240. Lanham, Md.: Lexington Books.

Najam, Adil. 2003. "Dynamics of the Southern Collective: Developing Countries in Desertification Negotiations." *Global Environmental Politics* 4(3) (August): 128–54.

Najam, Adil, et al. 2002. "From Rio to Johannesburg: Progress and Prospects." *Environment* 44(7): 221–31.

Neto, Ricardo Bonalume. 1993. "MIT's Amazon Outpost." *Nature*, 9 September: 101.

"A New Era for the IWC." 1991. *Greenpeace Magazine* (October–December): 5.

Newman, D. J., G. M. Cragg, and K. M. Snader. 2003. "Natural Products as Sources of New Drugs over the Period 1981–2002." *Journal of Natural Products* 66(7): 1022–37.

Oak Ridge National Laboratory. 2006. "LBA." http://www-eosdis.ornl.gov/LBA/misc_amazon.html

Oberthür, Sebastian, and Thomas Gehring. 2005. "Reforming International Environmental Governance: An Institutional Perspective on Proposals for a WEO." In *A World Environment Organization*, edited by Frank Biermann and Steffen Bauer, 205–34. Aldershot: Ashgate.

Odén, Svante. 1968. "The Acidification of Air and Precipitation and its Consequences in the Natural Environment." *Ecology Committee Bulletin* 1. Stockholm: Swedish National Research Council.

Offe, Claus. 1984. *Contradictions of the Welfare State*, edited by John Keane. Cambridge, Mass.: MIT Press.

Olson, Mancur, Jr. 1965. *The Logic of Collective Action: Public Goods and the Theory of Groups*. Cambridge, Mass.: Harvard University Press.

Organization for Economic Cooperation and Development. 1977. *The OECD Programme on Long Range Transport of Air Pollutants: Summary Report*.

Organization for Economic Cooperation and Development. 1985. *Environmental Policy and Technical Change*. Paris: OECD.

Ostergard, Robert L., Jr., Matthew Tubin, and Jordan Altman. 2001. "Stealing from the Past: Globalisation, Strategic Formulation and the Use of Indigenous Intellectual Property in the Biotechnology Industry," *Third World Quarterly* 22(4): 643–56.

Oye, Kenneth A. 1986. "Explaining Cooperation Under Anarchy: Hypotheses and Strategies." In *Cooperation Under Anarchy*, edited by Kenneth A. Oye, 1–24. Princeton: Princeton University Press.

Oye, Kenneth, and James H. Maxwell. 1995. "Self-Interest and Environmental Management." In *Local Commons and Global Interdependence: Heterogeneity and Cooperation in Two Domains*, edited by Robert O. Keohane and Elinor Ostrom, 191–221. Newbury Park, Calif.: Sage.

Ozone Secretariat. n.d. "2002 Environmental Effects Assessment." http://ozone.unep.org/Public_Informatio n/4D_PublicInfo_FAQ.asp.

Ozone Secretariat. 2006. "Table: Status of Ratification as at 28.2.2006." http://ozone.unep.org/Treaties_and_Ratif ication/2C_ratificationTable.asp?choices =MP&submit2=Submit.

Page, Diana. 1989. "Debt-for-Nature Swaps: Experience Gained, Lessons Learned." *International Environmental Affairs* 1(4): 275–89.

Palmer, Geoffrey. 1992. "New Ways to Make International Environmental Law." *American Journal of International Law* 86 (April): 274–76.

Parson, Edward A. 2003. *Protecting the Ozone Layer: Science and Strategy.* Oxford: Oxford University Press.

Paterson, Matthew. 1996. *Global Warming and Global Politics.* London and New York: Routledge.

Paterson, Matthew. 2000. *Understanding Global Environmental Politics: Domination, Accumulation, Resistance.* London: Macmillan.

Payne, Rodger A. 1996. "Nonprofit Environmental Organizations in World Politics: Domestic Structure and Transnational Relations." *Policy Studies Review* 14(1–2) (Spring–Summer): 171–82.

Pearce, Fred. 2000. "A Cool Trick." *New Scientist* 8 (April):18

Pearson, Charles S. 1985. *Down to Business: Multinational Corporations, the Environment, and Development.* Washington D.C.: World Resources Institute.

Pepall, Jennifer. 1998. "Putting a Price on Indigenous Knowledge." International Development Research Centre (7 July):

http://www.idrc.ca/books/reports/1996/3 0-01e.html.

Percival, Val, and Thomas F. Homer-Dixon. 1998. "Environmental Scarcity and Violent Conflict: The Case of South Africa." *Journal of Peace Research* 35(3) (May): 279–98.

Peterson, M. J. 1992. "Whalers, Cetologists, Environmentalists, and the International Management of Whaling." *International Organization* 46(1) (Winter): 147–86.

"Political Uncertainty Halts Bioprospecting in Mexico." 2000. *Nature* 408: 278.

Porter, Gareth. 1995. "Little Effect on Environmental Performance." *Environmental Forum* 12(6) (November–December): 43–44.

Porter, Michael E. 1990. *The Competitive Advantage of Nations.* New York: Free Press.

Porter, Michael E. 1991. "America's Green Strategy." *Scientific American* 264(4) (April): 168.

Potter, David. 1996. "Democratisation and the Environment: NGOs and Deforestation Policies in India (Karnataka) and Indonesia (North Sumatra)." In *NGOs and Environmental Policies: Asia and Africa*, edited by David Potter, 9–38. London and Portland, Ore.: Frank Cass.

Potter, David, ed. 1996. *NGOs and Environmental Policies: Asia and Africa.* London and Portland, Ore.: Frank Cass.

Price, Marie. 1994. "Ecopolitics and Environmental Nongovernmental Organizations in Latin America." *The Geographical Review* 84(1) (January): 42–58.

Princen, Thomas, and Matthias Finger. 1994. "Introduction." In Thomas Princen and Matthias Finger, *Environmental NGOs in*

*World Politics: Linking the Local and the Global*, 1–25. New York: Routledge.

Protocol Between the Government of Canada and the Government of the United States of America Amending the "Agreement between the Government of Canada and the Government of the United States on Air Quality." 2000.

Protocol to LRTAP Concerning the Control of Emissions of Nitrogen Oxides or their Transboundary Fluxes. 1988.

Protocol to LRTAP Concerning the Control of Emissions of Volatile Organic Compounds or Their Transboundary Fluxes. 1991.

Protocol to LRTAP on Further Reductions of Sulphur Emissions. 1994.

Protocol to LRTAP on Heavy Metals. 1998.

Protocol to LRTAP on Persistent Organic Pollutants. 1998.

Raines, Susan Summers. 2003. "Perceptions of Legitimacy in International Environmental Management Standards: The Impact of the Participation Gap." *Global Environmental Politics* 3(3) (August): 47–73.

Raustiala, Kal. 1997. "States, NGOs, and International Environmental Institutions." *International Studies Quarterly* 41: 719–40.

Raustiala, Kal, and David G. Victor. 1996. "Biodiversity Since Rio – The Future of the Convention on Biological Diversity." *Environment* 38(4): 18–20, 37–45.

Raven, Peter H., and Jeffrey A. McNeely. 1998. "Biological Extinction: Its Scope and Meaning for Us." In *Protection of Global Biodiversity: Converging Strategies*, edited by Lakshman D. Guruswamy and Jeffrey A. McNeely, 13–32. Durham, N.C.: Duke University Press.

Rawls, John. 1971. *A Theory of Justice*. Cambridge: Belknap Press of Harvard University Press.

Reaney, Patricia. 2000. "Deep Ocean Current Linked to Global Climate Change." *Reuters New Service*, 3 August.

Revkin, Andrew C. 2002. "Biologists Sought a Treaty; Now They Fault It." *New York Times*, 7 May: 1.

Richardson, Tim, Jiri Dusik, and Pavla Jindrova. 1998. "Parallel Public Participation: An Answer to Inertia in Decision-Making." *Environmental Impact Assessment Review* 18: 201–16.

Ridgeway, Collette. 1996. "Privately Protected Places." *Cato Policy Report* 18(2) (March–April): http://www.cato.org/pubs/policy_report/pr-xviii2-ridgeway.html.

*Rio Declaration on Environment and Development*. 1992.

Ripley, Randall B., and Grace A. Franklin. 1980. *Congress, The Bureaucracy, and Public Policy*, rev. edn. Homewood Il: Dorsey Press.

Risse-Kappan, Thomas. 1994. "Ideas Do Not Float Freely: Transnational Coalitions, Domestic Structures, and the End of the Cold War." *International Organization* 48(2) (Spring): 185–214.

Rittberger, Volker, and Michael Zürn. 1991. "Regime Theory: Findings from the Study of 'East–West' Regimes." *Cooperation and Conflict* 26: 171–72.

Roman, Joe, and Stephen R. Palumbi. 2003. "Whales Before Whaling in the North Atlantic." *Science*, 25 July: 508–10.

Rome, Abigail. 1999. "Amazon Adventure." *E* 10(2) (March): 48.

Ross, Michael. 2001. *Timber Booms and Institutional Breakdown in Southeast Asia*. Cambridge: Cambridge University

Press.

Rowlands, Ian H. 1995. *The Politics of Global Atmospheric Change*. Manchester and London: Manchester University Press.

Saab, Saleem S. 1998. "Move Over Drugs, There's Something Cooler on the Black Market – Freon." *Dickenson Journal of International Law* 16 (Spring): 634.

Sagar, Ambuj D., and Stacy D. VanDeveer. "Capacity Development for the Environment: Broadening the Scope." *Global Environmental Politics* 5(3) (August): 14–22.

Sands, P .J. 1991. "The Role of Non-Governmental Organizations in Enforcing International Environmental Law." In *Control over Compliance with International Obligations*, edited by William E. Butler, 61–68. Dordrecht: Martinus Nijhoff.

Sands, Philippe. 1995. *Principles of International Environmental Law*, vol. I. Manchester and New York: Manchester University Press.

Sarkar, Amin U. 1994. "Debt Relief for Environment: Experience and Issues." *Journal of Environment and Development* 3(1) (Summer): 123–36.

Schmandt, Jurgen, Hilliard Roderick, and Judith Clarkson. 1988. "Introduction to Part One." In *Acid Rain and Friendly Neighbors: The Policy Dispute Between Canada and the United States*, rev. edn., edited by Jurgen Schmandt, Judith Clarkson, and Hilliard Roderick, 3–6. Durham, N.C.: Duke University Press.

Schmandt, Jurgen, Hilliard Roderick, and Andrew Morriss. 1988. "Acid Rain is Different." In *Acid Rain and Friendly Neighbors: The Policy Dispute Between Canada and the United States*, rev. edn., edited by Jurgen Schmandt, Judith

Clarkson, and Hilliard Roderick, 7–30. Durham, N.C.: Duke University Press.

Schmidheiny, Stephan, and Federico J. L. Zorraquín. 1996. *Financing Change: The Financial Community, Eco-Efficiency, and Sustainable Development*. Cambridge, Mass.: MIT Press.

Schneider, Greg. 2001. "Taking No Chances: Disaster-Conscious Firms Treat Global Warming as a Reality." *Washington Post*, 26 June: E01.

Schreurs, Miranda. 1995. "Japan: Elite Newspaper Reporting on the Acid Rain Issue from 1972 to 1992." In *The Press and Global Environmental Change: An International Comparison on Elite Newspaper Reporting on the Acid Rain Issue from 1972–1992*, edited by William C. Clark and Nancy M. Dickson. Cambridge, Mass.: Center for Science and International Affairs, Kennedy School of Government.

Schreurs, Miranda. 2001. "Shifting Priorities and the Internationalization of Environmental Risk Management in Japan." In The Social Learning Group, *Learning to Manage Global Environmental Risks*, vol. I, 191–212. Cambridge, Mass.: MIT Press.

Sebenius, James K. 1992. "Challenging Conventional Explanations of International Cooperation: Negotiation Analysis and the Case of Epistemic Communities." *International Organization* 46(1): 358.

Secretariat of the Convention on Biological Diversity. 2006. *Global Biodiversity Outlook 2*. Montreal: CBD Secretariat.

Sell, Susan. 1996. "North–South Environmental Bargaining: Ozone, Climate Change, and Biodiversity." *Global Governance* 2: 97–118.

Sevilla, Roque. 1990. "Banks, Debt, and Development – II." *International Environmental Affairs* 2(2): 150–52.

Shaman Botanicals. 2000. "Shaman: About Us." http://www.shamanbotanicals.com/aumaster.htm.

Shaw, Roderick W. 1993. "Acid Rain Negotiations in North America and Europe: A Study in Contrast." In *International Environmental Negotiations*, edited by Gunnar Sjöstedt, 84–109. Newbury Park: Sage.

Sherman, K. 1992. "Large Marine Ecosystems." In *Encyclopedia of Earth System Science*, vol. II, 653–73. New York: Academic Press.

Shoumatoff, Alex. 1990. *The World Is Burning.* Boston: Little, Brown, & Company.

Simpson, R. David. 1999. "The Price of Biodiversity." *Issues in Science and Technology* 15(3): 65–70.

"Sinking CO." 2001. *Environment* 43(2) (March): 6.

Sinnar, Shirin. 1995–1996. "Mixed Blessing: The Growing Influence of NGOs," *Harvard International Review* (Winter): 54ff.

Sisky, Anthony. 2001. Project Coordinator. MIT. E-mail message received 6 June.

Slovic, Paul. 1991. "Beyond Numbers: A Broader Perspective on Risk Perception and Risk Communication." In *Acceptable Evidence: Science and Values in Risk Management*, edited by Deborah G. Mayo and Rachelle D. Hollander, 48–65. New York and Oxford: Oxford University Press.

Slovic, Paul, Baruch Fischhoff, and Sarah Lichtenstein. 1979. "Rating the Risks." *Environment* 21(3) (April): 14–20, 36–39.

Smart, Bruce. 1992. *Beyond Compliance: A New Industry View of the Environment.* Washington D.C.: World Resources Institute.

Snidal, Duncan. 1985. "The Limits of Hegemonic Stability Theory." *International Organization* 30(4): 579–615.

Snidal, Duncan. 1995. "The Politics of Scope: Endogenous Actors, Heterogeneity, and Institutions." In *Local Commons and Global Interdependence*, edited by Robert O. Keohane and Elinor Ostrom. London: Sage.

Socolow, Robert H. 2005. "Can We Bury Global Warming?" *Scientific American* (July): 49–55.

Soroos, Marvin S. 1991. "The Atmosphere as an International Common Property Resource." In *Global Policy Studies,* edited by S.S. Nagel. London: Macmillan.

Southgate, Douglas. 1997. *Alternatives for Habitat Protection and Rural Income Generation.* Washington D.C.: Inter-American Development Bank.

Spencer, Leslie. 1991. "The Not So Peaceful World of Greenpeace." *Forbes,* 11 November: 174.

Spiro, Peter J. 1994. "New Global Communities: Nongovernmental Organizations in International Decision-Making Institutions." *The Washington Quarterly* 18(1): 45–56.

Sprinz, Detlef, and Tapani Vaahtoranta. 1994. "The Interest-Based Explanation of International Environmental Policy." *International Organization* 48(1) (Winter): 77–105.

Steele, Giselle V. 1997. "Drowning in Sand: Environmental Effects of Desertification." *E* 8(1)(11 January): 15.

Stein, Arthur A. 1982. "Coordination and Collaboration: Regimes in an Anarchic World." In *International Regimes,* edited by Stephen D. Krasner, 115–40. Ithaca and London: Cornell University Press.

Steinberg, Paul. 2001. *Environmental Leadership in Developing Countries: Transnational Relations and Biodiversity Policy in Costa Rica and Bolivia.* Cambridge, Mass.: MIT Press.

Stewart, Robert B. 1988. "Negotiations on Acid Rain." In *Acid Rain and Friendly Neighbors: The Policy Dispute Between Canada and the United States,* rev. edn., edited by Jurgen Schmandt, Judith Clarkson, and Hilliard Roderick, 64–82. Durham, N.C.: Duke University Press.

Strange, Susan. 1996. *The Retreat of the State: The Diffusion of Power in the World Economy.* Cambridge: Cambridge University Press.

Susskind, Lawrence E. 1994. *Environmental Diplomacy: Negotiating More Effective Global Agreements.* New York and Oxford: Oxford University Press.

Swedish NGO Secretariat on Acid Rain. n.d. "Acidification." http://www.acidrain.org/pages/acidEutrophications/sub3_1.asp#Areas.

Tait, Maggie. 2006. "We were Rammed, says Greenpeace." *The Advertiser,* 9 January: 15.

Territo, Michele. 2000. "Note and Comment: The Precautionary Principle in Marine Fisheries Conservation and the U.S. Sustainable Fisheries Act of 1996." *Vermont Law Review* 24 (Summer): 1351ff.

Tesh, Sylvia Noble. 2000. *Uncertain Hazards: Environmental Activists and Scientific Proof.* Ithaca and London: Cornell University Press.

"Texaco Quits Anti-Kyoto Climate Change Group." 2001. *Reuters News Service,* 2 March.

Thapa, Brijesh. 1998. "Debt-for-Nature Swaps: An Overview." *International Journal of Sustainable Development and World Ecology* 5(4): 249–62.

Thomas, Alan. 1996. "NGO Advocacy, Democracy, and Policy Development." In *NGOs and Environmental Policies: Asia and Africa,* edited by David Potter, 38–65. London: Frank Cass.

Tønnessen, J.N., and A. O. Johnsen. 1982. *The History of Modern Whaling.* Berkeley: University of California Press.

Touraine, Alain. 1988. *Return of the Actor: Social Theory in Postindustrial Society.* Minneapolis: University of Minnesota Press.

Tufts Climate Initiative. 2006. "Who We Are." http://www.tufts.edu/tie/tci/WhoWeAre.html.

Tversky, Amos, and Daniel Kahneman. 1982. "Judgments of and by Representativeness." In *Judgment Under Uncertainty: Heuristics and Biases,* edited by Daniel Kahneman, Paul Slovic, and Amos Tversky, 84–98. Cambridge: Cambridge University Press.

Tversky, Amos, and Daniel Kahneman. 1991. "Loss Aversion in Riskless Choice." *Quarterly Journal of Economics* 106(4) (November): 1039–61.

"UN Convention to Combat Desertification." *M2 Presswire* (9 January) (Lexis/Nexis).

Underdal, Arild. 1997. "Patterns of Effectiveness: Examining Evidence from Thirteen International Regimes." Paper presented at the International Studies Association Annual Convention, Toronto, March.

UNDP. 1998. *Human Development Report 1998*. Oxford: Oxford University Press.

UNECE. 2006. "The 1991 Geneva Protocol Concerning the Control of Emissions of Volatile Organic Compounds or their Transboundary Fluxes." http://www.unece.org/env/lrtap/vola_h1.htm.

UNECE. 2006. "1999 Gothenburg Protocol to Abate Acidification, Eutrophication and Ground-Level Ozone." http://www.unece.org/env/lrtap/multi_h1.htm.

UNECE. 2006. "Status of Convention on Long-Range Transboundary Air Pollution and its Related Protocols (as of 13 January 2006)." http://www.unece.org/env/lrtap/status/Status%20of%20the%20Convention.pdf.

UNEP. 2005. "BACKGROUNDER: Basic Facts and Data on the Science and Politics of Ozone Protection." (November). http://ozone.unep.org/Public_Information/press_backgrounder.pdf.

UNEP. 2005. "Report of the Seventh Meeting of the Parties to the Vienna Convention for the Protection of the Ozone Layer and the Seventeenth Meeting of the Parties to the Montreal Protocol on Substances that Deplete the Ozone Layer." (16 December).

UNFCCC Secretariat. n.d. "Greenhouse Gas Emissions Data for 1990–2003." http://unfccc.int/essential_background/background_publications_htmlpdf/items/3604.php.

UNFCCC. 2005. Key GHG Data: Greenhouse Gas Emissions Data for 1990–2003 Submitted to the United Nations Framework Convention on Climate Change (November). Bonn: UNFCCC.

UNFCCC. n.d. "Kyoto Protocol, Status of Ratification." http://unfccc.int/files/essential_background/kyoto_protocol/application/pdf/kpstats.pdf.

Union of International Associations. 1993. *The Yearbook of International Organizations 1993–4*, vol. I. Munich: K.S. Saur.

*United Nations Convention on the Law of the Sea*. 1982.

United Nations Environment Programme. 1994. "Partnerships for Sustainable Development: The Role of Business and Industry." London: Flashprint Enterprises, for UNEP and the Prince of Wales Business Leaders Forum.

United Nations Environment Program. 1997. "Fact Sheet 8 – Financing Action to Combat Desertification." http://www.unep.ch/incd/fs8.html.

*United Nations Framework Convention on Climate Change*. 1992.

United States General Accounting Office. 1988. "Water Pollution: Stronger Enforcement Needed to Improve Compliance at Federal Facilities." Washington D.C.: GAO. GAO/RCED-89-144.

United States Public Law 92–219, sec. 8.

USAID. 2006. "Tropical Forest Conservation Act (TCFA) Program Descriptions." http://www.usaid.gov/our_work/environment/forestry/tfca_descs.html.

U.S. EPA. 2003. "Acid Rain Program 2003 Progress Report." http://www.epa.gov/airmarkets/cmprpt/arp03/summary.html.

Van Beers, Cees, and J. C. J. M. van der Bergh. 1999. "An Empirical Multi-Country Analysis of the Impact of Environmental Regulations on Foreign Trade Flows." *Kyklos* 50(1): 29–46.

VanderZwaag, David. 1999. "The Precautionary Principle in Environmental Law and Policy: Elusive Rhetoric and First Embrace." *Journal of Environmental Law and Practice* 8(3) (October): 355–75.

VanDeveer, Stacy D., and Ambuj D. Sagar. 2005. "Capacity Development for the Environment: North and South." In *Global Challenges: Furthering the Multilateral Process for Sustainable Development*, edited by Elisabeth Corell, Angela Churie Kallhauge, and Gunnar Sjöstedt, 259–73. London: Greenleaf.

Victor, David G. 1998. "'Learning by Doing' in the Nonbinding International Regime to Manage Trade in Hazardous Chemicals and Pesticides." In *The Implementation and Effectiveness of International Environmental Commitments*, edited by David G. Victor, Kal Raustiala, and Eugene B. Skolnikoff, 221–81. Cambridge, Mass.: MIT Press.

Victor, David G. 1998. "The Montreal Protocol's Non-Compliance Procedure." In *The Implementation and Effectiveness of International Environmental Commitments*, edited by David G. Victor, Kal Raustiala, and Eugene B. Skolnikoff, 147. Cambridge, Mass.: MIT Press.

Victor, David G. 1998. "The Operation and Effectiveness of the Montreal Protocol's Non-Compliance Procedure." In *The Implementation and Effectiveness of International Environmental Commitments*, edited by David G. Victor, Kal Raustiala, and Eugene B. Skolnikoff, 137–76. Cambridge, Mass.: MIT Press.

Victor, David G. 2001. The Collapse of the Kyoto Protocol and the Struggle to Slow Global Warming. Princeton: Princeton University Press.

Victor, David, Kal Raustiala, and Eugene B. Skolnikoff. 1998. *The Implementation and Effectiveness of International Environmental Commitments*. Cambridge, Mass.: MIT Press.

Vidal, John. 1995. "As the World Runs Dry … Next, Wars Over Water?" *World Press Review* 42(11) (November): 8ff.

*Vienna Convention for the Protection of the Ozone Layer*. 1985.

Vogel, David. 1993. "Representing Diffuse Interests in Environmental Policymaking." In *Do Institutions Matter?: Government Capabilities in the United States and Abroad*, edited by David Vogel, 237–71. Washington, D.C.: Brookings Institution.

Vogel, Joseph Henry. 1996. *The Successful Use of Economic Instruments to Foster Sustainable Use of Biodiversity*. Quito: Facultad Latinoamericana de Ciencias Sociales.

Von Neumann, John, and Oskar Morgenstern. 1947. *Theory of Games and Economic Behavior*, 2nd edn. Princeton: Princeton University Press.

Wallerstein, Immanuel. 1979. *The Capitalist World-Economy*. Cambridge: Cambridge University Press.

Waltz, Kenneth N. 1959. *Man, the State, and War: A Theoretical Analysis*. New York: Columbia University Press.

Wapner, Paul. 1995. "Politics Beyond the State: Environmental Activism and World Civic Politics." *World Politics* 47(3) (April): 311–40.

Wapner, Paul. 1996. *Environmental Activism and World Civic Politics*. Albany: SUNY Press.

Wapner, Paul. 1998. "Reorienting State Sovereignty: Rights and Responsibilities in the Environmental Age." In *The Greening of Sovereignty in World Politics*, edited by Karen T. Litfin, 275–97. Cambridge, Mass.: MIT Press.

Watson, Robert T., F. Sherwood Rowland, and John Gille. 1988. *Ozone Trends Panel: Executive Summary*. Washington, D.C.: NASA.

Watson, S. 1994. "Are Licensing Agreements Key to Technology Transfer?" *Legal Intelligencer*, 14 June: 13ff. (Lexis/Nexis).

Webb, Jason. 1998. "Scientists Clearing Up Clouds' Effects on Climate." *Reuters News Service*, 10 November.

Wetstone, Gregory S., and Armin Rosencranz. 1983. *Acid Rain in Europe and North America: National Responses to an International Problem: A Study for the German Marshall Fund of the United States*. Washington, D.C.: Environmental Law Institute.

"Whales in the Way of Sonar." 2006. *New York Times*, 7 March: 20.

Wheeler, David. 2002. "Beyond Pollution Havens." *Global Environmental Politics* 2(2): 1–10.

Whelan, Tensie. 1991. "Ecotourism and Its Role in Sustainable Development." In *Nature Tourism: Managing for the Environment*, edited by Tensie Whelan, 3–22. Washington D.C.: Island Press.

White, Robert M. 1993. "Introduction: Environmental Regulation and Changing Science and Technology." In *Keeping Pace With Science and Engineering: Case Studies in Environmental Regulation*, edited by Myron F. Uman, 1–7. Washington, D.C.: National Academy Press.

Wiener, Jonathan Baert. 1999. "On the Political Economy of Global Regulation." *Georgetown Law Journal* 87 (February): 749–94.

Willetts, Peter, ed. 1996. *The Conscience of the World: The Influence of Non-Governmental Organisations in the U.N. System*. Washington, D.C.: Brookings Institution.

Williams, Marc. 2005. "The Third World and Global Environmental Negotiations: Interests, Institutions, and Ideas." *Global Environmental Politics* 5(3) (August): 48–69.

Witze, Alexandra. 2005. "Antarctic Ozone Hole Set to Take 60 More Years to Recover." *Nature News* (online). http://www.nature.com/news/2005/051205/full/051205-9.html (8 December).

Wood, Megan Epler. 1991. "Global Solutions: An Ecotourism Society." In *Nature Tourism: Managing for the Environment*, edited by Tensie Whelan, 200–206. Washington, D.C.: Island Press.

World Bank. 2002. "Brazil to Triple Amount of Protected Amazon Rainforest over 10 Years." http://web.worldbank.org/WBSITE/EXTERNAL/NEWS/0,,contentMDK:20066968~menuPK:34457~pagePK:34370~piPK:34424~theSitePK:4607,00.html (5 September).

World Commission on Environment and Development. 1987. *Our Common Future*. Oxford: Oxford University Press.

World Resources Institute. 1992. *World Resources: A Report by the World Resources Institute and the International Institute for Environment and Development* 1992–1993. New York: Basic Books.

"Worldview – Whaling: Soviet Kills Could Affect Sanctuary Decision." 1994. *Greenwire*. 22 February.

Yohe, Gary W. 1979. "The Backward Incidence of Pollution Control – Some Comparative Statics in General Equilibrium." *Journal of Environmental Economics and Management* 6: 187–98.

Young, Oran R. 1989. "Science and Social Institutions: Lessons for International Resource Regimes." In *International Resource Management: The Role of Science and Politics*, edited by Steinar Andresen and Willy Ostreng, 7–24. London and New York: Bellhaven Press.

Young, Oran. 2001. "Inferences and Indices: Evaluating the Effectiveness of International Environmental Regimes." *Global Environmental Politics* 1(1) (February): 99–121.

Young, Oran R. 1999. *Governance in World Affairs*. Ithaca: Cornell University Press.

Young, Oran R., and Marc A. Levy (with the assistance of Gail Osherenko). 1999. "The Effectiveness of International Environmental Regimes." In *The Effectiveness of International Environmental Regimes*, edited by Oran R. Young, 1–32. Cambridge, Mass.: MIT Press.

Zebich-Knos, Michele. 1997. "Preserving Biodiversity in Costa Rica: The Case of the Merck-INBio Agreement." *Journal of Environment and Development* 6(2) (June): 180–86.

# Index